D1617575

Rule of Sympathy

Rule of Sympathy

Sentiment, Race, and Power
1750–1850

Amit S. Rai

palgrave

First published 2002 by PALGRAVE™
175 Fifth Avenue, New York, N.Y.10010 and
Houndmills, Basingstoke, Hampshire RG21 6XS.
Companies and representatives throughout the world.

PALGRAVE is the new global publishing imprint of St. Martin's Press LLC Scholarly and Reference Division and Palgrave Publishers Ltd. (formerly Macmillan Press Ltd.).

ISBN 0–312–29393–3 hardback

Library of Congress Cataloging-in-Publication Data
Rai, Amit, 1968-
Rule of sympathy : sentiment, race, and power, 1750–1850 / by Amit S. Rai.
     p.   cm.
   Includes bibliographical references and index.
   ISBN 0–312–29393–3
   1. Sympathy—History—18th century.   2. Race relations—History—18th century.   3. Social values—Europe—History—18th century.
4. Sympathy—History—19th century.   5. Race relations—History—19th century.   6. Social values—Europe—History—19th century.   I. Title.

BJ1533.S9 R35   2002
177'.7—dc21

                                                                          2001056141

A catalogue record for this book is available from the British Library.

Design by Letra Libre, Inc.

First edition: June 2002
10   9   8   7   6   5   4   3   2   1

Printed in the United States of America.

For Tara Rai and Chinu Mukherjee
In sympathy and solidarity.

Contents

Acknowledgments

This book would not have been possible without the support and encourage-ment of my parents, S. K. Rai and Meera Rai, and my sister, Leena Rai. I would not have embarked on this path without that first word of encouragement from my uncle, the late Professor V. K. Shrivastava. It has been the inspiring influ-ence of Shail Shrivastava that has kept me going even when I thought I had reached a dead end. For never losing faith in me, I thank Abha Choudhury.

I have had the privilege of studying with some amazing thinkers and doers. Dan Moshenberg, Kim Hall, and Eric Cheyfitz showed me the way out of a certain solipsism. Akhil Gupta, Ramon Saldivar, Silvia Yanagisako, Paula Ebron, Mary Louise Pratt, Pat Parker, Renato Rosaldo, and Purnima Mankekar taught me to be humble in the face of history's anomalies and cul-ture's contradictions. Kim Gillespie, Daniel Contreras, Kenneth Brewer, Jose Cazares, Hilton Obenzinger, Derrick Scott, Anahid Kasabian (and Maral and Leo!), Lee Medevoi, Josie Saldana, and David Kasanjian showed me how to pose the questions that matter. Don Scott, Steve Caton, Heidi Krueger, Jan Clausen, Greg Tewksbury, and Ann Snitow welcomed me and did what they could to create a climate of collegiality. Kian Tajbaksh taught me the how the rhythm of a (gui)tar can get one through when things mat-ter. I keep learning from the conversations I have had with Patricia Clough.

Prema Vora taught me what the yearning for justice means. John Matouk reminded me that one should always also be able to dance at the revolution. Aley Mathew inspired me to hold on to a broader vision of history, justice, and empowerment. Falu Bakrania sympathetically waded through an early version of this book, and prodded me into making it more focused. Ifeona Fulani lovingly taught me how to live with patience, survive with strength, and remember with joy. Amos Himmelstein offered friendship and generos-ity from the other side of the desk. Jasbir Puar shared the wisdom that comes with piebald hair and funky dancing. Anthony Ng taught me the power of hope during troubled times, and that the yearning for peace with justice can be a lived practice. Edie Meidev helped me to laugh at myself, and Stan kept me laughing at everything else.

Gary Lemons and Jacqui Alexander showed me how the written word could rise into spirit: in love, in solidarity, with strength, with justice. Rahul Shrivastava, Abhay Sardesai, and Shilpa Phadke gave me the comfort and challenge of a transformative friendship. Smita Kulshresta, Venky Rajan, and Kartik No. 1 gave me shelter from a bureaucratic storm, and then helped me to see beyond my world. Joby Gelbspan, Louisa Soloman, Clara Cuellar, Emily Kramer, Diane Roy, Taimur Khan, Ritu Shrivastava, Abhishek Jain, Ori Weisberg, Madhumita Patel, Pradeep Chorgadhe, Eric DeWald, and Morwenna Christensen have taught me to accept the responsibilities of learning from teaching. To all these people I am indebted for gifts that cannot simply be returned; I thank them for their generosity and caring.

I would like to thank the librarians at the National Archives of India (Delhi and Bhopal), the British Library, the New York Public Library, Stanford University Libraries, and NYU's Bobst Library.

I would also like to thank the reviewers and editors who have helped me at particular stages of this process: Ann Stoler's helpful and productive suggestions strengthened this manuscript; Eric Smoodin's early encouragement gave me the needed push to see the light at the end of the tunnel; and Kristi Long's prompt and professional editing helped bring this book to completion. The editorial staff at Palgrave—Meg Weaver, Erin Chan, and Roee Raz—have consistently been helpful and responsive. I also thank the librarians at the National Archives of India (Delhi and Bhopal), the British Library, the New York Public Library, Stanford University Libraries, and NYU's Bobst Library.

Bhopal, Brea, Brooklyn
Summer 2001

Preface

Through the Archives of Sympathy

Scenes of Sympathy

In his Preface to Frederick Douglass's autobiographical *Narrative* (1845), William Lloyd Garrison sent out a challenge to his readers. It was a call to action, a call to justice. For him, and hundreds of other (usually white and privileged) abolitionists in America, the Caribbean, and England, it was a call to sympathy.

> Reader! are you with the man-stealers in sympathy and purpose, or on the side of their down-trodden victims? If with the former, then you are the foe of God and man. If with the latter, what are you prepared to do and dare in their behalf? Be faithful, be vigilant, be untiring in your efforts to break every yoke, and let the oppressed go free. Come what may—cost what it may—inscribe on the banner which you unfurl to the breeze, as your religious and political motto—"NO COMPROMISE WITH SLAVERY! NO UNION WITH SLAVEHOLDERS!"

Sympathizing and acting, struggling for the freedom of enslaved African peoples, untiringly, benevolently, vigilantly: the zealous abolitionist since the late eighteenth century was the very figure of "active sympathy" and reforming benevolence. But sympathy always needs an object of pathos, and in abolitionist discourse the spectacle of the slave's suffering body, or the lamentable state of her mind would be that horrid but ideal object. As Garrison writes, fortunate are those "whose sympathy and affection [Douglass] has strongly secured by the many sufferings he has endured, . . . and who have been melted to tears by his pathos, or roused to virtuous indignation by his stirring eloquence against the enslavers of men!" Through such spectacles of sympathy, staged in poems, speeches, pamphlets, autobiographies, and mass meetings, literally tens of thousands of people were moved to lend their support to a struggle that was quite possibly the first international mass movement in the Western world, the struggle for abolition.

For modern readers in the twenty-first century, these words don't carry the same force as they did for the readers of Douglass's autobiography. To sympathize with the oppressed seems hopelessly quaint, decidedly Sixties. Today's liberals don't sympathize, at least not in the way of eighteenth-century evangelicals or nineteenth-century liberals did. After the everyday brutality of the Reagan-Bush-Thatcher era seemed to inure a whole generation of American and European youths to a variety of domestic and global violences, after the world witnessed the spectacle of American fighter planes dropping smart bombs and rather dumb lunch boxes on the peoples of Afghanistan in the wake of the tragedy of September 11, 2001, sympathy seems just "totally played out." Indeed, it has become something of a "bad" word in political and cultural discourse, bearing connotations of a patronizing, even colonizing benevolence. Humanitarian intervention is a case in point. In a recent *Nation* forum on humanitarian intervention,[1] Holly Burkhalter, the advocacy director of Physicians for Human Rights, argued that

> [w]e as citizens should demand that our President declare the principle that prevention and suppression of genocide and crimes against humanity, and punishment of those responsible, are of vital interest to the United States, and announce a program to make this pledge meaningful. (26)

Not as sanguine as Burkhalter, Mahmood Mamdani notes that humanitarian intervention has often fit too neatly "into a history of imperial intervention over the past several centuries." He asks, "Didn't slaving powers portray Africa as a state of nature where life was nasty, brutish and short and where slavery salvaged the lives of its victims, introducing them to the nobility of labor? And didn't colonial powers entering Africa toward the end of the nineteenth century claim to be stamping out slavery? In other words, hasn't every imperial intervention claimed to be humanitarian?" (22–24) A certain "suffering other," veiled and silent, presides over these debates—her specter speaks to an nearly occult relationship the West has with this other of pain: indeed, her class, gender, and colonial histories implicate the West in that very suffering. Let us keep in mind that modern humanitarianism took its rise in the course of the eighteenth century, and the benevolence and sensibility associated with it were thoroughly enmeshed in the rise of a certain bourgeois-colonial hegemony.[2] Coming to terms with this history involves understanding how the suffering other poses a fundamental—and urgent—

dilemma for us today: Shall we sympathize and ameliorate her suffering, or can another sensibility organize another praxis?

People on the left are generally inclined to substitute "solidarity" for "sympathy"—the former it seems linked to histories of international labor struggles,[3] and antiracist, anticolonial organizing. For Nietzsche, overwork, curiosity, and *sympathy* were our "modern vices."[4] Sympathy is often thought of as "soft," stupidly charitable, full of "good intentions," and just, well, too diffuse. Solidarity is firm, concentrated, unforgiving, relentless, courageous, and, as it were, "hard." At our most sardonic, we can have sympathy for the devil, but only solidarity links us to the "struggling masses."[5] But of course, in everyday usage there is a profound confusion and odd overlap between the two words. In the recent "Battle in Seattle" (November 1999), as thousands of (mostly white) environmentalists, youth activists, labor organizers, and even some anarchists rallied for over a week to stop the ongoing tyranny of the U.S.-backed World Trade Organization (WTO), the descriptions of the multiple struggles, affinities, and coalitions that were forming took up the politics of solidarity but often through the language of sympathy. For example, statements like the following were not uncommonly heard on Pacifica Radio's morning show "Democracy Now": "We have a deep sympathy for the miseries of the farmers of France and India, and it is in solidarity with their struggles that we have come to stop the WTO!" Such language has also become part of the dominant discourses of "Global assistance": In the wake of the recent cyclone disaster that killed thousands and left hundreds of thousands homeless in Orissa, India, expressions of "sympathy and solidarity" poured in from all over the world. The *Times of India*[6] reported that the "Australian, British, German, Italian, Canadian and Dutch governments pledged help and sent messages of sympathy to the families of victims" of the cyclone; and in a message to the Lok Sabha speaker, the interparliamentary union secretary-general, Anders B. Johnsson said, "I wish to convey to you and through you to your parliament and the people of India, the IPU's solidarity, sympathy and condolences in this tragic situation." My sense is that as practices, as discourses, as forms of sociality, sympathy and solidarity have a shared history. The former is the subject of this study, but the latter haunts it.

At the most general level, this book is about how people come to think about each other, about each other's suffering, and how people act through this sympathizing subjectivity. How is it that people come to identify with another's pain, act in solidarity with others in struggle, to cooperate with others, in communities, in social movements? What is the history of this force of human cohesion? Sympathy, I will argue, was a specific form of sociality that facilitated the elaboration of various forms of power-relations. I argue in the chapters that follow that sympathy as a practice of European civilizing congealed around a particular norm of humanity, and that history is tied to a story of domination that links class struggle to antislavery, abolition, and eventually colonialism. Simultaneously, I suggest, to the side of this history, always a bit awry, "something altogether different" was taking shape; other forms of sociality, other kinds of affiliations lingered on, and were transplanted, transformed, and developed. If sympathy was a practice elaborated out of a broader civilizing mission, there are moments throughout its history when the suffering object of sympathy—for example, the slave, the prostitute, the criminal, the insane, the colonial other—throws back the gaze of pity, redirecting it as, at once, a critique of Eurocentrism and an insistence on a shared history, and the demand of a more just future. These other histories are not retrievable in any simple sense for us today. But I believe that the ethical stakes of contemporary criticism must be located in reimagining, refashioning, renarrating these other forms of sociality.

Locating Sympathy

Let us pose some interrelated questions that may orient the reader of the pages that follow. If, in the discourse of abolition, the pained body of the enslaved, brutalized, dehumanized African man or woman is put on excessive display—how does this body come to function in this mobilization for justice? How, in what ways, did sympathy come to bear the burden of this work? If sympathy is filiated to justice in abolitionism, how is it that throughout the nineteenth century it is also just as closely associated with the project of colonialism? What were the cultural, epistemological, and historical forces that animated these transferences, displacements, and rearticulations and complicities in the figure of sympathy? How shall we remember this history of sympathy? How shall we narrate its history otherwise?

But then again, does sympathy have a history? For some, the rise of European humanitarianism as a historical phenomenon can be separated from the more universal question of pity and sentiment as timeless and constituent elements of the human and of the moral life. Friedrich Nietzsche disagreed; arguing against the "pernicious modern effeminacy of feeling," Nietzsche proposed a radical questioning of the "value of pity and of the morality of pity," one that would enable a new possibility, and through which "finally a new demand becomes audible." "Let us articulate this new demand: we need a critique of moral values, the value of these values themselves must first be called into question . . ." This critique led Nietzsche to assert that "there are no moral phenomena, there is only a moral interpretation of these phenomena. This interpretation itself is of extramoral origin."[7] Rethinking this basic insight through a certain feminist critique, what we are obliged to pose, in fact, is the very gendering of moral values as a fundamental historical problem.

My sense is that, if listened to with another ear, what becomes audible in the history of sympathy is the demand of the other for a certain justice. Michel Foucault once wrote, "A genealogy of values, morality, asceticism, and knowledge will never confuse itself with a quest for their 'origins,' will never neglect as inaccessible the vicissitudes of history. On the contrary, it will cultivate the details and accidents that accompany every beginning; it will be scrupulously attentive to their petty malice; it will await their emergence, once unmasked, as the face of the other."[8] Can we discern the face of the other in the details and accidents through which sympathy emerged in eighteenth-century Europe? If this history of sympathy is tied to the creation of dominant forms of citizenship in Europe throughout the nineteenth century, how do the non-citizen, the slave, the worker, the colonized, and the woman constitute this filiation?[9] Who is this other, this unmasked face whose truth is mired in petty malice? I seek to remember these others in all their force of difference as we seek to narrate the vicissitudes of history—in different modes of "sentimental" and Gothic literary representation, in the moral thought of a certain Enlightenment, in the flows of power legible in abolitionist, social reform, and missionary discourses.

Questions of Method

These are the questions that occupy me in this discursive and historical critique of sympathy. How shall we account for the emergence, indeed possibility of such "critique"? What analytics would expose its effects? In his 1978 lecture "What is Critique?," Foucault argued that in the analysis of dominations the line of questioning through which we approach the relay between knowledge and power can no longer be posed as what error or illusion knowledge has come to induce effects of domination manifested in the hegemony of this state, or that class. Rather,

> [t]he question instead would be: how can the indivisibility of knowledge and power in the context of interactions and multiple strategies induce both singularities, fixed according to their conditions of acceptability, and a field of [possibilities], of openings, indecisions, reversals and possible dislocations which make them fragile, temporary, and which turn these effects into events, nothing more, nothing less than events?[10]

Notice, first, that Foucault emphasizes both power and its reversal, or, better, its displacement. There is, therefore, an irreducible impulse for justice in Foucault's later thought. I consider this desire for justice indispensable for an effective critique of power and knowledge. Justice as an always immanent imaginative horizon that brings knowledge—or in this case a certain knowing sensibility—to crisis. Second—and this is what would crucially problematize the emancipationist impulse—any such "release," "reversal," or "opening" will always be complicitous with that dynamic which both "induces" certain temporary conjunctions of knowledge/power and fractures its concrete strategic field of possibilities.[11] If to critique the history of sympathy is to opt strategically for a justice beyond the "Enlightenment," that critique must come to terms with its own conditions of possibility, that is, a certain enlightenment. Negotiating this structure of complicity must be part of that desire for justice, for that desire not to be governed by sympathy, not in this way. Yet this desire operates from within that history, necessarily. As Gayatri Chakravorty Spivak, glossing Derrida, once put it, "'Operating necessarily from the inside, borrowing all the strategic and economic resources of subversion from the old structure, borrowing them structurally, that is to say without being able to isolate their elements and atoms, the enterprise of deconstruction always in a certain way falls prey to its own work.' . . . This is the greatest gift of deconstruction to question the authority of the investigating subject without paralyzing him, persistently transforming conditions of impossibility into possibility."[12]

In the chapters that follow, I pursue the experience of this (im)possible gift through different critical strategies. I analyze "sympathy" as what Jacques Donzelot once called a "moving resultant, an uncertain form whose intelligibility can only come from studying the system of relations it maintains with the sociopolitical level."[13] Thus, I construct a provisional historical outline, one that both relies on the seismic economic, cultural, and political shifts in Europe at the end of the eighteenth century, and critiques that moment as the supposed birth or origin of modernity and humanitarianism. The narrative I hope to disentangle has been inspired by critical strategies developed in the thought of Michel Foucault, Jacques Derrida, and Michel de Certeau; in the insurgent, transnational, and visionary critiques of Jacqui Alexander, Audre Lorde, Paul Gilroy, bell hooks, Ranajit Guha, Gyan Prakash, and Gayatri Chakravorty Spivak; in the feminists ruptures wrought through the works of Joan Scott, Judith Butler, Patricia Clough, Ann Stoler, Eve Sedgewick, Mary Poovey, and Chandra Mohanty. They have all taught me that writing history is a risky process. One must be vigilant of the categories and tools that history has bequeathed us: To practice a writing of history that is always open to a persistent critique, one that can recognize in its own failures other possibilities, and so other futures.

Michel de Certeau wrote in *The Writing of History* that today "the *relation* to the real has changed. And if meaning cannot be apprehended in the form of a specific knowledge that would either be drawn from the real or might be added to it, it is because every 'historical fact' results from a praxis, because it is already a sign of an act and therefore a statement of meaning. It results from procedures which have allowed a mode of comprehension to be articulated as a discourse of 'facts.'"[14] In this study, I try to avoid the straight line or closed circle that would fix the meaning of sympathy in a circuit that would run from, say, Jamaica through England, on to India and back to the Caribbean.[15] Instead, I have tried to reconstruct a more complicated, overlapping network of practices, communities, institutions, and discourses that are always haunted by the history of the other, by history's other.

An awareness of such haunting, that there is "something altogether different" behind the face of things, has also drawn me to a genealogical analysis of the career of sentiment in England and its colonies.[16] My aim in this genealogical analysis of sympathy as a mode of power is to problematize the very concept of historical and civilizational progress, as well as to extend the received relationship[17] between practice and discourse. Waking us from the anesthesia of naturalized sentiments, Michel Foucault remarked that "We believe that feelings are immutable, but every sentiment, particularly the noblest and most disinterested, has a history. We believe in the dull constancy of instinctual life and imagine that it continues to exert its force indiscriminately in the present as it did in the past" (87). Using discursive practice as a historiographical tool, Foucault was able to write the history of prisons, madness, clinics, and sexuality as genealogies. Such genealogies recorded "the singularity of events outside of any monotonous finality; it must seek them in the most unpromising places, in what we tend to feel is without history—in sentiments, love, conscience, instincts; it must be sensitive to their recurrence, not in order to trace the gradual curve of their evolution, but to isolate the different scenes where they engaged in different roles. Finally, genealogy must define even those instances when they are absent, the moment when they remained unrealized."[18] Genealogy, being without "constants" (87), rejects the metahistorical deployment of ideal significations and indefinite teleologies (the supposed goal of humanity, humanization, civilization, for instance). Moreover, genealogy opposes itself to the search for "origins" (77) because the pursuit of the origin is an attempt to capture the exact essence of things, their purest possibilities, and their carefully protected identities; because this search assumes the existence of immobile, transhistorical, transcendent forms (such as sympathy or humanitarianism) that precede the external world of accident and succession. "However," Foucault continues, "if the genealogist refuses to extend his faith in metaphysics, if he listens to history, he finds that there is 'something altogether different' behind things: not a timeless and essential secret, but the secret that they have no essence and that their essence was fabricated in a piecemeal fashion from alien forms" (78). To approach the history of sympathy genealogically then is to situate discourses and practices in contexts that effectively disrupts linear, progressivist narratives of the emergence of European humanitarianism. The genealogies that follow suggest that the other is that ghosted presence that shadows the birth of the enlightened human.

But, as I signaled above, such refusals and reversals will remain just that until an historical discourse can come to terms with its own complicities—those traces that "bear evidence of former structurings and forgotten histories." All of the sympathy or solidarity with the other that I may have cannot transcend the essential instability of the historical enterprise. This is what Michel de Certeau once warned:

> Historians are in an unstable position. If they award priority to an "objective" result, if they aim to posit the reality of a former society in their discourse and animate forgotten figures, they nonetheless recognize in their recomposition the orders and effects of their own work. The discourse destined to express what is *other* remains *their* discourse and the *mirror* of their own labors. Inversely, when they refer to their own practices and examine their postulates in order to innovate, therein historians discover constraints originating well before their own present, dating back to former organizations of which their work is a symptom, not a cause. . . . Thus founded on the rupture between a past that is its object, and a present that is the place of its practice, history endlessly finds the present in its object and the past in its practice. Inhabited by the uncanniness that it seeks, history imposes its law upon the faraway places that it conquers when it fosters the illusion that it is bringing them back to life.[19]

To write another memory of sympathy, sympathetically, is to locate oneself necessarily within this uncanniness, this essential strangeness. It is that enabling space of complicity through which we begin to imagine in the past the possibility of another future.

The Structure of the Argument

This book is a social and historical critique of sympathy in British discourse in the late eighteenth and early nineteenth century. Although initially associated with "feminized" or effeminate forms of sentimental discourse (the romance, the novel, the Gothic), sympathy came to function as a key "technology" of gender and race in new evangelical social movements, such as abolitionism and missionizing. I analyze this shift in the gendering of sympathy as it became a form of European power, that is, as it was deployed in discursive and material practices. Crucially, these practices functioned through processes of identification. To sympathize with another, one must identify with that other. But sympathy, as I show, was a paradoxical mode of power. The differences of racial, gender, and class inequalities that increasingly divided the object and agent of sympathy were precisely what must be bridged through identification. Yet without such differences, which were differences of power, sympathy itself would be impossible: In a specific sense, sympathy produces the very inequalities it decries and seeks to bridge. I argue that this paradoxical mode of power transformed the ways in which people came to think of how best to manage, order, and govern individuals and populations in the late eighteenth century. By critically adapting Michel Foucault's work on "governmentality," I narrate the development of sympathy as a set of related practices, or protocols of surveillance, normalization, and subject production (identity formation) in discourse, institutions, religion, and government. The use of sympathy as a form of governmentality was nowhere more conspicuous than in the mobilizations and reforms that dominated the political, economic, and social agenda in Britain from the late eighteenth century on. As a mode of power, sympathy tied together subjects, families, communities, classes, nations, races, and colonies in a kind of acrobatics of identification and differentiation. Sympathy, in other words, as a principle of sociality and cohesion. Moreover, as a form of subjectivity sympathy was instrumental in launching projects of marking off populations in need of benevolence, and thus of normalizing subjects into better citizens, in the home, for the nation, for the empire. Sympathy, then, as a mechanism of differentiation and normalization. During this period, sentiment, literature, art, benevolence, pity, charity, justice, education, pleasure, amusement, discipline, and amelioration were all concepts that relied in one way or another on the practice of sympathy. *Rule of Sympathy* analyzes this reticulated field of signs, subjectivities, discourses, practices, and institutions as a "dialectic"—in the sense of "the movement of relations among different procedures on the same stage, and not in the sense of the power assigned to a particular place to totalize or 'surmount' these differences."[20] I argue that sympathy was central in the overthrow of colonial slavery, the project of evangelizing India, and the "redeeming" of the laboring classes in England. In all these mobilizations, across these disparate cultural contexts, I argue that social sympathy was a way of establishing affinities as relations of power. I piece together this history of sympathy by considering its diverse deployment in literary and moral philosophical discourse, social and religious mobilizations, class(ed) reformism, and territorial expansion.[21] *Rule of Sympathy* analyzes this imbricated field in order to tell another history of European bourgeois sympathy, that is the history of sympathy's other.

Rule of Sympathy is divided into four chapters. In the first two chapters, I trace the emergence of sympathy as a practical form of self-governing by focusing on the "sentimental" subject of sympathy in moral philosophical discourse. In chapter one, "Sympathetic Governmentality: The Traces of Religion and the Family," I situate my history of sympathy in relationship to forms of governing, drawing on Michel Foucault's theory of governmentality.

I argue that Foucault's brilliant displacement of the state in analyses of rule after mercantilism is constituted by the exclusion of the family-as-model from his theory of governing populations. I suggest that the family, as both model and target of disciplinary and security regimes of power, exerted a very particular force on the social imaginary of governing after 1750. Thus, I urge a rethinking of the relationship between strategies of domination, the family and the emergence of sympathy. In chapter two, "The Rules of Sympathy," gendered figurations of sentimentalism, the aesthetic theory of the sublime, and medical theories of sympathy guide my discussion of the dislocations and displacements of sympathy in the moral philosophy of David Hume and Adam Smith and the aesthetic theory of Edmund Burke. Teasing out the civilizational anxieties around difference, inequality, and justice that haunt the scenes of sympathy in these texts, I argue that another demand is audible, another principle of sociality is promised and betrayed in the play of identification and differentiation, one that could be named solidarity. In chapter three, "'Some Inscrutable Appeal': Race, Gender, and the Closure of Sentimentalism," I locate the sentimental and gothic novels of the eighteenth century in a trajectory that relates questions of gender and race in Charlotte Brontë's *Jane Eyre* with, for instance, nature, class, and property in what many critics call Europe's "first novel," Richardson's *Pamela.*

In the last chapter, "Theaters of Horror," I show how sympathy was central in the project of humanizing the Slave, and civilizing the Other—sympathy was the midwife at the birth of European humanitarianism. Here, I analyze political, evangelical, abolitionist, and missionary discourses in terms of the rhetoric of sentimentalism and the production of normalized subjects of empire. I trace this multiple genealogy of sympathy, horror, and sentiment as a mode of governmentality and a rhetorical style in the parliamentary debates around the abolition of the slave trade (1804–1807) and the renewal of the British East India Charter (1813). I draw forth the "petty malice," secret concessions, and strategic silences that constitute these debates, and show how evangelical reformism had come to rely on a certain "gothic" practice of sympathetic identification. Linking analyses of the works of Anthony Benezet, John Wesley, and Thomas Coke, with the ex-slave narratives of Olaudah Equiano, Mary Prince, and Ottobah Cugoano, I historicize their moment in terms of massive slave revolts, colonial consolidation in India and colonial fragmentation in America, and, of course, the French Revolution. My analysis in this chapter is informed by counter-memories of sympathy in the ex-slave narratives. I insist that if sympathy was a form of European power, then it did not go unchallenged; the question of justice in slave communities was posed through practices that were both negotiations with and ex-centric to European forms of sympathy. Moving through and beyond the archive, I imaginatively reconstruct those tactics that never enjoyed the "precondition . . . of having their own place (*un lieu propre*)" on the stage of power.[22] It is this necessarily ambivalent form of engagement that I take up in this chapter.[23]

✎   ✎   ✎

I end this preface with a word on what this book is not, or, better, what it does not attempt to do. First, in *Rule of Sympathy* I do not attempt to tell the history of Evangelicalism in the Caribbean, England, or India. That is a much larger project, but one that impinges on all aspects of this work. Rather, I focus on specific Nonconformist sects (for example, Methodists and Baptists), marking their particular historical contexts and the use and elaboration of sympathetic relations. Second, this study doesn't comprise all of Europe. The important contexts of, for example, eighteenth-century French sentimentalism or early nineteenth-century German romanticism do not receive the full treatment they deserve. Instead, I try to situate a kind of colonial circuit that in some senses passes through Europe but whose nexus is in Britain. Finally, my aim in this study was not to archive "native culture" or "slave communities" in terms of their resistances and/or complicities with European sympathy. Again, that is a very different project, one which, frankly, I am not much interested in. What I have tried to do, however, is consider the ways in which a form of elite sociality—that is, European sympathy—was transformed, manipulated, reversed, and displaced by those who spoke in voices and through tactics that take us beyond simply archiving the other of sympathy.

And yet, to archive sympathy. One of the etymological roots of the term archive, the Greek *arkheion,* means house, magisterial residence, public office, and also town hall; it derives from *arkhé,* "government," and *arkhein,* "to rule."[24] Perhaps to tell the history of sympathy as it was fashioned into a relation of governing, as it was bodied forth in diffuse practices of sociality that no rule could entirely enclose or comprehend, is to imagine a form of storytelling that traverses metropoles and colonies, town halls and fields, the oral and the textual, the past and other futures? Why, after all, tell the story of sympathy in this way? Why tell the history of European self-fashioning through the circuitous routes of others? In writing this book, most of all, I think, I wanted to live another memory. Again I follow others here. Gyan Prakash, drawing on Nietzsche, has recently remarked that such an imaginative reconstruction of another past enables a critical, disjunctive, heterogenous history "from which we *might* spring."[25] The following pages, then, are written in this spirit of another memory of self-fashioning, another wisdom of the body and its pain, pleasures, longings, sensualities, another time for love, struggle, and community.

Chapter One

Sympathetic Governmentality

The Traces of Religion and the Family

I begin with a set of orienting questions. In what ways was sympathy a style of rule? How did sympathy draw on earlier practices of governing while attracting and propagating new kinds of sensibilities, knowledges and relations of power seemingly exogenous to it? What is at stake here is how we conceptualize the very role of humanitarianism in the new capitalist-colonial order in England and the colonies. Given the temporal coincidence between the rise of abolition and capitalism, historians have asked, Was humanitarian sympathy a way of diverting criticism from the "enormities" of industrialization? Or was it a genuine response to the suffering of slaves, Indians, and then, later, workers? Was the sympathy of abolitionist men and women (who were, to a remarkable degree, intimately connected to the ever-widening circuits of industrial and finance capital) a "highly selective response to labor exploitation," as David Brion Davis once argued?[1] Not only the role of humanitarianism but its very structure, practice, and discursive reticulations are at stake here.

I consider the possibilities opened by these questions in the context of Michel Foucault's reformulation of notions of state and power as "governmentality." For, in an essential way, sympathy was about better governing: governing the self, the other, one's family, society, and nation such that a new and preeminent principle of cohesion would ensure the stability of the new dispensation. In what follows, I trace Foucault's elaboration of the arts of governing populations, arguing that his relegation of the model of the family in political practice is predicated on a kind of secularist bias, one that cannot account for the emergence of and transformations in Evangelical paternalism. This is especially pronounced when we turn to contexts of racial domination in the West Indies or India. Since I elaborate the colonial contexts of sympathetic governance at length in subsequent chapters, here I elaborate the specific implications of Foucault's argument.

Displacing the State:
Governmentality and Modes of Power

In a lecture delivered in February 1978, Foucault argued for a shift in analyses of the state. "We all know," he said, "the fascination which the love, or horror, of the state exercises today; we know how much attention is paid to the genesis of the state, its history, its advance, its power and abuses, etc." Not surprisingly, there is a general tendency to overvalue the problem of the state, "one which is paradoxical because apparently reductionist: it is the form of analysis that consists in reducing that state to a certain number of functions, . . . and yet this reductionist vision of the relative importance of the state's role nevertheless invariably renders it absolutely essential as a target needing to be attacked and a privileged position needing to be occupied." Foucault counters, "But the state, no more probably today than at any other time in its history, does not have this unity, this individuality, this rigorous functionality, nor, to speak frankly, this importance; maybe, after all, the state is no more than a composite reality and mythicized abstraction, whose importance is a lot more limited than many of us think. Maybe what is really important for our modernity—that is, for our present—is not so much the étatisation of society, as the 'governmentality' of the state."[2] Such a shift entails a massive estrangement of analyses of power; instead of a centered locus of legitimate violence, one is able to pose questions that dehisce this unity, and re-member other sources and dynamics of force relations, other sites of counter-discourse, and ex-centric practices. Let us follow Foucault further in his elaboration.

In sixteenth- and seventeenth-century Europe, Foucault asserts, the art of government linked the prince (or ruler) to the people through the modality of a science of the police, Polizeiwissenschaft (although, as Colin Gordon makes clear, the English word "policy" would better translate this concept),[3] and a metaphorics of the government of the family, termed economy. Through an epistemic rupture, the "word 'economy,' which in the sixteenth century signified a form of government, comes in the eighteenth century to designate a level of reality, a field of intervention, through a series of complex processes that I regard as absolutely fundamental to our history."[4] This signals a shift in the definition of government: Instead of leading to the form of the common good, it is now the right manner of disposing of things so as to lead to an end that is "convenient" for each of the things that are to be governed (95)—a new kind of finality, one which resides in the things to be managed, is born. What this enables is a proliferation of the instruments of government—instead of only laws, a range of multiform tactics are developed.[5] Significant for our understanding of eighteenth-century regimes of racial and economic domination, Foucault asserts it is under mercantilism that new savoirs of state, or "rationalizations of the exercise of power as a practice of government," proliferate.

But mercantilism[6] was caught within two incompatible logics: the "inordinately vast, abstract, rigid framework of the problem and institution of sovereignty," that sought a way to allow the ruler to accumulate wealth, and an art of government that relied on a model "which was too thin, too weak, and too insubstantial, that of the family" (98). It was the destiny, as it were, of "population" to break this deadlock. Emerging at the conjuncture of a number of macrological processes (demographic shifts, an abundance of money for some, expansion of agricultural production, not to mention, and, typically Foucault doesn't, abolition, colonial expansion, and the exploitation of natural and human resources around the globe), the problem of population made possible the "derestriction" of the art of government by "finally eliminating" the family as model and the recentering of the notion of economy (99). The family "now disappears as the model of government, except for a certain number of residual themes of a religious or moral nature. What, on the other hand, now emerges into prominence is the family considered as an element internal to population, and a fundamental instrument in government" (99). I simply mark a strategic exclusion: "residual themes of a religious or moral nature."[7]

This new savoir (absolute knowledge) of state, then, with statistics as its science and population as its target, incorporates policing techniques of discipline and security. Indeed, discipline was never more important to manage a population, because managing a population not only concerns the "collective mass of phenomena, the level of its aggregate effects," it also entails the tactical administration of populations in their depths and details. For Foucault, this proliferation of the tactics of governmentality "renders all the more acute the problem of the foundation of sovereignty . . . and all the more acute equally the necessity for the development of discipline . . ." (102).

> Accordingly, we need to see things not in terms of the replacement of a society of sovereignty by a disciplinary society and the subsequent replacement of a disciplinary society by a society of government; in reality one has a triangle, sovereignty-discipline-government, which has as its primary target the population and as its essential mechanism the apparatuses of security. . . . I wanted to demonstrate the deep historical link between the movement that

overturns the constants of sovereignty in consequence of the problem of choices of government, the movement that brings about the emergence of population as a datum, as a field of intervention and as an objective of governmental techniques, and the process which isolates the economy as a specific sector of reality, and political economy as the science and the technique of intervention of the government in that field of reality. Three movements: government, population, political economy, which constitutes from the eighteenth century onwards a solid series, one which even today has assuredly not been dissolved. (102)

If Western modernity is constituted through this triangulation of subjection (and subjection here should be understood as both that which subjects, or constrains, and that which enables subjectivity), if population emerges as a problem only at the moment when the family as model is displaced, Foucault's argument, as a history of "our" present, opens up a field of analysis that (1) reposes the question of the state and its power at the level of its conditions of possibility; (2) disperses both in terms of multiform tactics, and its heterogeneous target; (3) rejoins knowledges (savoirs of state, political economy, statistics, psychology, history, ethnology, moral philosophy, etc.), and various strategies of power (security, discipline, sovereignty, biopolitics) with the emergence of the subject (as a member of specific, fixable, knowable, proper families, populations, civilizations, nations, races)—within an overall analysis of disciplinary regimes of governmentality.

In "Society must be Defended," Foucault outlines the implications of this strategy clearly:

In order to conduct a concrete analysis of power relations, one would have to abandon the juridical notion of sovereignty. That model presupposes the individual as subject of natural rights or original powers; it aims to account for the ideal genesis of the state; and it makes law the fundamental manifestation of power. One would have to study power not on the basis of the primitive terms of the relation but starting from the relation itself, inasmuch as the relation is what determines the elements on which it bears: instead of asking ideal subjects what part of themselves or what powers of theirs they have surrendered, allowing themselves to be subjectified [*se laisser assujetir*], one would need to inquire how relations of subjectivation can manufacture subjects. Similarly, rather than looking for the single form, the central point from which all forms of power would be derived by way of consequence or development, one must first let them stand forth in their multiplicity, their differences, their specificity, their reversibility: study them therefore as relations of force that intersect, interrelate, converge, or, on the contrary, oppose one another or tend to cancel each other out. Finally, instead of privileging law as a manifestation of power, it would be better to try and identify the different techniques of constraint that it brings into play.[8]

As we shall see, an analysis of sympathy on the terrain of Euro-colonial governmentality necessarily entails a tireless solicitation—both an appeal to and a displacement—of the subject and its identifications. But moreover, this analysis of the new arts of governing populations and subjects necessitates a radical rethinking of our contemporary practices of historiography. We would be obliged, I think, to situate relations of force, those quotidian webs of discourse and materiality that are really the sinews of the subject, as the objects of our analyses, if not our desire. We must trace carefully, meticulously the multiplicity, the differences, the specificity, and the reversibility of these relations across the ruptures and continuities in regimes of domination. Indeed, such a strategy, Foucault suggests, would enable us to understand anew the very present of our Western modernity.

Reframing Governmentality:
Colonialism, Religion, and the Family

And yet we know today that Western modernity was never itself, and it was never less so than under the laughing gaze of Michel Foucault. If we are able to push Foucault in other directions, it will be because those possibilities will have always already haunted his text. Almost as though revenants from a history he could never name were come to life again. Which would, of course, not leave Foucault's text unsullied or pure, it may even blur it to the point of nonrecognition.

In an attempt to think at this limit, I would suggest that Western governmentality, as Foucault understood it, in fact constituted itself through a number of different overlapping modalities that effected a certain "tropicalization."[9] First, a global apparatus of security created a kind of relay of power, discourse, and institutional practices between metropole and colony. This relay of domination grew more and more hysterical as well as total, at least in its aspirations, after the Indian Mutiny of 1857 and the Morant Bay uprising in 1865. Second, the elaboration of racial and sexual discipline organized subjectivity around an ethic of purity. These were, in effect, pedagogies of colonial masculinity and femininity coiled around the "horror" of miscegenation and the "infection" of otherness. As we shall see, this horror assumed a near absolute status in the wake of the strategic redeployment of utilitarianism and evangelicalism on the terrain of the colony. And, finally, the emergence of grids of (proto)ethnographic *savoir,* which, building on eighteenth-century (mis)conceptions of "national character," in the nineteenth, taxonomized other peoples through the elaboration of a racist biology, and the deployment of a normative (that is, Western) Civilization. These multiform and mobile tactics of government created a style of domination that seemed perfectly adapted to the essence of the other. Of course, these stratified essences were themselves produced through a metalepsis (taking an effect for a cause): The "genius" or "character" of "regional" populations produced through ethnographic practices became the seemingly solid foundation for empire. But if the self-consolidating *Others* of Western democracy—for example, Oriental despotism or African slavery—became key *instruments* in colonial governmentality, this process itself figured a specifically colonial mode of governance (which would have profound implications for the ways in which workers were to be governed). This discourse on despotism and slavery was also the site of possibly the most ironic tranfer(ence)s of power: The colonial state legitimized its own system of sometimes forced, sometimes waged slavery by assimilating Oriental despotism to itself as "paternal despotism" (this was John Stuart Mill's phrase for British colonial rule).[10]

Such are the possibilities that a rethinking of Foucault enables. But as we turn to specific historical contexts, we must be as critical of the tools we use as we are of the objects of our criticism. Thus, although the implications of a critical genealogy of global governmentality are indeed immense, here I would like to highlight two overlapping problematics that persistently haunt Foucault's analysis, that of secularization and the family. Interrogating religious contexts and family discourses as key cites for the construction of gender inequality and the renegotiation of citizenship allows us to take a critical distance from Foucauldian thought even as we strategically engage aspects of that very thought. Needless to say, a certain complicity is irreducible here.

Now, the elaboration of the police, Foucault insists, emerges at the very moment of a kind of "secular critique" of power. Governmentality, oddly enough, is born with the decision "not to be governed," or as Foucault more carefully phrases it in another lecture,[11] "how not to be governed like that, by that, in the name of those principles, with such and such an objective in mind and by means of such procedures, not like that, not for that, not by them" (28). This question itself is bound up, even as a refusal or displacement, in the obscure history of the "art of governing men."

There was an explosion in two ways: first, by displacement in relation to the religious center, let's say if you will, secularization, the expansion in civil society of this theme of the art of governing men and the methods of doing it; and then, second, the proliferation of this art of governing into a variety of areas—how to govern children, how to govern the poor and beggars, how to govern a family, a house, how to govern armies, different groups, cities, States and also how to govern one's own body and mind. . . . So, this governmentalization, which seems to me to be rather characteristic of these societies in Western Europe in the 16th century, cannot apparently be dissociated from the question "how not to be governed?" . . . I mean that, in this great preoccupation about the way to govern and the search for the ways to govern, we identify a perpetual question which would be: "how not to be governed like that, by that, in the name of those principles, with such and such an objective in mind and by means of such procedures, not like that, not for that, not by them." And if we accord this movement of governmentalization of both society and individuals the historic dimension and breadth which I believe it has had, it seems that one could approximately locate therein what we could call the critical attitude. (27–28)

Let us note first that this moment of governmentalization also marks the moment of emergence of the critical attitude for Foucault. Foucault gives us a hint of this productive confusion when he argues that among the historical "anchoring" points for the emergence of critique (the others being jurisprudence or law, and truth or the authority of dogma) is, in fact, the Bible: " . . . from Wycliffe to Pierre Bayle, critique developed in part, for the most part, but not exclusively, of course, in relation to the Scriptures. Let us say that critique is biblical, historically" (30). If so, then could we say that the evangelicalization of European society and politics in the eighteenth and nineteenth century, as well as the extensions, reversals, and displacements of this process in the abolitionist and missionary discourses, were at least in part critical responses to the governmentalization of colony and metropole? I want to tease out the implications of this complication, but in a very specific sense: I will argue in what follows that sympathy named "a spiritual art," which must be situated in a certain refusal or challenge to the right of the (colonial or racist) state, the role of the (utility maximizing) citizen, and the authority of dogma; *at the same time,* as one of the residual "arts of governing," the sympathetic relation received a fresh impetus in the eighteenth century through the elaboration of bourgeois civil society and the expansion of colonial regimes of racial domination, and was thus integrated into overall strategies of governmentality. We can see this contradictory history clearly in the rise of missionary colonialism in India in the late eighteenth and early nineteenth centuries. What is too often forgotten in this history is that missionizing and Christianity in general were key sites of conflict *within* the colonial apparatus. Thus, with the rise of British dominance in Bengal in the latter half of the eighteenth century, an entirely new form of Christian agency was unevenly integrated into various practices of governing (or "improving") the self, colonial peoples, the family, sexuality, commerce, and the nation—and this fundamentally transformed the relationship among Christian colonizer, heathen native, and the colonial project.

Second, turning to the question of the family, we are again confronted by the long shadow of Foucault. Following his own work on the history of sexuality and population, scholars have largely corroborated Foucault's arguments on the creation and proliferation of "sexual knowledge" in Europe from the late eighteenth century on.[12] Staying within the French context for a moment, Jacques Donzelot has argued that under "the *ancien régime,* there was a continuity between public power and familial power, on in any case, an implicit homology. . . . This position of the family would gradually disappear in the nineteenth century . . . as a consequence of transformations brought about by individuals or groupings who were entirely representative of the new, so-called bourgeois, order."[13] Donzelot goes on to outline a whole matrix of practices that would transform the family from both the inside—"from the propagation within it of medical, educative, and relational norms whose over-all aim was to preserve children from the old customs"—and the outside—by the modification of family law. In terms of this later transformation:

> The ancient and monolithic authority of the father gave place to a dual regime, which took the form of a simple alternative: either the system of tutelage, or that of the contract. The former is for social categories that combine a difficulty in supplying their own needs with resistances to the new medical and educative norms. In essence, tutelage means that these families will be stripped of all effective rights and brought into a relation of dependence vis-à-vis welfare and educative agents. The contractual system—for the others—corresponds to an accelerated liberalization of relations, both within and outside the family. Here, norms are joined . . . to a liberal law that fluidifies the family.[14]

That the family became "an element internal to population, and a fundamental instrument in government" cannot be doubted today. But one could also understand the term tutelage and the entire apparatus of philanthropic intervention that Donzelot names social economy as new form of "paternalism." What I am suggesting is that the family was not "eliminated" (nor was it reduced to a "residual theme"—itself a telling phrase)[15] as a model of government. And this for two crucial reasons. First, as Lynn Hunt pointed out in the case of the social imaginary of Revolutionary France, the discourse of the family as model for rule continued to have salience even under circumstances where the "Father-King" was no longer present (as in Republican France).[16] Second, there is the question of the very formation of European subjectivity in and through discourses of colonial paternalism. As Ann Stoler asked in her study of Foucault and the colonial order of things, "Why, for Foucault, [do] colonial bodies never figure as a possible site of the articulation of nineteenth-century European sexuality? And given this omission, what are the consequences for his treatment of racism in the making of the European bourgeois self?"[17] Extending this suggestive line of questioning, I will argue that in the colonial ordering of the West Indies and India, paternalism as a model, the family as an object, and "domestic affection" as an instrument were all central to the practices of governing populations. Moreover, the arguments around "benevolent despotism" in India or the paternalism of the West Indian plantation owner had important implications for how industrial and agricultural laborers were going to be dealt with. In other words, paternal sentimentality demarcated an entire field of global intervention through a taxonomy of the affections, and this discursive practice was itself a pedagogy of colonial subject formation: Sympathy was both a model and instrument of governmentality. Can one say that the eventual defeat of Whig oligarchic paternalism (and we must radically qualify such a "defeat" when for much of the nineteenth century the landed gentry were clearly the dominant class), and the displacement of practices of rule associated with it, created new outlets in the emergence of sympathy as a form of governmentality?

Consider the relationship between the family and nationhood in certain colonial discourses. Ann McClintock has marked the ideological complicities in the relationship among nation, family, and power thus:

> The family trope is important for nationalism in at least two ways. First, it offers a "natural" figure for sanctioning national *hierarchy* within a putative organic *unity* of interests. Second, it offers a "natural" trope for figuring national time. After 1859 and the advent of social Darwinism, Britain's emergent national narrative took shape increasingly around the image of the evolutionary family of man. The family offered an indispensable metaphoric figure by which national difference could be shaped into a single historical genesis narrative. Yet a curious paradox emerged. The family as a *metaphor,* offered a single genesis narrative for national history while, at the same time, the family as an *institution* became void of history and excluded from national power. The family became, at one and the same time, both the *organizing figure* for national history and its *antithesis.*[18]

Following this line of argumentation, Gyan Prakash has noted how, in Gandhian nationalism, kinship and territoriality "were bound together to constitute India as a radically different ethical order from the modern West. Rejecting the brute force, machinery, greed, and violence associated with Western modernity, Gandhi envisioned India as a family bound by love."[19] For Prakash, governmentality-as-kinship articulated anticolonial nationalism's unique "alternative principle of governance."

Extending the implications of these argument, I would suggest that Foucault's own elimination of the family from the history of Western governmentality is an effect of a certain tradition of national(ist) historiography. On the contrary, the continued salience of the family as it was imbricated with the new art of governing populations is why, precisely, it is the site of paradox and ambivalence. Through discourses and strategies Foucault maps out, and through others he eliminates (religion, for instance), the family became at once a laboratory of subjection (producing/policing subjects and populations), a model of racial governance, and, perhaps not so strangely, the site of numerous contradictory counter-strategies. If the family, as pastoral utopia, was a refuge from the "unfeeling" cash-nexus colonizing the world, it also was the model of romantic and even utilitarian social critique and reform. Uncannily transforming from pastoral utopia to a site of domestic horror, the patriarchal family was also the model of political tyranny. As John Stuart Mill famously put it in his "protofeminist" tract, *The Subjection of Women,* "Not a word can be said for despotism in the family which cannot be said for political despotism."

> In domestic as in political tyranny, the case of absolute monsters chiefly illustrates the institution by showing that there is scarcely any horror which may not occur under it if the despot pleases, and thus setting in a strong light what must be the terrible frequency of things only a little less atrocious. Absolute fiends are as rare as angels, perhaps rarer: ferocious savages, with occasional touches of humanity, are however very frequent: and in the wide interval which separates these from any worthy representatives of the human species, how many are the forms and gradations of animalism and selfishness, often under an outward varnish of civilisation and even cultivation, living at peace with the law, maintaining a creditable appearance to all who are not under their power, yet sufficient often to make the lives of all who are so, a torment and a burthen to them![20]

That Mill could speak with seeming authority on despots, savages, and humanity in both the domestic and political arenas was due, in large part, to his own experience as an employee of the British East India Company. Through all his vicissitudes, Mill never lost sight of that fundamental insight of utilitarian thought (which was itself drawn from eighteenth-century moral sense philosophy) that the greatest good is founded on the stability of the domestic affections. Both at home and in the colonies what was at stake in the discourse of the family was the creation of a particular kind of citizen. Indeed, if we turn for a moment to other colonial contexts, Foucault's elimination of the family from the question of governmentality becomes even more fraught. In her recent study, *States of Sympathy: Seduction and Democracy in the American Novel,* Elizabeth Barnes argues that

> [s]ympathetic identification—the act of imagining oneself in another's position—signified a narrative model whereby readers could ostensibly be taught an understanding of the interdependence between their own and others' identities. In a time when American national as well as individual identity was in question, it is not surprising that American literature brought such issues as identification, unification, diversity, and autonomy so directly to the

fore. Sympathetic identification—one of the foremost elements of sentimental literature—works to demonstrate, even to *enact,* a correspondence or unity between subjects. In American literature sympathetic identification relies particularly on familial models. Readers are taught to identify with characters in such a way that they come to think of others—even fictional "others"—as somehow related to themselves.[21]

As a performance of identification, sympathy relates subjects through a "familial" bond of citizenship; the fashioning of such a citizen, indeed such a nation, through sympathy and sentimentalism set the parameters of the hegemonic field of the patriarchal state (Barnes, 13). In eighteenth-century American political, philosophical, and literary discourses "sympathy—the act of imagining oneself in another's position—is contingent upon familiarity." If the reader is to engage in sympathetic identification, others must be shown to be like the reader. In a sense, sympathy is both the expression of familiarity and the vehicle through which familiarity is created. Sympathetic identification emerges in eighteenth-century America, then, as the definitive way of reading literature and practicing human relations. As Barnes notes, for disgruntled colonists, it defines national interests as well: "To read sympathetically becomes synonymous with reading like an American." In the variety of literary, philosophical, and political texts she analyzes, we see the extent to which sentiment and sympathy pervade early national culture; in all three genres, sociopolitical issues are cast as family dramas, a strategy that ultimately renders public policy an essentially private matter. Which also implied that private matters should be a concern for public policy. Barnes notes that the conversion of the political into the personal, or the public into the private, "is a distinctive trait of sentimentalism; its influence is made plain in the postrevolutionary and antebellum eras where *family stands as the model for social and political affiliation.* In American fiction and nonfiction alike, familial feeling proves the foundation for sympathy, and sympathy the foundation of democracy. For American authors, a democratic state is a sympathetic state, and a sympathetic state is one that resembles a family."[22]

I believe, with the proper provisos, one can adapt Barnes's argument for a British context. It was in England, after all, that the cult of sentimentalism, sympathetic humanitarianism, and the moral philosophy of sympathy first took hold in the late eighteenth century. But in almost all these contexts, one cannot help but notice the profound impact and continuing influence of religious, specifically Evangelical thought on British modes of governmentality after 1750—such that even when the modern scientific spirit seemed finally to have become dominant (let us say, somewhat arbitrarily, around 1865) the givenness of the normative human was itself partly an effect of a crucial religious genealogy. (I elaborate the contours of this religious genealogy in the following chapters.) Now, this other context of constructing a viable transition from sovereignty and mercantilism necessitates a thoroughgoing displacement of any opposition between governmentality and the family. Indeed, as Foucault's later work enables us to see so well, the family, as the central incubator of sympathy (and sentimentalism more broadly), is absolutely crucial for the art of governing—without the one, the other could not be named.

In the chapters that follow, I analyze the triangulation that links histories of race, metaphors of family, and practices of governmentality through a form of universal, humanized kinship: sympathy. I hope to show how the familial model of power is reticulated with *savoirs* of state: sympathetic discourses on the connections between property, marriage, kinship structure, race, class, family, and religion. In short, what this means in terms of our re-situating governmentality is that (1) the family continued to be a powerfully effective model of government, even as new techniques of managing populations used the family as an instrument of discipline. The explosion in population through the course of the long eighteenth century, with its concomitant rise in illegitimacy and prenuptial sex in England, is certainly tied to the targeting of the family as an object of new disciplines and pedagogies[23]—indeed, in what follows, I will attempt to think the phantom life of this "moral or religious" trace as the structural unconscious of governmentality. (2) In differing colonial contexts (South Asia, and the Caribbean, for instance) the family, traversed as it is with gender, sexual, class, racial, and caste pedagogies, has exerted a profound force not only on the national political imaginary but also on the very structures of that polity, so much so that no effective analysis of power relations can risk neglecting it. The challenge in all this is to trace carefully the ways in which these nascent global regimes of capitalist accumulation both adapted and transformed the family (as model and object of governance) through new and ambivalent forms of subjection. Tracing the effects of these proliferating circuits enables us to think beyond the state/community binary, and to begin to chart specific community practices that exist in disjunctive relation to the practices of governmentality. As I will show, the family became the strategic site for the emergence of a general attitude of evangelical critique (abolitionism, social and educational reformism, missionary discourses) both within Europe and its (often feminized) "possessions."

Let us summarize the argument and conclude. Adapting Foucault's narrative of the emergence and proliferation of a new savoir of state, one that had statistics as its science and population as its target, and that incorporates policing techniques of discipline and security, I have argued for a certain displacement and rethinking. If with the defeat of mercantilism we can say that the family was rearticulated and redeployed in techniques of discipline and security, in certain religious or nonsecular discourses and practices (such as Evangelicalism, and, by extension, antislavery and missionary colonialism), the family assumed an importance that would have profound implications for practices of governmentality. For instance, in the sympathetic relation. As we shall see, for evangelists, abolitionists, missionaries, reformers, novelists, and moral philosophers, the family was the preeminent work space for the functioning of sympathy. As it became a vehicle for new pedagogies of control and the elaboration of citizenship, a historically crucial shift took place: The sympathetic relation, as the first of all domestic affections, became a model and an instrument for a newly atomizing class-society and a rapidly consolidating empire (and not always, as we shall see, in opposition to market socialization). Finally, the metaphor of family also became part of counter-discourses, critiques, and strategic displacements. As "a spiritual art," sympathy could be a kind of refusal or challenge to capitalist norms, colonial culture, or even Anglican hegemony. This conceptual framework, then, operating under the double displacement of a gender and nonsecular critique, opens the possibility for understanding the role of sympathy both as an art of governing and a mode of critique; both as an emergent practice of sociality and the production of a new citizen-subject. It enables, in other words, another memory of sympathy.

Chapter Two

The Rules of Sympathy

The piecemeal fashioning of a global apparatus of colonial governmentality was nowhere more prolific than in the mobilizations and reforms that dominated the political, economic, and social agenda in Britain toward the end of the eighteenth century. This social agenda emerged through the rhetoric and practice of sympathy. In the next two chapters, I seek to give a social and discursive overview of the role of sympathy in the late eighteenth century. I analyze sympathy as a mode of European power, as a discursive practice that was a pedagogy of identification. To sympathize with another, one must identify with that other: In the struggle against slavery, for instance, sympathy was both instrument and object, both script and performance in the formation of a new kind of national, racialized, gendered subject—in both the colony and the metropole. For most abolitionists the act of sympathizing was the enabling condition for the overthrow of slavery. *But it was a paradoxical mode of power.* The difference of race, and often of gender that divided the object and agent of sympathy was precisely that which must be bridged, effaced even, through a certain process of identification. Yet without such differences, which were inequalities of power, sympathy could not function; one might say that sympathy produced the very inequality it sought to bridge. In this chapter, I argue that these paradoxes, and the multiple forms of power that they entail, are legible in the torsions and shifts in the sympathy of eighteenth-century philosophy. I focus on the way in which sympathy is deployed in the emerging discipline of aesthetics as a kind of useful labor of the terrorized imagination and body; or as it is posited as a universal, natural instinct that founds society and social relations (which are themselves thought of as relations of sympathy). In the texts of moral philosophy, I track how the sympathetic procedure broaches questions of benevolence, justice, social good, and utility. I mark how the undecidable frontier between nature and culture, that sympathy both bridges and demarcates, is propriated, or made proper, homogeneous, and stable. In this process, sympathy becomes a kind of discipline; through a consideration of the "time" of sympathy, I connect this history of sympathy to the rise of market and utilitarian discipline. But, and at the same time, this gesture of propriation is marked by a certain call of "something else altogether," one that obliges us to consider the more general text of other histories. I turn first to a provisional narrative that situates the rise of sentiment, pity, and the sensual in three areas of European thought, that is, moral philosophy, aesthetics, and medical discourse.

The Emergence of Sympathy

From the fifteenth century on,[1] the European concept of sympathy (in Italian, Spanish, Portuguese, French, and somewhat later, in English) referred primarily to a "(real or supposed) affinity between certain things, by virtue of which they are similarly or correspondingly affected by the same influence, affect or influence one another (esp. in some occult way),[2] or attract or tend towards each other" (Oxford English Dictionary). Throughout this period, sympathy named that "relation between two bodily organs or parts such that disorder, or any condition, of the one induces a corresponding condition in the other." Through a kind of hidden, or occult metaphorization of pain, sympathy relates body parts (the arm and the leg) or organs (the heart and the stomach), and not only, and sometimes not even primarily, two human subjects. Etymologically rooted in the Greek concept of *sumpatheia,* "to feel with,"[3] or "having a fellow feeling," sympathy will always be haunted by the call to suffer for or with another. But a proleptic principle is also part of its impulse: When we sympathize with another's suffering, we anticipate that we may suffer similarly in the future. For instance, in the *Rhetoric,* Aristotle defined pity as that "feeling of pain caused by the sight of some evil, destructive or painful, which befalls one who does not deserve it, and which we might expect to befall ourselves or some friend of ours, and moreover to befall us soon. . . . And . . . we feel pity whenever we are in the condition of remembering that similar misfortunes have happened to us or ours, or expecting them to happen in the future."[4] This sense of a threatening future and this return of the past would come to assume a new social function in the practice and pedagogy of eighteenth-century sympathy: To sympathize with another was also to think, to project, and of course to calculate on one's own spiritual and material future.

In the rapidly industrializing contexts of eighteenth-century England, there was a growing preoccupation with the concept of sympathy among writers in moral philosophy, aesthetics, medicine, and literature (I turn to the literary contexts of sympathy in the next chapter).[5] This preoccupation took hold at a moment when Britain's imperial fortunes were on the rise. In the aftermath of the 1688 revolution, Britain emerged in the eighteenth century as the world's leading commercial power; by mid century, London had become the largest center of international trade, the premier port and warehouse of the world, and witnessed the forging of some spectacular fortunes.[6] Accompanying this rise to global dominance we also witness transformations in the conceptualization, scope, and practice of state power, the elaboration of complex institutions of civil society, and the emergence of a vibrant public sphere.[7]

It is in this context we must situate the rise of sympathy as a key technology of governmentality in late eighteenth-century England. As Thomas McCarthy notes, much of the growing preoccupation with sympathy was an attempt to counter Thomas Hobbes's (1588–1679) claim that human beings are fundamentally, or naturally selfish. For instance, Anthony Ashley Cooper, third Earl of Shaftesbury (1671–1713), in his *Inquiry Concerning Virtue, or Merit* (1699), argued for the inherent link between self-interest and public interest by means of what he called the "natural affections."[8] The molding of such an "artless" nature through sympathetic attachments would enable a fusing of an increasingly individuated self to a "civilization" unraveling at the cash nexus. But the naturalness of sympathy could also be an invocation or harkening back to something entirely *un*civilized—when MacKenzie's simple *Man of Feeling* (1771) inveighs against the degradations of the "coin of the world," he also implicitly questions norms of civilization.[9] If the sympathetic subject was the most natural, she was also, and for precisely that reason, dangerous—she was often blunt, awkwardly truthful, even uncultured, too close, that is, to the uncivilized state, to the darkness of the primitive. Perhaps the profound resiliency of this mode of power has to do with the range of concept-clusters in which it was imbricated. McCarthy notes at least three:

> One cluster of concepts emphasized the importance of feeling and included "enthusiasm," "ardor" and "passion." Another group, attempting to describe heightened intellectual capacity, included "genius," "invention," "instinct" and "knowledge." Terms emphasizing "the moral sense," especially as part of the century-long effort to rebut Hobbes, include "fellow-feeling" and "disinterested." There is an enormous overlapping element among these terms and there are terms which defy categorization, such as "projection" and one of the period's most important terms, "sensibility." The subtle, multiplex, even diffuse, nature of sympathy is its most characteristic feature. (4) This complex field of meanings and connotations, linking sympathy to "sensibility" and "sentiment," was thought of by contemporary writers as a "variety of weak

thought that will not bear analysis, that escapes discussion, that is not to be analysed by reason or rational debate."[10]

But as Markman Ellis argues, this complex semantic layering is due to the variety of discourses and practices that sympathy and sentiment is embedded in; thus, sympathy was an organizing principle in: the history of ideas (moral sense philosophy); the history of aesthetics (taste); the history of religion (latitudinarianism, Evangelicalism, and the rise of philanthropy); the history of political economy (civic humanism); the history of science (physiology and optics); the history of sexuality (conduct books and the rise of the domestic woman); and the history of popular culture (periodicals and popular writing).[11]

Moral Philosophy and the Practice of Sympathy

Emerging, thus, at the intersections of these discursive formations, and during a period when England's expanding colonial, mercantilist economy was adjusting to a free-trade regime of accumulation,[12] sympathy must be understood as a vehicle of culture and a way of doing politics—on the eve of an era when both would come to be objects of violent hegemonic struggle. Indeed, sentiment was a key technology in this struggle itself: If sentiment "has a special appeal to middle-class England at a time of economic growth and rising standards of living," its function "was to express the middle-class need for a code of manners which challenged aristocratic ideals and fashions."[13] This struggle is legible in the traces of other voices in the discourse of eighteenth-century moral philosophy, a discourse that seems preoccupied with the role of social sympathy. Extending Lockean empiricist psychology into the realms of aesthetics and social thought, moral philosophers sought to ground reason and morality in observable human emotions, which were written, as it were, on the body (we shall return to the question of the body below). As McCarthy notes, David Hume's *Treatise of Human Nature* (1739) drew close connections between sympathy and morality, asserting that sympathy is the chief source of moral distinctions; this text subsequently became one starting point for the fascination with sympathy that later swept the century. As Hume writes, "The sentiments of others can never affect us, but by becoming, in some measure, our own." By making the other present to us through sympathy—knowing, and being moved by her—one can act as a proper moral being. *In The Theory of Moral Sentiments* (1759), which "opened the floodgate to the rising tide of interest in the sympathetic imagination," Adam Smith writes of "the experience of sympathy as an epistemological and an aesthetic problem." That is, Smith demonstrates that sympathy represents more than simply feeling; it is a critical and aesthetic doctrine (2).[14]

Moral philosophical discourse of this period was fascinated with what one writer called the "divine impulse" of sympathy.[15] For sympathy not only joined subject and object in an acrobatics of identification, it founded an entire "moral economy," as Keshub Chunder Sen, the famous Hindu reformer, would put it in the late nineteenth century. The profound value of this process was that it was at once a displacement and an extension: a displacement of man's duty toward God, and an extension of civility.[16] As such, moral sense philosophy constantly underscores its allegiances to at least one of its progenitors, namely Christian theology. Informed by such biblical texts as Job 31:13–15,[17] moral sense thinkers drew explicit connections between the fulfillment of Christ and the humanitarian imperative. An American clergyman put the connection in this way at the very dawn of the nineteenth century:

> If a sensible and intelligent being be too great or too distant to receive benefit, or injury from us, as is necessarily the case with the Deity, affection then, in a good and virtuous mind, is limited to love, to dutiful respect, to rejoicing in his existence, and happiness. But the amiable qualities of men like ourselves we may be justly said to *enjoy,* by the powerful intercommunion of *sympathy.* A principle . . . which disposes the mind to *feel along with others,*—participating in their happiness, sharing in their griefs, and reciprocating all their sensibilities; and which is, indeed, the true amalgam of society. Sympathy . . . is evidently a fruitful source of many of our strongest and tenderest emotions. . . . It is a kind of mental attraction which communicates the action of different minds to each other, and is among the principal sources both of our pleasures, and our virtues. . . . [Sympathy] exhibits its influence chiefly in congratulation with the happy, and compassion for the distressed; and entering both with the one and the other into all the reasonable and moderate sensibilities. As it inclines men to assume the tone of the society in which they may happen to be . . . , it may be regarded as the great principle of imitation, both in domestic, and in civil life; the charm of social, and the mould of national manners. The forms of politeness in civilized society pay homage to this principle, and demonstrate its tendency to promote all the courteous and benevolent virtues. . . . It goes far towards making up a perfect moral character.[18]

One could take this passage as fairly representative of the role of sympathy in the discourse of moral philosophy. It articulates the complex chain of ideas that form sympathetic identification. First of all, sympathy is a "principle," a universal, *natural* force of attraction; the principle of sympathy is both an intimation of the transcendent divine and a natural human process (notice, too, how the occultism in the OED definition of sympathy is assimilated to a rationalist Christianity, a violence to which we will return). As McCarthy argues, moral thought presumed that "a common bond of humanity exists which makes the process of sympathy more natural, if not inevitable" (33). But if it is a principle of nature, it is equally the "great principle of imitation," in other words, of sociality, of culture, of civilization. Indeed, in moral philosophy sympathy functions in such a way as to render the distinction between nature and culture absolutely indeterminate—sympathy is the condition of possibility for both.

By feeling sympathetically, that is by "reciprocating" all the "sensibilities" of an other, by *embodying* the emotions of that other, by answering the call of the suffering other, a man or woman at once moves toward moral perfection (hence toward the divine), toward an aesthetic sensibility (hence toward the Beautiful), toward domestic order (hence toward civilization), and civic integration (hence toward communal, national, or even racial accord). Sympathetic identification, as pedagogical "mold," ties together the aesthetic and the political, the domestic and the national, the public and the private, the divine (soul) and the merely human (body), and of course the self and other: an "involvement so elemental between self and Other so as not merely to bring about emotional identification with and understanding of the Other, but to move and transform the sympathizing self incalculably, if temporarily . . . some sort of 'dissolution of boundaries,' a blurring of self and Other, is necessary in order not simply to achieve knowledge and understanding of another, but actually, somehow, to experience the Other."[19] The process of sympathy, further, involves both the intellect and the emotions; properly performed it should be legible on the very body of the sympathetic subject: one should be able to read immediately the tracks of another's tears or the beams of joy from laughing eyes, the discomfiting of the body, the sighing, the belabored breathing—all as the sympathetic quivering of the divine soul. In this way the sensual body became a key instrument linking the humanized mind to a benevolent deity. Following an argument recently made by Talal Asad, I would suggest that, as an "embodied practice," sympathy forms the "precondition for varieties of religious experiences";[20] in evangelical reformist spirituality, the sympathetic relation, as a bodily practice, became an essential discipline that enabled one to commune with god. Moreover, by filiating sympathy to concerns around the body, eighteenth-century thinkers articulated a crucial discursive overlap: the emergence of aesthetic enquiry and new medical theories of sensation and sensibility.

Sympathy and the Body

Aesthetics, Terry Eagleton declared, "is born as a discourse of the body."[21] From its early formulation in the work of the German philosopher Alexander Baumgarten (in his *Aesthetica* [1750]), the term referred primarily not to art, but "to the whole region of human perception and sensation, in contrast to the more rarefied domain of conceptual thought." Eagleton comments on this distinction:

> The distinction which the term "aesthetic" initially enforces in the mid-eighteenth century is not one between "art" and "life," but between the material and the immaterial: between things and thoughts, sensations and ideas, that which is bound up with our creaturely life as opposed to that which conducts some shadowy existence in the recesses of the mind. It is as though philosophy suddenly wakes up to the fact that there is a dense, swarming territory beyond its own mental enclave which threatens to fall utterly outside its sway.[22]

The dense, swarming region of the body would enter the enclave of Western philosophy through the contemplation of pain or pleasure. In the British empiricist tradition, as Steven Bruhm points out, John Locke had reified and moralized the distinction between pleasure and pain: "Things then are Good or Evil, only in reference to Pleasure or Pain."[23] But a new tradition in both literature and philosophy was founded in the eighteenth century, one which moves away from "a distinction between pleasure and pain, toward the beginnings of a pleasure in pain, and more problematically, toward an aesthetic pleasure in someone else's pain."[24] The body, and all its sensations, took on different moral, political, and epistemological implications, as the concept of aesthetics validated the body's existence in the material world, privileging sensation as the source of knowledge, and further blurring the distinction between pleasure and pain that Locke had assumed.[25] Bruce Burgett characterizes this shift as the "disestablishment of the body" in the eighteenth century: "No longer one of many phenomena ordered through pre-existing political, ethical, and theological systems, the body becomes the noumenal grounding of existence itself—a point of origin upon which political, ethical, and theological systems are then erected. The body . . . is transformed from a 'sign of' into a 'foundation for civil society.'"[26]

The most famous articulation of this shift, at least in the British tradition,[27] was in Edmund Burke's *A Philosophical Enquiry into the Origin of our Ideas of the Sublime and the Beautiful* (1757). Speaking both within and outside Lockean empiricist psychology, Burke attempted to show that anything that "conveyed ideas of 'pain or terror' to the mind yet brought with it no actual physical danger . . . prompted emotions of sublimity in the viewer. . . . Natural objects that were vast, powerful, obscure, dark, towering, or irregular were often sublime in the extreme: when viewed from a safe distance, they produced pleasure because they excited 'the passions' without causing real danger."[28] I return to Burke's *Enquiry* below; for the moment let us mark the role assigned to that which produces "pain or terror" in his aesthetics—sublime pleasure arises from the necessary distance of the horrifying spectacle, and so elevates the "viewer."

As we shall see in the next chapter, Gothic fiction exploited this theater of cruelty, the scene of pain. But always from a safe distance, just close enough for a good look. "The history of pain . . . is in many ways a history of looking; it is a narrative of watching a pained object while occupying a contradictory space both within and outside that object. And within that narrative is a multitude of discourses that mediate the way a culture—or indeed an individual— experiences pain at any given time or place."[29] As we turn to abolitionist discourses on the Caribbean and missionary discourses on India in subsequent chapters, we will witness such scenes of suffering, and the pained body. Indeed, the necessary distance of sympathy, and the imaginative bridging of it through a kind of identification—the double movement of the gaze of sympathetic power—would be the effective paradox of the sympathetic relation in both abolitionism and missionary discourse.

But the body had another provenance, one that tied sensation, pain, and the bodily organs to the sympathetic response; as if harking back to the etymological roots of the term, eighteenth-century medical discourse also explained the workings of the body through sympathy. As Bruhm notes, until the early 1750s, pain was understood through the model provided by Descartes, who asserted that the body's reaction to pain was purely mechanical, a simple reflex action. Following the Cartesian dualism of "thought" and "extension," medical theories posited the soul as activating the brain's pineal gland, which in turn secretes animal spirits to direct the body toward the proper nerve response and subsequent protective behavior.[30] According to such theories, one has a greater propensity for sensibility and imagination the more "exquisite" or "delicate" one's nerves are. As Albrecht von Haller put it in 1758, " . . . as the Deity seems to have implanted in our minds a kind of Sense respecting Morals, when we approve of some actions, and disapprove of others, almost instantly, and without previous reasoning . . . so, methinks, the analogy will appear very easy and natural, if we suppose our minds so formed and connected with our bodies, as that, in consequence of a stimulus affecting any organ . . . they shall immediately excite such emotions . . . as may be most proper to remove the irritating cause."[31]

Around mid century, physicians began to look critically at the reflex model of pain and its attendant behaviors.[32] Not coincidentally, during this same period we witness the rise of a massive reformation in the management of physical sentience that would eventually transform the cultural imaginary. As Foucault pointed out in *Discipline and Punish,* in utilitarian judicial theory sweeping changes in the procedures of punishment sought to reduce pain and corporeal affliction, thereby replacing torture and flogging with more humane, gentler methods of correction.[33] Such programs of social reform were often organized by medicine, which became the master discourse in defining the healthy body against the painful body and of demarcating the threshold of the sensible. For the newly medicalized bodies of the later eighteenth century—those bodies that were made to speak their "truths" by conventions of the medical gaze and as sites for "the production of symptoms and signs within determinate frameworks of signification"[34]—the relationship between morality, piety, sentiment, and the corporeal was, indeed, intimate, even if thoroughly contradictory.[35] Physicians began to conceptualize "sensibility" as the coordinating principle of bodily integrity, providing the basis for the overall integration of the body function; in this framework, sympathy "was no more than the communication of feeling between different bodily organs, manifested by functional disturbance of one organ when another was stimulated."[36] For the Scottish physician Robert Whytt (b. 1714), for instance, the Cartesian mechanism was too systematic and general; moreover, it did not account for the role that emotional disposition seemed to play in the behavior of symptoms. In his *Essay on the Vital and Other Voluntary Motions of Animals* (1751), Whytt dispersed Descartes's centralized, alienated soul. Arguing that "the soul was not sequestered in the fortress of the pineal gland," he hypothesized that the soul extends from the brain down the spinal column, through the nerve endings, and to all parts of the body.[37] Nerves, said Whytt, "are endued with feeling, and . . . there is a general *sympathy* which prevails through the whole system; so there is a particular and very remarkable *consent* between various parts of the body"; and "there is a still more wonderful sympathy between the nervous systems of different persons, when various motions and morbid symptoms are often transferred from one to another, without any corporeal contact."[38] Drawing on the work of Foucault, John Mullan, and Dorinda Outram, Bruhm clearly outlines this relation between sympathy and the body.

> What comes to be valorized by late eighteenth-century moralists as "sympathy," then, is physiologically based. Galenic medicine had discussed sympathy, but only as the product of moving humours throughout the body. . . . Whytt firmly connects the term "sympathy" not just to the bodily organs, but to a kind of mutual awareness that these organs share with each other. With Whytt—and a group of physicians doing similar work at Montpellier, France—sentience in general and pain in particular are no longer monologic reflexes. Rather, corporeal feeling becomes part of an internal integrity, wholeness, and unity of the body, one that can be rendered visible by the physician's penetrating gaze.[39]

And of course the figure of consenting organs in a well-ordered, harmonious, and sympathetic body would provide a powerful metaphor for the social body as well. Indeed, especially after the terrors of the French Revolution, the image of the body as naturally sympathetic became an important model both for the patriarchal family and for the body politic. The democratic impulse of universal human sympathy "underwrote democratized communal sentience. At the level of the medical body, sympathy, especially for the distressed sufferer, makes society possible."[40] As we shall see, for both David Hume (1711–1776) and Adam Smith (1723–1790) sympathy would be a fundamental means of not only communicating with others but of ensuring the proper, that is the natural functioning of society.

Moreover, as numerous studies have shown, meditations on the delicacy of the body and its susceptibility to pain were often also occasions to construct essential differences between both the sexes and civilizations: At the very moment when "sex as we know it was invented," sympathy, sensibility, and benevolence would come to characterize and delimit the "nature" of gender and England's civilizational status.[41] Needless to say, a whole matrix of power converged here around the figuration of women's bodies, which was also a marker for the transformation in practices of masculinity. As numerous writers have noted, the first half of the eighteenth century saw the emergence of the modern system of gender and sexual relations in England and the rest of northwestern Europe. But after 1750, "maternal love became a major topic for 'enlightened' writers, most of whom again were men"; writers such as Rousseau "envisioned a 'natural' woman educated to please her husband, bear his children, and care for the family, a woman successfully removed from the social sphere and returned to the domestic duties for which nature intended her, a woman sensitive and loving, a woman dependent on and obedient to male authority."[42] Randolph Trumbach argues that "What it meant to be female or male and the connection of gender roles to sexual behavior were both undergoing a revolution that was part of the appearance of that first modern Western culture . . . called the Early Enlightenment." The behavior and status of women were being modified by new ideals of romantic marriage, conjugal companionship, and the tender care of children. As Donzelot notes, for the bourgeois woman a certain alliance between her role as mother and the protective apparatuses of the new medicine gradually insulated the bourgeois family against outside influences. "This was an alliance profitable to both parties: with the mother's help, the doctor prevailed against the stubborn hegemony of that popular medicine of the old wives; and on the other hand, owing to the increased importance of maternal functions, he conceded a new power to the bourgeois woman in the domestic sphere. . . . By augmenting the civil authority of the mother, the doctor furnished her with a social status. It was the promotion of the woman as mother, educator, and medical auxiliary that was to serve as a point of support for the main feminist currents of the nineteenth century."[43] But the behavior and status of men were more markedly transformed by the new meaning attached to sexual relations between males. "In Europe before

1700, adult men had had sexual relations with both women and adolescent males. . . . These sexual relations between men and boys did not . . . carry with them the stigma of effeminacy or of inappropriate male behavior as they began to do after 1700 and have continued to ever since in modern Western societies."[44]

The modality of this revolution in gender and sexuality was a certain discourse around "nature." As Bruce Burgett, Robyn Weigman, and others have suggested, one effect of founding civil society on new technologies of the body "lies in the body's newfound ability to naturalize social and political inequalities through reference to the corporeal self-evidence of anatomical 'differences' like sex and race."[45] In these discourses, nature is always already gendered. Thomas Laqueur, in his groundbreaking work *Making Sex,* notes that although in France social-contract theory postulated a nearly sexless body, undifferentiated in its desires, interests, or capacity to reason, it nevertheless gendered nature and the "natural body": " . . . the end result is that women are absent from the new civil society for reasons based in 'nature.' A biology of sexual incommensurability offered these theorists a way of explaining . . . how in the state of nature and prior to the existence of social relations, women were already subordinated to men. . . . Ironically, the genderless rational subject engendered opposite, highly gendered sexes."[46] Similarly, for Scottish moral philosophers, nature was gendered feminine, and so legitimated as natural "the real world of male dominion of women"[47] and their practical exclusion from the emerging public sphere. These differences, again, were legible on bodies of sentiment.

This very notion of women's natural susceptibility to pain and suffering became an index of civilization, giving new meaning to both human misery and human history. Citing the work of the Scottish Enlightenment thinker John Millar on the *Origin of the Distinctions of Ranks* (1793), Laqueur notes that the "special qualities of female sexual desires become in the eighteenth century a key element in the understanding of the meaning of human history. . . . Thus civilization in Millar's account leads to an increasing differentiation of male and female social roles; conversely, a greater differentiation of roles and specifically greater female 'delicacy and sensibility' are signs of moral progress."[48] As W. J. Bate noted in his 1945 essay, "The Sympathetic Imagination in Eighteenth-Century Criticism," moral philosophy posited the existence of "a natural and instinctive sympathy for one's fellow man . . . and that, because of its primary importance in the constitution of man, identification by sympathy, which is through the imagination, characterizes the highest moral and aesthetic exertion."[49] Yet, before the constitution of "man," sympathy was a feminine pedagogy; and of course it is not fortuitous that as this genealogy was both repressed and incorporated, sympathy was more and more assimilated to the twin projects of civilization and nation-building.

What I am suggesting is that there was a certain disciplining of sympathy it-self such that its feminized, non-rational, even occult excesses were normal-ized through a pedagogy of the abstract human. In the pages that follow, I will pursue the implications of this elision.[50]

I conclude with a brief summary and some general observations. I have at-tempted to outline the emergence of sympathy as it related and articulated three areas of English (and Scottish) thought, that is, moral philosophy, aes-thetics, and medical discourse. As I have shown, the body of sympathy was central to all of these discourses. Through sympathy, subjects came to imag-ine themselves as *embodying* the emotions of a suffering other; doing so they partook of the natural, and so divine, impulse of humanity, and one that was pleasurable even if painful. Such was the fabrication of the new subject of sympathy, a thoroughly paradoxical one, we might add. If, on the one hand, sympathy draws a man or woman toward moral perfection, toward an aes-thetic sensibility, toward domestic and civic integration, on the other, as a kind of bridge across social, civilizational, and gender differences (or inequal-ities), sympathy also could undermine the moral and aesthetic norms and so-cial order of the status quo. Who is to say where one's sympathy should stop? This role as an agent of a kind of proliferating social bond was, at least in part, its role in abolitionism. Finally, then, I end with a word on the elision of "race" in the historiography of sympathy. The great value, I think, of follow-ing the circuits of sympathy through different European and colonial con-texts is that one is obliged to remember that in the eighteenth century the (sometimes suffering, but most often supposedly happily savage) other was always also the racialized other (coupled later in the nineteenth with the classed other). Even texts that seem thoroughly removed from colonial con-texts, such as Burke's *A Philosophic Enquiry into the Origin of Our Ideas of the Sublime and Beautiful* (1757), or Hume's *Inquiry Concerning The Principles of Morals* (1752), are in fact pervaded by questions of race, civilization, and power. In what follows, I pursue this archeology of racial difference as it was articulated with other forms of difference, such as gender and class inequali-ties. My final intention here is that another story be told of the rise and pro-liferation of practices of sympathy. It is to that story I now turn.

The Sublime, the Beautiful, and the Sympathetic in Burkean Aesthetics

Musing on the essence of the "beautiful," Edmund Burke wrote: " . . . it is usual to add the endearing name of *little* to every thing we love. . . . A great beautiful thing, is a manner of expression scarcely ever used; but that of a great ugly thing, is very common. There is a wide difference between admi-ration and love. The sublime, which is the cause of the former, always dwells on great objects, and terrible; the latter on small ones, and pleasing; we submit to what we admire, but we love what submits to us; in one case we are forced, in the other we are flattered into compliance."[51] Burke's hugely influential ideas on aesthetics provided generations of philosophers and litterateurs with a mode of expressing concepts of the beautiful, the terrible, and the sublime. More, it provided a whole style of being and communicating with others and the world.[52] But such modes of expression are never innocent; as we can sense with Burke's assertion that "we submit to what we admire, but we love what submits to us," aesthetic representations were also about relations between things, people, ideas, and so always also about relations of power. In what follows, I track these relations of power through Burke's conceptions of beauty, sublimity, and sympathy.

For Burke the object of love, which he terms a "mixed passion," is the beauty of the (other) sex. Unlike mere brutes, who pursue their mates through that "more unmixed" passion of generation, that is, lust, "man, who is a creature adapted to a greater variety and intricacy of relation, connects with the general passion [of generation], the idea of some social qualities, which direct and heighten the appetite which he has in common with all other animals . . ." These "social," or "sensible qualities" create in humans a preference that "fixes" or settles lust: "Men are carried to the sex in general, as it is the sex, and by the common law of nature; but they are attached to particulars by personal beauty. I call beauty a social quality; for where women and men, and not only they, but when other animals give us a sense of joy and pleasure in beholding them, (and there are many that do so) they inspire us with sentiments of tenderness and affection towards their persons; we like to have them near us, and we enter willingly into a kind of relation with them, unless we should have strong reasons to the contrary."[53]

Such social affections are tied closely to ideas of sympathy. In a decidedly Lockean vein, sympathy in the *Enquiry* arises out of the "the mechanical structure of our bodies"; through it, "we enter into the concerns of others . . . we are moved as they are moved, and are never suffered to be indifferent spectators of almost any thing which men can do or suffer." Through the sympathetic relation a subject participates in a "sort of substitution, by which we are put into the place of another man, and affected in many respects as he is affected." But the sympathetic subject may substitute herself in a scene of either pain or pleasure; if the former, sympathy "may partake of the nature of those which regard self-preservation, and turning upon pain may be a source of the sublime"; in the latter, sympathy partakes of the social affections (such as beauty).[54]

But the question of pain seems to interest Burke the most as he comes to consider sympathy; indeed, he seems to take a certain delight in it, or rather he argues that we all do.

> I am convinced we have a degree of delight, and that no small one, in the real
> misfortunes and pains of others; for let the affection be what it will in ap-
> pearance, if it does not make us shun such objects, if on the contrary it in-
> duces us to approach them, if it makes us dwell upon them, in this case I
> conceive we must have a delight or pleasure or some species or other in con-
> templating objects of this kind. . . . The prosperity of no empire, nor the
> grandeur of no king, can so agreeably affect in the reading, as the ruin of the
> state of Macedon, and the distress of its unhappy prince.[55]

Pain, then, even as it may activate the instinct for self-preservation, if properly approached, can elevate us. As Bruhm has argued, in the *Enquiry* pain
can be an actual moment of "sentient transference" through sympathy, in that
the observer could put himself in the place of the actual sufferer of pain;
through an act of the imagination, the subject's body becomes interchange-
able with the victim's.[56] Negotiating the complex terrain of the private and
the public, Burke suggests that the delight one gets out of another's pain "hin-
ders us from shunning scenes of misery; and the pain we feel, prompts us to
relieve ourselves in relieving those who suffer."[57] In some basic, physiological
sense, which, oddly, is also part of its public, or social function, another's pain
is immediately legible on the mind and body of the observer. And yet if the
pain of terror (or the terror of pain?) is to have a truly elevating effect on the
observer a space—a temporal and physical distance—is also necessary.

Such as in the case of the sublime. Recall that for Burke the sublime "always dwells on great objects, and terrible"; indeed, terror is central to an experience of the sublime. From Burke onward, this aesthetics of terror would
come to exert an enormous fascination over the modern imaginary. First of
all, Burke's *Enquiry* helped redefine the concept of the sublime. As James T.
Boulton remarks, in the *Enquiry* sublimity undergoes some crucial changes:
whereas in prior aesthetic discourse the sublime is essentially a style of writing, with Burke it becomes a mode of aesthetic experience found in literature and far beyond it. By contrast, the sublime acquires a more rigid
definition as a quality in objects that excites such an experience. Boulton
notes that in "the time of Boileau 'sublime' is a term primarily for literary
critics; later, sublimity is a subject for psychological study by philosophers
interested in the relation between human emotions and sublime objects."[58]
The sublime, which originally meant "set or raised aloft, high up" (OED),
became a technique of actually elevating the soul through some kind of
painful observation. Holding that pleasure and pain are "each of a positive
nature, and by no means dependent on each other,"[59] Burke argues that

> [w]hatever is fitted in any sort to excite the ideas of pain, and danger, that is
> to say, whatever is in any sort terrible or . . . operates in a manner analogous

to terror, is a source of the sublime; that is, it is productive of the strongest possible emotion which the mind is capable of feeling. I say the strongest emotion, because I am satisfied the ideas of pain are much more powerful than those which enter on the part of pleasure. . . . Nay I am in great doubt, whether any man could be found who would earn a life of the most perfect satisfaction, at the price of ending it in the torments, which justice inflicted in a few hours on the late unfortunate regicide in France. . . . When danger or pain press too nearly, they are incapable of giving any delight, and are simply terrible; but at certain distances, and with certain modifications, they many be, and they are delightful, as we every day experience.[60]

For Burke, then, pain and danger, sickness and death are ideas that give rise to the strongest passions of which humans are capable, but can be a source of pleasure elevating one to that ultimate of sensations, sublimity. Sublime terror becomes almost a kind of deterrent force that warns us away from the temptations of pleasure. A "passion similar to terror . . . must be a source of the sublime, though it should have no idea of danger connected with it." Only such a danger-less terror could produce sublimity. "But if the sublime is built on terror, or some passion like it, which has pain for its object; it is previously proper to enquire how any species of delight can be derived from a cause so apparently contrary to it."[61] Burke explains this seemingly perverse "delight" in terms of inactivity and labor.

> Providence has so ordered it, that a state of rest and inaction, however it may flatter our indolence, should be productive of many inconveniences; that it should generate such disorders, as may force us to have recourse to some labour. . . . Melancholy, dejection, despair, and often self-murder, is the consequence of the gloomy view we take of things in this relaxed state of body. The best remedy for all these evils is exercise or *labour;* and labour is a surmounting of *difficulties,* an exertion of the contracting power of the muscles; and as such resembles pain, which consists in tension or contraction. . . . Labour is not only requisite to preserve the coarser organs in a state fit for their functions, but it is equally necessary to these finer and more delicate organs, on which, and by which, the imagination, and perhaps other mental powers act.

Just as "common labour" (which for Burke is a "mode of pain") exercises our "grosser organs," "a mode of terror is the exercise of the finer parts of the system." And as long as pain and terror are not "actually noxious," "they are capable of producing delight; not pleasure, but a sort of delightful horror, a sort of tranquility tinged with terror."[62] The exclusion of pleasure from the economy of the sublime seems symptomatic here of an anxiety around perversity. Hence, the recuperation of "delightful horror" as a kind of useful labor. Delight and pain, then, are linked to a kind of temporalization through work and fear. As I noted above, Aristotle had placed a certain concern for futurity at the heart of the sympathetic relation. This sense of time would become absolutely central in eighteenth-century theories of social relations, such as aesthetics and ethics. For Burke, no delight can compare to the prospect of a pain "which we *may* be made to suffer" in its "effect on the body and mind," and that is because, like the body, the sensibilities "must be shaken and worked" if they are to be in "proper order." Thus, not only does terror activate in us a fear of what might happen, but the very projection of the self into a situation of pain becomes a kind of labor that staves off future "inconveniences" like melancholy, dejection, despair, and even suicide. This temporalization is also crucial to the pedagogy of sympathy; it assumes an enormous importance when we consider it in relationship to the inculcation of market discipline through a future-oriented, utility calculating sensibility (I will return to this capitalist temporality in my consideration of Adam Smith). In Foucauldian terms, we might say that the Burkean sublime becomes a practice of the self that entwines terror and pleasure, in a discipline of futurity.

Yet, we should not lose sight of the fact that this theory of sublimity was articulated at a historical moment when colonial issues were becoming more and more central to Britain's self-understanding; the notions of the sublime emerged within a Europe that was increasingly faced with an otherness that needed to be valued and re-valued aesthetically, politically, economically. Sara Suleri, in *The Rhetoric of English India*,[63] notes that one of the genealogies of nineteenth-century discourse of colonial terror is in fact Burke's notion of the sublime (exploited in the works of missionaries and colonial administrators and in such texts as Thomas Babington Macaulay's "Lord Clive," and the colonial fiction of Wilkie Collins, H. Rider Haggard, Rudyard Kipling, and Joseph Conrad, to name but a few).[64] Contextualizing Burke's moments in terms of British colonialism, Sara Suleri notes:

> The year 1757 [a year that saw the establishment of British power in Bengal], in which *A Philosophic Enquiry into the Origin of Our Ideas of the Sublime and Beautiful* was first published, is by historical accident, a turning point in the narrative of the East India Company's survival in Bengal. Exactly one hundred years before the Indian Mutiny of 1857 and the Company's final dissolution, Robert Clive's victory at the Battle of Plassey not only ensured the Company's control over Bengal but has further been conventionally regarded as the symbolic beginning of British imperialism in the subcontinent.[65]

In terms of colonial discourse, the sublime would come to function as a conduit between "the delusional aspects" of imperialism and the "very solidity of history," one that appears to suggest "a continually stable hold on what the proper course of events may be."[66] In the nineteenth century, the terror of this history being contaminated by delusion is written as a domestication of the colonial encounter—"into the familiarity of every day facticity, so that terror becomes the norm rather than the exception."[67] The quotidianization of colonial terror was precisely what abolitionists and missionaries would struggle against in their efforts to remake the enslaved, colonized body the sight/site of sublimity. For such men and women, the colony came to be seen as a theater of horror.

But if the sublime dwells on great and terrible objects, which produce a certain fear, what of those objects that incite horror? If sublime terror elevates our minds, what is its relationship to the grotesque that inspires horror? As we shall see, these questions relate Gothic aesthetics to abolitionism and utilitarian social reformism. Initially, in Burke, terror, horror, and the sublime were linked. Among the examples that Burke gives as an experience of sublimity is the confrontation between racialized and sexed subjects:

> Perhaps it may appear on enquiry, that blackness and darkness are in some measure painful by their natural operation. . . . Mr. Cheselden has given us a very curious story of a boy, who had been born blind, and continued so until he was thirteen or fourteen years old. . . . Among many remarkable particulars that attended his first perceptions, and judgements on visual objects, Cheselden tells us, that the first time the boy saw a black object, it gave him great uneasiness; and that some time after, upon accidentally seeing a negro woman, he was struck with great horror at the sight.[68]

Burke posits a force inherent within female blackness, and the European boy, who seems to be a universalist metonym for humanity, cannot but help his biological reflex of horror.[69] It is, of course, no simple coincidence that a black woman should incite such fear in the boy. We know that by the end of the eighteenth century, between fifteen thousand and twenty thousand people of African descent were living in London—the living fact of blackness embodied in these people and their exclusion from English propriety was a matter of something more than aesthetics. Indeed, in the coming years, the "natural operation" of blackness would be compounded by the human horror of savagery and barbarism in the colonies.

Interestingly, this linkage between terror and horror is severed in certain forms of Gothic aesthetics (roughly 1790–1830). For instance, the novelist Ann Radcliffe (1764–1823), in an essay posthumously published in 1826, argued that:

They must be men of very cold imaginations with whom certainty is more terrible than surmise. Terror and horror are so far opposite, that the first expands the soul, and awakens the faculties to a high degree of life; the other contracts, freezes, and nearly annihilates them. I apprehend that neither Shakespeare nor Milton by their fictions, nor Mr. Burke by his reasoning, anywhere looked to positive horror as a source of the sublime, though they all agree that terror is a very high one; and where lies the great difference between terror and horror, but in uncertainty and obscurity, that accompany the first, respecting the dreader evil?[70]

What seems crucial here is that the sublimity of terror is appropriated to the "higher faculties"—by which Radcliffe means no doubt not only the social affections but also the power of imagination; as if master of some "occult" region above us, terror rules its empire through uncertainty and obscurity. That some possible future pain lurks around the corner is the surmise that would be the modality of sublime terror (a temporality not unlike sympathy, we should note). Horror, however, is moored to an epistemology of certainty, the surety of pain, and a temporality of immediacy, giving off a clarity of vision; horror would function through knowledge, immediacy, and the body. Mark, then, how beginning as a discourse of the body, the aesthetics of terror came to superintend a new split between the imagination and the sensual (hence also between "high" and "low" forms of art). As the sublime was appropriated by the "higher forms of culture" (such as realist literature or painting) they became part of a regime for the productive exercise of the "higher faculties"; the body in pain came to be seen as that which could not be tolerated, as that which must be filtered through "anatomico-metaphysical" and "technico-political" registers, and so constituted by "a whole set of regulations and by empirical and calculated methods relating to the army, the school and the hospital, for controlling or correcting" the body's operations.[71] As the body became both object and target of multiple grids of power, so a new, more prolix "art of the human body" was born. In this massive history, the sympathetic relation seems to play a minor role. A seemingly atavistic, almost archaic form of sociality, one that tied human beings together through a kind of almost magical "mental attraction," sympathy seemed incapable of "obtaining effects of utility" at the level of the body.[72] But what if sympathy was the condition of possibility for that relentless, "uninterrupted, constant coercion" that assured "the constant subjection of its forces and imposed upon them a relation of docility-utility"? What if a mode of social ethics came to legitimate, and even to extend this very coercion? In the eighteenth century, a key discourse in the production of docile subjects was "moral sense philosophy."

The Rules of Sympathy:
Hume, Smith, and Moral Philosophy

One of the central aims of eighteenth-century moral sense philosophy was to provide an enlightened, rational (usually Christian) foundation for a moral (i.e., law governed) ontology of the subject-citizen.[73] As Markman Ellis notes, the parameters of the discussion of moral philosophy during this period were "that systems of virtue were established in mankind by the spiritual authority of God, that ethical judgments are made by an intuitive, aesthetic moral sense, and that they are subject to an empirically observed and analytic reason."[74] As such, the elaboration of the discourse can be situated within the history of disciplining the subject in terms of the piecemeal dismantling and refashioning of outmoded systems of hierarchy; of the consequent rise of civil society and the public sphere, and the quotidianization of capitalist, market-oriented social relations; of the overall Evangelical awakening in Western Europe, and the proliferation and diffusion of different modes of Christian religiosity in the eighteenth century; of the "rationalization" of the various legal apparatuses in England and the "normalization" of bourgeois kinship ties; and, of course, the gradual consolidation of European global dominance by the turn of the century. As I remarked earlier, this also was the moment of the emergence of modern humanitarianism; proliferating at an amazing rate as the century progressed, "benevolent institutions" were founded in quick succession: Westminster Hospital (1719), Guy's Hospital (1725), London Hospital (1740), Lock Hospital (1746), and Queen Charlotte Lying-in Hospital (1752); the late eighteenth century saw the founding of the Climbing Boys Charity (for chimney sweeps), the Royal Humane Society (for the dissemination of knowledge of techniques for the resuscitation of those supposed drowned), the Society for the Discharge and Relief of Persons Imprisoned for Small Debts; and, of course, abolition and missionary societies such as the Quakers's London Meeting of Sufferings (1783) and the Church Missionary Society (1795).[75]

All these seismic changes in European society and economy were governed by a new regime of ethical truth that has marked our modernity ever since. Jeffrey Minson, in his study of Foucault's genealogical critique, argues against the "regime of ethical truth which dominates social, political, cultural, legal and economic discussion in the liberal-capitalist democracies," whose humanist and Enlightenment foundation is a certain "moral ontology of human personality": "By this is meant the kind of ethical thinking which locates the *fons et origo* of moral value in one or more personal attributes, whose possession is deemed part of the definition of what it is to be human. By possessing a 'free' will or the capacity for conscious reflection, the person—a unity of body and soul—appears as the embodiment of absolute value and the foundation of moral judgement. The ultimate test of any action, law or institution hinges on whether, or to what extent, it respects this human personality, i.e., recognises and permits the unrestricted exercise of these essential human attributes" (3).

This essential human subject of moral philosophy gradually becomes a node in the reconfigured networks of power after the collapse of absolutism. Another name for this transformation of England into Britain (in the wake of the flight of James II [1688], the subjugation of Ireland [roughly 1692], and the union with Scotland [1707]) in contemporary scholarship is "liberal governmentality." In her history of "the modern fact," Mary Poovey has argued, "Operating in civil society and through the market, liberal governmentality depended (depends) on self-rule rather than rule by coercion; eliciting voluntary compliance through the mechanisms of discrimination and emulation essential to rule by fashion. . . . [A]s the monarch ceased to be the primary guarantor or steward of knowledge and as the old machinery of fashion took up some of the burdens of both (self-) rule and knowledge production, theorists reconsidered the kind of knowledge useful for government. Administering self-rule in a market society involved understanding human motivations, including the desire to consume, rather than simply measuring productivity or overseeing obedience. As a consequence, the knowledge that increasingly seemed essential to liberal governmentality was the kind cultivated by moral philosophers: an account of subjectivity that helped explain desire, propensities, and aversions as being universal to humans as a group."[76] Through her provocative readings of both Hume and Smith, Poovey goes on to show that the practice of moral philosophy was devised in the image of Baconian natural philosophy but designed as an account of human motivation. As such, it was partially integrated as a modality of liberal governmentality. Like "natural philosophers, experimental moralists claimed to describe particulars and to extract from them the general laws or regularities that informed them, especially those laws that explained the virtuous behaviors that made individuals social (governable)" (175). Faced with the dilemma of having to preserve a certain Christian notion of free will without relinquishing the broader aim of generating universal laws, eighteenth-century moral philosophers formulated general laws that were supposedly both prescriptive as well as descriptive. Although Poovey points out, quite rightly, that this "would not have been a meaningful distinction" for these writers, what she misses, I think, is that this disjuncture had specific effects of power that can in fact be charted historically as well as discursively. This is what I aim to do in my reading of David Hume's *Inquiry Concerning The Principles of Morals* and Adam Smith's *Theory of Moral Sentiment.*

Before I turn to these texts, however, I want to return briefly to my critique of Foucault's theory of governmentality. In chapter one, I outlined Foucault's theory of the emergence and proliferation of "a new savoir of state," one which had "statistics as its science and population as its target, and which incorporates policing techniques of discipline and security." I argued that in certain discourses and practices such as those surrounding the family and religion (and, by extension, Evangelical antislavery and missionary colonialism), the family, in a kind of transfiguration, became crucial as both model and instrument in tactics and overall strategies of power. One such tactic was sympathy.[77] In what follows, I hope to show how for eighteenth-century moral philosophers, the family was the preeminent work space for the functioning of sympathy. As it became a vehicle for new pedagogies of control and the elaboration of citizenship, sympathy was both recathected with and reconnected to expanding relations of power: The sympathetic relation, as the first of all domestic affections, became a model and an instrument for a newly atomizing class-society and a rapidly consolidating empire. Finally, the metaphor of family also became part of counter-discourses, critiques, and strategic displacements. As "a spiritual art," sympathy could also, and not without contradictions, be a kind of refusal or challenge to capitalist norms, colonial culture, or Anglican hegemony. As we shall see, for both Hume and Smith, if the family was a model for social relations of sympathy, it was also a target for normalizing and naturalizing heterosexual, patriarchal domination. The figure of woman as other will intersect here with the constitutive exclusion of all those savages and barbarians who in a few short years will be made to call out for justice, enlightenment, and the Word.

"A parent flies to the relief of his child":
Hume and The Nature of Sympathy

Published in 1752, David Hume's *Inquiry Concerning The Principles of Morals*[78] attempts to understand how people come to that "final sentence . . . which pronounces characters and actions amiable or odious, praiseworthy or blamable; that which stamps on them the mark of honour or infamy, approbation or censure; that which renders morality an active principle and constitutes virtue our happiness, and vice our misery" (6). By analyzing the reasoning and sentiment founding morality, Hume hopes to illuminate "some internal sense or feeling which nature made universal in the whole species" (6). Let us trace the emergence of this universal sense in Hume's text.

Hume begins by making clear his own sympathies. He contends that "no qualities are more entitled to the general will and approbation of mankind than beneficence and humanity, friendship and gratitude, natural affection and public spirit, or whatever proceeds from a tender sympathy with others and a generous concern for our kind and species. These, wherever they appear, seem to transfuse themselves, in a manner, into each beholder, and to call forth, in their own behalf, the same favorable and affectionate sentiments which they exert on all around" (10–11).[79] Later in the text, Hume will name this principle "sympathy and humanity," or simply "sympathy." A number of intersecting discourses barely legible here will reemerge throughout the *Inquiry;* let us repose them as questions: What is the relationship between "humanity" and sympathy? Who is of "our kind and species"? What is "natural" about sympathy? If sympathy is natural, how, in what way is it also the "trans-fusing" bond of society? Of culture? What are the effects of sympathetic identification? What does sympathy "call" us to? These questions will regulate my analysis of Hume's text.

To return to Hume's argument: Why is it, then, that sympathy is entitled to universal approbation? Hume argues that "whatever proceeds from a tender sympathy" in fact adds to the happiness and satisfaction of the broader society. Both Hume and, as we shall see, Adam Smith, follow the teaching of Francis Hutcheson (1694–1746), who was Professor of Moral Philosophy at Glasgow from 1730 to 1746 (Hume was his pupil). In a series of related works that mark a shift toward empiricism and systematizing,[80] Hutcheson had argued against egoists that moral action and moral judgment are both disinterested, and against rationalists that they both depend on natural feelings. He held that since benevolence aims at producing happiness or preventing unhappiness, and since a wide benevolence is approved more than a narrow, the morally best action is that which, in his words, "procures the greatest happiness for the greatest numbers."[81] Hume follows Hutcheson in believing that people are basically benevolent; he, too, contends that a principle of utility marks the good works of tender benevolence, and feelings of pleasure in beauty are one of the effects of such benevolence. But, as D. D. Raphael and A. L. Macfie point out, Hume moves beyond Hutcheson by giving an explanation of moral motivation, moral laws, and disinterested approval in terms of a theory of sympathy (13); sentiments were communicated through sympathy, and so it could provide an analytic model by which the operations of sentimentalism could be described.[82] For Hume, imagining the feelings, the misery, of another person elicits our sympathy because the misery of another gives the observer an interest in the circumstances of that person: "I feel a sympathetic motion in my breast, conformable to whatever I imagine in his."[83]

> . . . it seems undeniable that nothing can bestow more merit on any human
> creature than the sentiment of benevolence in an eminent degree, and that a

part, at least, of its merit arises from its tendency to promote the interests of our species and bestow happiness on human society. We carry our view into the salutary consequences of such a character and disposition; and whatever has so benign an influence and forwards so desirable an end is beheld with complacency and pleasure. The social virtues are never regarded without their beneficial tendencies, nor viewed as barren and unfruitful. The happiness of mankind, the order of society, the harmony of families, the mutual support of friends are always considered as the result of the gentle dominion over the breasts of men. (14)

Social sympathy is productive, not barren. Once again, it is future oriented action; it is also collective and not simply individualizing. It gives pleasure through an association with the beautiful. Moreover, *everything in civilization depends on this natural and social virtue:* order, family, friendship, the human species.[84] But is the sympathetic movement of the heart natural, that is given, or is it something we *should* engage in? The text equivocates. "In general," writes Hume, "it is certain that wherever we go, whatever we reflect on or converse about, everything still presents us with the view of human happiness or misery and excites in our breast a sympathetic movement of pleasure or uneasiness" (48). This "sympathetic movement" functions everywhere it seems, universally, naturally. And yet, "Sympathy . . . is much fainter than our concern for ourselves, and sympathy with persons remote from us much fainter than that with persons near and contiguous; but for this very reason it is necessary for us, in our calm judgements and discourse concerning the characters of men, to neglect all these differences and render our sentiments more public and social" (55).[85] It would seem that sympathy, although natural and "universal" (56), is also that which *should* be an open, public principle of sociality, and one that would enable us to "neglect," transcend "all these differences" that constitute the social itself. I emphasize this conditional tense because it marks a key vacillation in Hume's text: from the explicative to the pedagogical, the *Inquiry* is animated by a desire simultaneously to arrive at some universal, homogeneous, and homogenizing principle of morality, and also to attend to a call of sympathy, which would be in effect the call of suffering, and also of difference and otherness, the call of the other. What are we to make of this odd movement?

Now Hume assumes a certain relation of correspondence, if not identity, among an individual's "sentiment of benevolence," "the interests of our species," and the "happiness" of human society. As such, the temporality of the sympathetic movement ties it to a calculable, comprehensible future. The correspondence between individual sympathy and social interests figures both individual and society as homogeneous—Hume marginalizes differences between and within individuals (that is inequalities of power,

histories of [unconscious and material] repression, divided interests) as ec-
centric to the functioning of social sympathy. I say "marginalizes" because
Hume everywhere finds himself obliged to refer to these inequalities, he cannot simply exclude them.

Hence the importance of justice. For Hume, the particular needs or convenience of a community will determine the laws governing justice; but like
Kames before him,[86] he attempts to go further by arguing that nothing can
legislate the human "instinct" for justice. Justice (by which he means a particular, that is European, arrangement of property) tends to "promote utility and
to support civil society," but like "hunger, thirst, and other appetites" arises
"from a simple original instinct in the human breast, which nature has implanted for like salutary purposes. If the latter be the case, it follows that property, which is the object of justice, is also distinguished by a simple, original
instinct . . ." (31–2). Natural sympathy is that instinct, as Hume makes clear:

> The social virtues of humanity and benevolence exert their influence imme-
> diately by a direct tendency or instinct, which chiefly keeps in view the sim-
> ple object, moving the affections, and comprehends not any scheme or
> system, not the consequences resulting from the concurrence, imitation, or
> example of others. A parent flies to the relief of his child, transported by that
> natural sympathy which actuates him. (120)

Let us keep certain connections foremost in mind. For Hume, sympathy is
a natural, unmediated human, universal instinct because it propagates, or is
useful for, the species; that is, without sympathy there would be no society,
no humanity, no more human beings (a clear repudiation of the Hobbesian-
Lockean school of social thought). But at the same time, sympathetic acts
are the object of human (or cultural) approbation, and so can become examples to be imitated. To put it in a Foucauldian register, sympathy corresponds to certain norms, and as a discursive practice it has a certain
pedagogical function. Also—and one cannot simply escape this circle—
since nature has apportioned "her" gifts unequally, the useful instinct for
sympathy gives off, as it were, justice that promotes "utility" and supports
(bourgeois) "civil society."

But that is not all. As the last passage quoted makes clear, for Hume, the
family, and heterosexual relations more generally, is the privileged site and
metaphor for the presentation of sympathy. It is this role of the family that
is absolutely crucial to moral philosophical accounts of sympathy. If, say, the
"mind [were] so enlarged and so replete with friendship and generosity that
every man [had] the utmost tenderness for every man,"

> Every man . . . being a second self to another, would trust all his interests to
> the discretion of every man without jealousy, without partition, without dis-

tinction. And the whole human race would form only one family where all would lie in common and be used freely, without regard to property; but cautiously too, with an entire regard to the necessities of each individual, as if our own interests were most intimately concerned. (16)

Although such is not the case in "the present disposition of the human heart," "still we may observe that the case of families approaches toward it; and the stronger the mutual benevolence is among the individuals, the nearer it approaches, till all distinction of property be . . . lost and confounded among them. Between married persons, the cement of friendship is by the laws supposed so strong as to abolish all division of possessions, and has often, in reality, the force ascribed to it" (17). Again, a gesture of homogenizing and naturalizing, in other words a force of what Jacques Derrida calls propriation[87] animates this figuration of sympathetic kinship and marital ties. Marx notes how the revolution in social relations (the rationalization of laws, for instance) and productive forces (the massive legislative enclosures that turned "waste" and common land into private property) gave "the urban industries the necessary supplies of free and rightless proletarians" (*Capital, Vol. I,* 895); similarly, later scholars have told the history of how, by 1800, the rationalization of the law had sacrificed the economic security of daughters, wives, and widows in favor of the consolidation of power and property in another locus.[88]

It is this more "general textuality,"[89] that Hume's text obscures by homogenizing, propriating differences of power in the family. But there are intimations of these differences, these other histories everywhere in the *Inquiry.* Consider the figuration of the chaste woman, who appears in more than one passage. In Section VI, Part 1, entitled "Of qualities useful to ourselves," Hume argues that one owes a duty to society and to oneself to remember and practice those qualities which have an "immediate tendency to promote the interests of society": honesty, fidelity, truth. "Perhaps this consideration," he adds, "is one *chief* source of the high blame which is thrown on any instance of failure among women in point of chastity. The greatest regard which can be acquired by that sex is derived from their fidelity; and a woman becomes cheap and vulgar, loses her rank, and is exposed to every insult, who is deficient in this particular. The smallest failure is here sufficient to blast her character. A female has so many opportunities of secretly indulging these appetites that nothing can give us security but her absolute modesty and reserve. . . . If a man behave with cowardice on one occasion, a contrary conduct reinstates him in his character. But by what action can a woman whose behavior has once been dissolute be able to assure us that she has formed better resolutions and has self-command enough to carry them into execution?" (63) Of course, honesty, fidelity, and truth in women are precisely what would assure the stability of property relations within a patrilineal, patriarchal society. Relating such passages to earlier definitions of "social approbation," society, property, and justice, one gets a clearer sense of the specificity of these terms, in spite of Hume's insistence on their universality.

Finally, I quote at length a passage that, through the fantasy of the human, relates sympathy to justice, colonialism, and gender. Keep in mind that this passage comes in a section entitled "Of Justice," written in the year 1752.

> Were there a species of creatures intermingled with men which, though rational, were possessed of such inferior strength, both body and mind, that they were incapable of all resistance and could never, upon the highest provocation, make us feel the effects of their resentment, the necessary consequence, I think, is that we should be bound by the laws of humanity, to give gentle usage to these creatures, but should not, properly speaking, lie under any restraint of justice with regard to them, nor could they possess any right or property exclusive of such arbitrary lords. Our intercourse with them could not be called society, which supposes a degree of equality, but absolute command on the one side, and servile obedience on the other. Whatever we covet, they must instantly resign. Our permission is the only tenure by which they hold their possessions, our compassion and kindness the only check by which they curb our lawless will; and as no inconvenience ever results from the exercise of a power so firmly established in nature, the restraints of justice and property, being totally *useless*, would never have place in so unequal a confederacy.
>
>   This is plainly the situation of men with regard to animals; and how far these may be said to possess reason I leave it to others to determine. The great superiority of civilized Europeans above barbarous Indians tempted us to imagine ourselves on the same footing with regard to them and made us throw off all restraints of justice, and even of humanity, in our treatment of them. In many nations, the female sex are reduced to like slavery and are rendered incapable of all property, in opposition to their lordly masters. But though the males, when united, have in all countries bodily force sufficient to maintain this severe tyranny, yet such are the insinuations, address, and charms of their fair companions that women are commonly able to break the confederacy and share with the other sex in all the rights and privileges of society. (21–22)

Animals, Indians, women: This passage, it seems to me, presents a number of difficulties for Hume's argument specifically and for our consideration of the discourse on sympathy more generally. Notice, first, that the laws of humanity are divorced from the laws of justice; thus, inequality in this particular case does not emerge from nature's caprice but is a social relation of force: those possessed of strength inferior to us are necessarily our subjects, slaves even. Also, those very "insinuations, address, and charms" that are the characteristic signs of women's dubious agency under patriarchal "slavery" must be contrasted with those supposedly womanly virtues that promote the interests of society, namely honesty, fidelity, and truth. It would seem that for Hume, if a woman is to share in all the rights and privileges of society, she must in some sense unsex herself (I am reminded of that odd figure who seemed to bridge the gulf between nature and culture, Richardson's Pamela; I turn to her in my next chapter). But Hume also asserts that there are laws that bind these unequal social relations, not the laws of justice, but the laws of humanity, benevolence, compassion, kindness, that is, of sympathy. What binds animals, the colonized, the enslaved and women to European men is the law of humanity. Oddly, then, the laws of humanity adjudicate relations between humans (i.e., European men) and all the others, the not-quite-humans. But even here the humans might be tempted to cast off their humanity, hence a certain equivocation: "The great superiority of civilized Europeans above barbarous Indians tempted us to imagine ourselves on the same footing with regard to them and made us *throw off all restraints of justice, and even of humanity, in our treatment of them.*" If the laws of humanity can be thrown off by those who have arrogated to themselves the title of human, perhaps neither justice, nor humanity can be said to be natural to humanity. My sense is that this indecision is in fact a sign of something else, a displacement of an anxiety, the history of which would take us to the limits of sympathetic discourse.

This space of indecision opens the possibility of hearing another call—of difference, of otherness, of inequality that shadows this discourse. As we have seen, Hume was not a stranger to such concerns. As is well known, in a notorious footnote to his essay "Of National Characters" (published in a revised form in 1753), he had dismissed Francis Williams, the poet, in these harsh terms:

> I am apt to suspect the negroes, and in general all other species of men (for there are four to five different kinds) to be naturally inferior to the whites. There never was a civiliz'd nation of any other complexion than white, nor even any individual eminent either in action or speculation. No ingenious manufactures amongst them, no arts, no sciences. On the other hand, the most rude and barbarous of the whites, such as the ancient Germans, the present Tartars, have still something eminent about them, in their valour, form of government, or some other particular. Such a uniform and constant difference could not happen, in so many countries and ages, if nature had not made an original distinction between these breeds of men. Not to mention our colonies, there are Negroe slaves dispersed all over Europe, of whom none ever discovered any symptoms of ingenuity; tho' low people, without education, will start up amongst us, and distinguish themselves in every profession. In Jamaica indeed they talk of one negroe as a man of parts and learning; but 'tis

likely he is admired for very slender accomplishments, like a parrot who speaks a few words plainly.[90]

Note here how a radical—even biologically racial—difference functions to exclude the "Negroe" from civilization. The point here, of course, is to understand this racial context in its relationship to Hume's moral philosophy. We must affirm that such a position was a structural possibility of Hume's theory of sympathy. I have been arguing, indeed, that sympathy needs this abjected other, as the constitutive exclusion that would cohere its own fantasy of identity. And yet we are obliged immediately to add that it was precisely sympathy that would be a crucial counter-strategy in abolitionist discourses.

And slave narratives. What would have shocked Hume, perhaps, was that the "parrots" had learned not only to speak a few words, but they could do so with a certain panache. Consider, for instance, the reply made to Hume by Quobna Ottobah Cugoano in his *Thoughts and Sentiments on the Evil of Slavery and Commerce of the Human Species*. Cugoano, an ex-slave originally from Ghana, was sold into slavery, transported to the West Indies, and in 1772 was taken to England, where he eventually achieved freedom; by 1784 he was employed as a servant by the fashionable painters Richard and Maria Cosway, through whom he met many prominent politicians, artists, and writers, including William Blake. Originally published in 1787, *Thoughts and Sentiments* is a jeremiad written in the style of an Evangelical sermon. Invoking both the sympathy of his readers and excoriating them for their role in slavery, his text is at once inside and outside the language of eighteenth-century social sentiment. Cugoano explicitly refutes Hume, insisting that there can only be one law for all of humanity—not one law for the powerful and another for the weak. Quoting from Numbers 25:16, and Matthew 7:12,[91] Cugoano argues that:

> Wherefore because of the great wickedness, cruelty and injustice done to the Africans, those who are greatest in the transgression give an evident and undubious warrant to all other nations beholding their tyranny and injustice to others, if those nations have any regard to their own innocence and virtue, and wish to maintain righteousness, and to remain clear of the oppression and blood of all men; it is their duty to chastize and suppress such unjust and tyrannical oppressors and enslavers of men. . . . The life of a black man is of as much regard in the sight of God, as the life of any other man; though we have been sold as a carnage to the market and as a prey to profligate wicked men, to torture and lash us as they please, and as their caprice may think fit, to murder us at discretion.[92]

Here Cugoano, speaking in some of the same idioms as Hume insists that justice and virtue must be tied together, and that humanity demands equality. For Hume, sympathy is a natural, universal instinct, and so unequal relations of power would place the subjugated beyond the pale of humanity, somehow beyond instinct. But Cugoano's insistence on the necessary connections between power, humanity, and equality displace Hume's naturalized grid of power, and cause us to think another relationship between justice and humanity (we will return to Cugoano's narrative in the next chapter). Resituating these displacements we see far-flung differences of force introjecting a movement and an anxiety of non-identity within the human, the social(ized) body of moral philosophical discourse. And sympathy would be parasitic on this difference. There could be no sympathy without differences in power.

In this analysis, I have argued that Hume's *Inquiry Concerning the Principles of Morals,* posits a universal instinct of social sympathy or humanity; it relates questions of justice and the social good to utility, not only through self-interest (as a later Utilitarian tradition will argue), but also through benevolence and social "virtue." Hume manages this crisis of identity between universal nature and social ethics by positing a homogeneous society and individual through which sympathy does its good works. But this same gesture of homogenization is marked by a certain call of otherness, one that obliges us to consider the more general text of other histories. It is in that space that I would situate the insistence of Cugoano's call for humanitarian sympathy and justice. Hume answers and betrays this call of sympathy through procedures of propriation, and thus of normalization. But isn't this call, our answer, and the history of betrayal an essential part of the very practice of sympathy?

In the Shadow of the Spectator: Smith and the Economy of the Human Affections

Let us pursue this question through a consideration of Adam Smith's *Theory of Moral Sentiment.* Smith follows both Hume[93] and Hutcheson in founding his moral theory on sympathetic approbation, but through a much more complex economy of merit, intention, conscience, representation, and pleasure. As Raphael and Macfie note, "For Hume, sympathy is a sharing of the pleasure or pain produced in a person affected by an action. For Smith, sympathy can be a sharing of *any* feeling and its first role in moral approbation concerns the motive of the agent. . . . A benevolent action [for Smith] is not only proper but meritorious. The judgment of merit expresses a double sympathy, both with the benevolent motive of the agent and with the gratitude felt by the person benefited" (13). Indeed, as perhaps the last major philosopher of sensibility in the Western tradition, Smith's *Theory* was considered a definitive articulation of the concept of "sympathy as the arbiter for moral judgment."[94] I turn now to an analysis of this sympathetic economy. In my analysis, I pursue Smith's elaboration of what is essentially a triangular economy of pain, sympathy, approbation or censure; I also continue to track in this economy the obsession around nature and society, of which the family seems to be a symptom; returning to questions of time and discipline, I situate sympathy in the *Theory* in terms of both the rise of disciplinary modes of power and capitalist humanitarianism, or what one critic has called commercial sentimentalism,[95] as strategies of propriation; finally, I solicit the dissonance in those moments of difference that Smith would silence through this propriation.

Let us begin with perfection, or more accurately with Smith's "perfect man." For Smith,

> The man of the most perfect virtue, the man whom we naturally love and revere the most, is he who joins, to the most perfect command of his own original and selfish feelings, the most exquisite sensibility both to the original and sympathetic feelings of others. The man who, to all the soft, the amiable, and the gentle virtues, joins all the great, the awful, and the respectable, must surely be the natural and proper object of our highest love and admiration. (152)

The perfect man (and the gender of this man is already a question) is in command of his selfish feelings that are original, or, better, primary. Recalling Hutcheson, and foreshadowing Bentham, Smith writes, "Every man feels his own pleasures and his own pains more sensibly than those of other people. The former are the original sensations; the latter the reflected or sympathetic images of those sensations. The former may be said to be the substance; the latter the shadow" (219). Shadowing this original self is a sensibility of the other, or better, a sense of the other's sensibility and the other's selfishness. There will be much to say about this shadow, or shade, but for the moment let us note further that for Smith the virtues of softness, amiability, gentleness and greatness, awfulness, and respectability are always gender complements. The first set will be linked at crucial moments in the text to humanity, benevolence, effeminacy, society, indulgence, civilization, and woman, while the second to generosity, self-denial, sacrifice, self-government, virility, savagery, and man (22). Perfection consists in the proper balance of these characteristics, and perfection seems to be open to every man; perfection naturally elicits sympathetic approval from the general observer, that other who Smith will name the impartial spectator. No man is perfect without the love, reverence, admiration of this spectator. The scene of sympathy will also always be an open spectacle, open, that is, to the gaze of the impartial spectator, who himself remains the secret double of every man.

But as we shall see this Everyman is in fact not also every woman, nor even every man. A first question then: Is there a principle of femininity (through a certain figuration of woman) that is appropriated, made proper for masculinity in the discourse of sympathy, and moral philosophy more generally? I suggest that a certain kind of emotionalism was rearticulated and appropriated to European masculinity through the practice of sympathy. As I remarked earlier, the first half of the eighteenth century was the defining moment in terms of modern gender and sexuality. Trumbach writes,

> After 1700, in the cities of England, France and the Netherlands . . . [the] traditional system of male homosexual behavior was replaced by a new standard of sexual relations between males. Most men were now thought to desire sexually only women and this exclusive desire was largely what gave them masculine status. . . . Women were not whores because by their nature they were intended for the domestic joys of motherhood. This was the new ideal. It differed from the old ideal, which held that every woman was at heart a rake, with her sexual desires more powerful and less controlled than those of men. By 1750, the families of gentlemen were affected powerfully by the new ideal. The romantic marriage began to replace the arranged. A married couple hoped to share one another's constant company after marriage rather than going out separately into the social world.[96]

Through this historical lens we can understand better, perhaps, Smith's repetition (which I take as a sign of a certain insistence) of the words naturally, natural. The natural was a pedagogy of sympathy through which gender was transformed in early modern England.

I want to set the scene of Smith's argument a bit more carefully. Smith begins by describing a spectacle of sympathy, and points out that since "we have no immediate experience of what other men feel, we can form no idea of the manner in which they are affected, but by conceiving what we ourselves should feel in the like situation."

> Though our brother is upon the rack, as long as we ourselves are at our ease, our senses will never inform us of what he suffers. They never did, and never can, carry us beyond our own person, and it is by the imagination only that we can form any conception of what are his sensations. Neither can that faculty help us to this any other way, than by representing to us what would be our own, if we were in his case. It is the impressions of our own senses only, not those of his, which our imaginations copy. By the imagination we place ourselves in his situation, we conceive ourselves enduring all the same torments, we enter as it were into his body, and become in some measure the same person with him, and thence form some idea of his sensations, and even feel something which, though weaker in degree is not altogether unlike them. His agonies, when they are thus brought home to ourselves, when we have

thus adopted and made them our own, begin at last to affect us, and we then tremble and shudder at the thought of what he feels. (9)

For Smith, this process (is it natural? is it social?) is the source of "our fellow-feeling for the misery of others" (10). This fellow-feeling with the other's misery, an occasion for pity or compassion, becomes the privileged, though specific, example of a more general sensibility: "Sympathy . . . may now . . . be made use of to denote our fellow-feeling with any passion whatever" (10). As with Hume and Kames, sympathy is crucial for all relations within society, the most fundamental unit of which is the family. "After himself, the members of his own family, those who usually live in the same house with him, his parents, his children, his brothers and sisters, are naturally the objects of his warmest affections. They are naturally and usually the persons upon whose happiness or misery his conduct must have the greatest influence. He is more habituated to sympathize with them" (219).[97] Mark the strange juxtaposition between what is natural and what is habitual. As the family is naturally the object of (the father's) sympathy, so the state is the next obvious candidate for our affections (and notice that there is no absolute rupture between these two scenes of sympathy, between the order of the family and the order of the state): "The state or sovereignty in which we have been born and educated, and under the protection of which we continue to live, is, in ordinary cases, the greatest society upon whose happiness or misery, our good or bad conduct can have much influence. It is accordingly, by nature, most strongly recommended to us" (227). If we consider the history of nationalism and the family in Europe after 1800, which I alluded to in the last chapter, we can get a sense of the political valences of this narrative: sympathy as natural habituation (!) in the home is both a pedagogy of sociality and a discipline of the nation. (As it would also be a laboratory for empire later in the nineteenth century.)

As I pointed out above, representing the agonies of the body is central to the work of sympathy; thus, the example of our brother on the rack emphasizes the effects of pain on the observer.[98] Also, there are at least two bodies that must be present at the scene of sympathy. This other body, the body of the sympathizer must visibly register certain effects, through trembling, shuddering, and so on (10). Sympathetic identification, as an embodied form of subjectivity then, writes itself on the body.[99] For the sympathizer to be present to the pain of the other the imagination must operate through representations; and the effects of these representations, as they are brought home to us, must be legible on the body. This complex semiotics of sympathy owes an inestimable debt to representation, although—and this is absolutely crucial— Smith will neglect the ethical implications of representation throughout the rest of his text, assimilating, (ap)propriating sympathy finally to the natural.[100] Let us follow the mechanics of this propriation.

Now, as we have seen, representation brings the other's pain home to us. The other takes up residence in our home, as it were, and so we "become in some measure the same person with him." "In all such cases, that there may be some correspondence of sentiments between the spectator and the person principally concerned, the spectator must, first of all, endeavour, as much as he can, to put himself in the situation of the other, and to bring home to himself every little circumstance of distress which can possibly occur to the sufferer. He must adopt the whole case of his companion with all its minutest incidents; and strive to render as perfect as possible, that imaginary change of situation upon which his sympathy is founded" (21). Moreover, this homecoming of the other parallels for Smith a certain synchrony between the other and the sympathizer: "To see the emotions of their hearts, in every respect, beat time to his own, in the violent and disagreeable passions, constitutes his sole consolation" (22).[101]

Imaginative representation "must," or should present "every little circumstance" of the other's situation; in other words, the sympathetic procedure demands something approaching a complete knowledge of the other's situation. No where will Smith consider that in comprehending the other what is lost is, precisely, otherness. As Levinas once put it, "When the Other enters into the horizon of knowledge, it already renounces alterity."[102] But again the conditional is crucial here, because in the very next passage Smith notes that "the emotions of the spectator will still be very apt to fall short of the violence of what is felt by the sufferer. Mankind, though naturally sympathetic, never conceives, for what has befallen another, that degree of passion which naturally animates the person principally concerned" (21). In what way is "mankind" naturally sympathetic if sympathy can only function through an imaginative representation that "must" or should comprehend the "minutest incidents" in the other's situation, a comprehension that will often "fall short"? Do people have a responsibility to sympathize with the pain or joy of the other or is it an innate function (which would imply that sympathy is absolutely irresponsible, absolutely ex-centric to the order of reason, knowledge, morality)? It would seem, from Smith's own formulations, that sympathy naturally triggers a highly acrobatic form of psychic, bodily identification. But then does representation or nature trigger this gymnastics of identification? I suggest the impossibility of this line of questioning—situated as it is on the border separating representation and nature, and the body and the mind—leads Smith to qualify his notion of sympathy with such phrases as "some measure" and "some correspondence," and necessitates a crucial admission: an irreducible difference will always also be part of the sympathetic relation. Paradoxically, for the observer to correspond to, and with the other, this gap of difference (both space and time) must in some measure be closed. Hence, Smith's repeated metaphors of "bringing the other home" and "beating time with the other." We are still within that circuit of difference and sameness that I traced in Hume's theory of sympathy.

Yet for Smith, sympathy names a much more complex relation of human-ness to virtue. In Smith's thought every affection must be in proper proportion to the cause that excites it. "In the suitableness or unsuitableness, the proportion or disproportion which the affection seems to bear to the cause or object which excites it, consists the propriety or impropriety, the decency or ungracefulness of the consequent action" (18). Contra Hume, Smith does not primarily locate this question of the propriety of actions and the suitability of affections in utility. "Originally . . . we approve of another man's judgement, not as something useful, but as right, as accurate, as agreeable to truth and reality: and it is evident we attribute those qualities to it for no other reason but because we find that it agrees with our own. . . . The idea of the utility of all qualities of this kind is plainly an after-thought, and not what first recommends them to our approbation" (20). A judgment or an affection agrees with truth and reality only when there is harmony and correspondence, that is a certain pleasurable beauty, between the cause and the action. As if demarcating that strange terrain beyond utility, beauty, and pleasure (and so a certain aesthetics of virtue), secondary concerns in the *Inquiry Concerning The Principles of Morals* become central to the project of *The Theory of Moral Sentiment*.[103] Yet this correspondence with beauty in itself does not constitute virtue according to Smith. There is, in fact, "a considerable difference between virtue and mere propriety," because to act with the "most perfect propriety" requires nothing more than "that common and ordinary degree of sensibility or self-command which the most worthless of mankind" possesses. Virtue, by contrast, "is excellence, something uncommonly great and beautiful, which rises far above what is vulgar and ordinary" (25). To be virtuous, then, is to rise above the "mob" (47) of humanity, the "rude vulgar of mankind" (25); and the more that virtue approaches perfection the more completely can the "impartial spectator" sympathize with all our judgments and passions (26). There is no virtue without the sympathetic approbation of this other self. But the rude vulgar, first of all, must be transcended. Following Hume, Smith posits, and then, in later editions, significantly qualifies the natural benefits of sympathy in forming esteem for the rich and the great. As Rafael and Macfie point out, "We admire the rich and the great because we take sympathetic pleasure in their enjoyments. The admiration or respect is perfectly natural and contributes to the stability of society. By 1789, however, . . . Smith was less complacent and followed that discussion with a new chapter on 'the corruption of our moral sentiments' by the disposition to admire the rich and the great" (17).

I will attempt to tease out the class implications of Smith's notion of virtue below, but let us for the moment pause over this impartial spectator, whom Smith introduces in the very first section of the text. In the next section of the *Theory*, Smith considers the "Degrees of the different Passions which are consistent with Propriety," treating respectively passions that originate in the body, passions that originate "from a particular turn or habit of the Imagination," unsocial and social passions, and, finally, selfish passions. Throughout this section the proper intensity of our emotions is determined by reference to "the cool and impartial spectator,"[104] who legislates on all matters of "truth and reality." Writing of the social Passions, Smith alludes to a "redoubled sympathy":

> Generosity, humanity, kindness, compassion, mutual friendship and esteem, all the social and benevolent affections, when expressed in the countenance or behaviour, even towards those who are not peculiarly connected with ourselves, please the indifferent spectator upon almost every occasion. His sympathy with the person who feels those passions, exactly coincides with his concern for the person who is the object of them. The interest, which, as a man, he is obliged to take in the happiness of this last, enlivens his fellow-feeling with the sentiments of the other, whose emotions are employed about the same object. We have always, therefore, the strongest disposition to sympathize with the benevolent affections. (38–39)

The scene of sympathy, now, names a triangular economy. The indifferent spectator, who turns out to be not indifferent at all, gazes silently as one subject shows kindness to another in need. The spectator sympathizes with the agent and the object of this relation (but, "as a man," his sympathies supposedly had already been activated by the one in need). This sympathy pleases both the agent and the object, but also, and perhaps most importantly the indifferent spectator. It is the sympathetic pleasure or approbation of this last "subject" that becomes the key reference for all proper actions, indeed for all virtue: " . . . all the other passions of human nature, seem proper and are approved of, when the heart of every impartial spectator entirely sympathizes with them, when every indifferent bystander entirely enters into, and goes along with them" (69). Only when, therefore, our passions coincide with the impartial spectator, who stands in for the universal human, can we say that something like propriation takes place. Unlike in Hume, propriation here is an effect of the spectator as a force of universalization.

Now this universalist propriation has a specific temporal dimension. One that looks both ahead and backward. "And when he looks backward to the motive from which he acted, and surveys it in the light in which the indifferent spectator will survey it, he still continues to enter into it, and applauds himself by sympathy with the approbation of this supposed impartial judge" (85).[105] And when we make a decision to act, it is always in reference to this spectator, even if the reference is occult, hidden from view, or even secret. "Whatever judgement we can form concerning [our own sentiments and motives] must always bear some secret reference, either to what are, or to what, upon a certain condition would be, or to what, we imagine, ought to be the judgement of others. We endeavour to examine our own conduct as we imagine any other fair and impartial spectator would examine it" (110). Even in secret, the impartial spectator judges our past actions, and watches over our future behavior.

But again who is this spectator? What function does he serve in Smith's text? As should be clear, the impartial spectator becomes something like one's conscience, which for Smith is in fact the mirror of society—or the looking-glass of the other.

> Were it possible that a human creature could grow up to manhood in some solitary place . . . he could no more think of his own character, of the propriety or demerit of his own sentiments and conduct, or the beauty or deformity of his own mind, than of the beauty or deformity of his own face. All these are objects which he cannot easily see, . . . and with regard to which he is provided with no mirror which can present them to his view. Bring him into society, and he is immediately provided with the mirror which he wanted before. Our first ideas of personal beauty and deformity, are drawn from the shape and appearance of others, not from our own. We soon become sensible, however, that others exercise the same criticism upon us. We are pleased when they approve of our figure. . . . We examine our persons limb by limb, and by placing ourselves before a looking-glass . . . endeavour . . . to view ourselves at the distance and with the eyes of other people. . . . We suppose ourselves the spectators of our own behaviour, and endeavour to imagine what effect it would, in this light, produce upon us. This is the only looking-glass by which we can, in some measure, with the eyes of other people, scrutinize the propriety of our own conduct. (110–12)[106]

Notice how the other, as s/he comes to occupy that privileged space of impartial spectator, becomes the modality through which a consideration of the effects of our actions is introjected into our consciousness; if one can say that a certain sympathetic identification takes hold here of the socialized subject, this entire process must be situated within a history of normalization. Recall that Smith had grounded sympathy in an imaginative act of representation, which would bring knowledge of the other home to us. But here we see that this home is already inhabited—by the other. In other words, there can be no originary, or natural representation that sympathy can take hold of—sympathy is an effect of the "appearance of others." Propriety, duty, and virtue, as well as our ideas of beauty and rightness, then, are reflections in the mirror of society, itself made up of countless others who exercise a power of judgment over us.[107] It is as a target and, later, instrument of these multiple relations of power that our subjectivity is formed. This is crucial: the other of sympathy, that supposedly impartial other whose sympathy we constantly solicit, is always also a modality of socialization, of subject-formation in a particular regime of truth; this sympathetic spectator invites or, better, incites us to recognize our moral obligations.[108] Sympathy, then, as a mode of a certain discipline (I return to this below).

Now readers will recall that Michel Foucault tied his analysis of disciplinary procedures to a new way of "administering time." For Foucault, two of the "great 'discoveries' of the eighteenth century"—"the progress of societies and the genesis of individuals"—were correlative with the "new techniques of power, and more specifically, with a new way of administering time and making it useful, by segmentation, seriation, synthesis and totalization." Thus, the "disciplinary methods reveal a linear time whose moments are integrated, one upon another, and which is orientated towards a terminal, stable point; in short, an 'evolutive' time." At the same time, administrative and economic techniques of control "reveal a social time of a serial, orientated, cumulative type: the discovery of an evolution in terms of 'progress.'"[109] My concern here is the relationship between these tactics of discipline, and a certain futurity that humanitarian principles such as sympathy inculcated in their subjects. Thomas L. Haskell, in his analysis of capitalism and humanitarianism, pointed out that what "altered cognitive style in a 'humanitarian' direction was not in the first instance the ascendancy of a new class, or the assertion by that class of a new configuration of interests, but rather the expansion of the market, the intensification of market discipline, and the penetration of that discipline into spheres of life previously untouched by it."[110] My suggestion, is that, first, and most broadly, sympathy was crucial in altering the style of cognition for European subjects from the middle of the eighteenth century on; coupled not only with the impact of technological changes in travel, war, communication but also in institutions and political organizations, sympathy expanded the conventional limits within which people felt responsible enough to act.[111] Second, it did this by the incitation of a future oriented drive, one whose "terminal, or stable point" was the docile, market oriented citizen; and lastly, as the apotheosis of the human affections, sympathy was a sign of civilization and an instrument in all those minute and massive projects of progress. I will return to these arguments in the pages to come.

Read from another perspective, however, the very agent of this progressive sympathy, the impartial spectator, could be a reminder of a repressed other (and a harbinger, as we shall see, of a future terror). The spectator, as the subject's double, could be seen as a force of what Freud would later call the self-regarding faculty. As he so succinctly puts in "The 'Uncanny,'" "The idea of the 'double' does not necessarily disappear with the passing of the primary narcissism, for it can receive fresh meaning from the later stages of development of the ego. A special faculty is slowly formed there, able to oppose the rest of the ego, with the function of observing and criticizing the self and exercising a censorship within the mind, and this we become aware of as our 'conscience.' . . . The fact that a faculty of this kind exists, which is able to treat the rest of the ego like an object—the fact, that is, that man is capable of self-observation—renders it possible to invest the old idea of a 'double' with a new meaning and to ascribe many things to it, above all, those things which seem to the new faculty of self-criticism to belong to the old surmounted narcissism of the earliest period of all" (387–388). (I should say what I find truly uncanny is the amazing rhetorical overlap, repetition with a difference, between Freud and Smith here.)[112] As we have seen, for Smith the spectator represents in some sense both society in general and all the others that make it up. But that is not all the indifferent spectator comes to represent. He comes to herald the presence of the divine in the human.

Writing on the possibility of duty, Smith relates our capacity for sentiment and judgment to an "all-wise Author of Nature":

> The all-wise Author of Nature [in earlier editions, this being is called the "great judge" or "Great Judge"] has . . . taught man to respect the sentiments and judgements of his brethren. . . . He has made man, if I may say so, the immediate judge of mankind; and has . . . created him after his own image, and appointed him his vicegerent upon earth. . . . They are taught by nature, to acknowledge that power and jurisdiction which has thus been conferred upon him, to be more or less humbled and mortified when they have incurred his censure, and to be more or less elated when they have obtained his applause. But though man has . . . been rendered the immediate judge of mankind, he has been rendered so only in the first instance; and an appeal lies from his sentence to a much higher tribunal, to the tribunal of their own consciences, to that of the supposed impartial and well-informed spectator, to that of the man within the breast, the great judge and arbiter of their conduct. (128–130)

What does it mean to be taught by nature? In what sense can nature teach humans? Are the lessons of nature still natural? If they are natural, why must we be taught them? This series of questions returns us to that undecideable frontier that is supposed to separate culture from nature. Now if we consider the phrasing of earlier editions, the connection I am arguing for becomes rather more apparent: the all-wise Author of Nature implants a representative in each human heart in the form of an impartial spectator—this great judge is in fact a miniaturized double of God. A universal, transcendent being, living (sometimes in secret, and sometimes even in hibernation, as it were) in our hearts, who sees but is not seen, enables each man and woman to oppose and rise above the selfish passions. Hence, the possibility of impartiality. But earlier Smith had situated this impartiality in the necessary reference to society and the other. A certain shuttling, then, between a concept of the impartial spectator that would be an effect of society and the other, and that of a great judge formed by an all knowing God of nature, between the other of culture who materializes relations of power, and the Other of Nature, who transcends all men—this movement structures Smith's argument.

One can see that for Smith (and this is common to all moral philosophical discourse in the eighteenth century) sympathy is a gift one gives to another, but one that, as gift, and despite anything the other might do, immediately yields a certain profit, a return, a pleasure in/to oneself. Derrida has this to say about the gift, if there is such a thing:

> From the moment the gift would appear as gift, as such, as what it is, in its phenomenon, its sense and its essence, it would be engaged in a symbolic, sacrificial, or economic structure that would annul the gift in the ritual circle of the debt. The simple intention to give, insofar as it carries the intentional meaning of the gift, suffices to make a return payment to oneself. The simple consciousness of the gift right away sends itself back to the gratifying image of goodness or generosity, or the giving-being who, knowing itself to be such, recognizes itself in a circular, specular fashion, in a sort of auto-recognition, self-approval, and narcissistic gratitude.[113]

One is tempted to say, on the basis of this suggestive reading of the gift, that as soon as there is the phenomenon of sympathy, as such, there is no sympathy, that as soon as the sympathetic relation enters consciousness, sympathy has already come to an end. But we must keep in mind that, in the eighteenth century, sympathy as discourse (rather than as phenomenon), or as a practice of governmentality was indissociable from the ritual circle of debt linking the subject to bourgeois sociality. But not without remainder. And in fact the giver of sympathy is not a subject without an other, even when there is such a "return payment" of goodness. The agent of sympathy is always constituted through a relational procedure, or, better, struggle, that will always also compromise her wholeness. This must be remembered: The gift of sympathy is also part of a certain economy of violence. What Derrida's analysis also reminds us of, however, is that an analysis of the practice of sympathy must take thought to another horizon of possibility. My conclusion will attempt to approach one such horizon.

Here I close my consideration of *The Theory of Moral Sentiment* by returning to the question of difference—sexual, national, civilizational—and the general textuality of another history. My sense is that for Smith the development of moral sentiment is always also a narrative of European masculinity. But this formulation is rather too general to be actually of any help in understanding the specific political valences of this narrative. We must gauge these valences in the act of interpretation.

Let us end, then, with a representation of imperfection. Borrowing from Hume but much more explicitly from Kames,[114] Smith argues that, although for "civilized nations, the virtues which are founded upon humanity are more cultivated than those which are founded upon self-denial and the command of the passions," among "savages and barbarians it is quite otherwise."

> Among rude and barbarous nations, it is quite otherwise, the virtues of self-denial are more cultivated than those of humanity. The general security and happiness which prevail in ages of civility and politeness, afford little exercise to the contempt of danger, to patience in enduring labour, hunger, and pain. Poverty may easily be avoided, and the contempt of it therefore almost ceases to be a virtue. The abstinence from pleasure becomes less necessary, and the mind is more at liberty to unbend itself, and to indulge its natural inclinations in all those particular respects. (204–205)

Smith articulates rather well the close relationship between a certain ideal of gentility, as liberty, pleasure, and wealth, and the identity of civilized humanity. Indeed, civilized humanity is most properly represented by European gentility. Not surprisingly, then, according to Smith savages cannot express sympathy.

> Every savage undergoes a sort of Spartan discipline, and by the necessity of his situation is inured to every sort of hardship. . . . All savages are too much occupied with their own wants and necessities, to give much attention to those of another person. A savage, therefore, whatever be the nature of his distress, expects no sympathy from those about him, and disdains, upon that account, to expose himself, by allowing the least weakness to escape him. The savages in North America, we are told, assume upon all occasions the greatest indifference, and would think themselves degraded if they should ever appear in any respect to be overcome either by love, or grief, or resentment. . . . The weakness of love, which is so much indulged in ages of humanity and politeness, is regarded among savages as the most unpardonable effeminacy. (205)

Notice first of all the semantic sliding between "civilized nations" (204) and "ages of humanity" (205): It is almost as if time and space collapse, or better fold in on themselves when the civilizational other is at stake. The practice of sympathy, in other words, renders visible a normalizing "anthropology" and a teleological historicism. To be at liberty to sympathize with another, furthermore, one must be free from want, from poverty, which would seem to imply that sympathy is less a question of nature than a matter of material, social positioning. Needless to say, Smith is contradicting himself here. But this contradiction points to what will be an important lesson of the political movements of sympathy: sympathy is always a modality of power—to exercise sympathy is always to be in some sort of position of privilege, however limited, however imaginary. In Smith this modality is narrativized through a peculiar relay between sympathy, effeminacy, and poverty: the savage, who is in a constant state of need and hardship, cannot love, cannot show affection, cannot feel. Now it seems a certain figuration of the feminine merges with Smith's notions of virtue and civilization. Which does not mean savages are completely devoid of virtue—they in fact embody (in an extreme degree) the qualities of masculinity: "The hardiness demanded of savages diminishes their humanity; and, perhaps, the delicate sensibility required in civilized nations sometimes destroys the masculine firmness of the character" (209). The "perhaps" and "sometimes" contrasts with the simple assertion of the non-humanity of the savage. As I have argued throughout this chapter, such muted differences narrate "race,"[115] rank, femininity, and masculinity through a complex play of otherness, sameness, and propriation. Thus, the narrative of masculinity that I alluded to earlier can be charted in these subtle, marginal references to womanly virtues ("Humanity is the virtue of a woman, generosity of a man" [190]), the effeminacy of civilized nations, fashionable and vain women (115), the "more fearful sex" (208). Finally, for Smith these differences constitute essences which not even the violence of torture can annul:

> This difference gives occasion to many others that are not less essential. A polished people being accustomed to give way, in some measure, to the movements of nature, become frank, open, and sincere. Barbarians, on the contrary, being obliged to smother and conceal the appearance of every passion, necessarily acquire the habits of falsehood and dissimulation. It is observed by all those who have been conversant with savage nations, whether in Asia, Africa, or America, that they are all equally impenetrable, and that, when they have a mind to conceal the truth, no examination is capable of drawing it from them. . . . The torture itself is incapable of making them confess any thing which they have no mind to tell. (208)

As I suggested above, sympathy is thought of as the very apotheosis of the human affections; and civilization is the name of that process of refinement and gradual completion of this human. I wonder what this impenetrable other has to say to Smith's impartial spectator? If the falsehood attributed to the one is the correlate of the truth-full-ness of the other? As civilization shears itself of the supposedly chaotic, intolerable freedom of savagery, the impartial spectator, as the representative of the Great Judge, appropriates that power to himself. Perhaps through some "occult process," the strength, brutality, indeed, essential masculinity of the savage is transferred to the sympathetic spectator, and thus is naturalized another kind of dissimulation? And yet these dissimulations, legible in notes, on the margins, in seemingly non-essential arguments, tell of another history.

The history of British slavery, for instance. Smith himself felt that slavery was an inefficient means of organizing productive forces, and so was against it. Later in the century, voices such as Cugoano and Olaudah Equiano (Gustavus Vasa) would speak in the idioms of sympathy and sentiment to seek justice. The impenetrable savage would demand to be recognized as a human, an apt object of sympathy. The ambivalences of such a project are profound and we will return in subsequent chapters to its fraught structure and rhetoric. For now, I want to end this consideration of moral philosophy with a passage from Equiano's *The Interesting Narrative of the Life of Olaudah Equiano, or Gustavus Vassa, the African, Written by Himself.* It reminds us, I think, that European "civilization" was brought back to itself by the other, that savage who supposedly "expects no sympathy from those about him."

> Are there not causes enough to which the apparent inferiority of an African may be ascribed, without limiting the goodness of God, and supposing he forbore to stamp understanding on certainly his own image, because "carved in ebony?" Might it not naturally be ascribed to their situation? When they come among Europeans, they are ignorant of their language, religion, manners, and customs. Are any pains taken to teach them these? Are they treated as men? Does not slavery itself depress the mind, and extinguish all its fire, and every noble sentiment? But, above all, what advantages do not a refined people possess over those who are rude and uncultivated? Let the polished and haughty European recollect that his ancestors were once, like the Africans, uncivilized, and even barbarous. Did Nature make *them* inferior to their sons? And should *they too* have been made slaves? Every rational mind answers, No. Let such reflections as these melt the pride of their superiority into sympathy for the wants and miseries of their sable brethren, and compel them to acknowledge, that understanding is not confined to feature or colour. If, when they look round the world, they feel exultation, let it be tempered with benevolence to others, and gratitude to God, "who hath made of one blood all nations of men for to dwell on all the face of the earth; and whose wisdom is not our wisdom, neither are our ways his ways.[116]

Writing with passion but also with pathos, Equiano's rhetoric is poised between demand and plea. He would compel Europeans into sympathy. That "sympathy for the wants and miseries of their sable brethren" could be the legitimizing strategy for the civilizing mission is part of the historical irony that we must also remember. I will return to that history in subsequent chapters.

In Conclusion

My reading of moral philosophic and aesthetic discourse has sought to follow the movement of the sympathetic operation. As we shall see, sympathy does not operate in the same way in other discourses; we would be obliged to speak, rather, of mutually ramifying "rationalities."[117] Below I try to schematize the axioms of moral philosophy's sympathetic rationality; what follows, then, is a kind of map of the rules of (im)possibility for the sympathetic procedure.

The rule of agent/object

In the scenario of moral philosophy and aesthetics, there must be at least two, non-identical subjects of sympathy: the active, often empowered and privileged sympathizer, and the seemingly passive, disempowered and often suffering object of sympathy. In the moral philosophical texts I have looked at, both in Hume's simpler and Smith's more elaborate structures, an essential difference of subjectivity and physical space is basic to sympathy. But agency is limited to the cognizing subject, or, in Smith, to the judging, disciplining spectator; the agency of the object seems hardly ever considered. As we have seen, in other discursive modes, for instance in slave narratives, the object is authorized, if not empowered, with a certain agency through and limited by this sympathy; the sympathetic relationship sets up a kind of contract of justice between the two subjects. (I will trace this agency, which is only implicit and in fact mostly obfuscated in the discourse of moral philosophy, in my analysis of *Jane Eyre* and *Pamela* and the slave narratives).[118]

This relationship or kinship is characterized by an exchange of some kind of emotion (pain or pleasure). The one calls for sympathy, the other, if he is properly humanized, gives it. To give sympathy in exchange for the call of suffering is a central pedagogy of the procedure. It is predicated on a certain identification, termed "taking the place of" or a "sort of substitution" between agent and object.

This exchange aims both to diminish (if not obliterate) the difference between agent and object, but also to mark this very difference as a target of some sort of action of justice (betterment, amelioration, understanding, but even approval, fellow-feeling, affinity, pity, etc.). Properly performed and executed, sympathy should obliterate its own conditions of existence.

Let us reiterate a basic aporia: Difference must be both produced and effaced in the sympathetic operation.[119]

The rule of representing the body

Sympathy involves the agent in and through a certain epistemology and bodily practice of alterity. For the sympathetic operation to function, a true, disinterested representation (i.e., objective knowledge or absolute comprehension) of the other's emotion must enliven the imagination and activate the bodily senses of the agent.[120] Sympathy does not function only, or even primarily in the order of reason. For these representations to be effective, they must tap into our very natures, our very bodies. Sympathy should be legible on the bodies of both subjects. The sympathetic relation writes its effects, as it were, on the body. The sympathetic movement is preeminently sensual. This movement, moreover, is an agency of the great judge, the divine creator, the Deity.

A second aporia: the sympathetic operation is based on representation, but sympathy is itself lodged in our (physiological and divine) nature.

The rule of sympathetic nature and civilizing sympathy

Representations that elicit sympathy naturally trigger our humanity; these representations work because human nature is innately susceptible to their influence. Except for animals, some women, and savages, sympathy founds our, that is human, nature. Our sympathetic nature is a signature of God the Creator, the Maker, the Designer, and Judge.

At the same time that sympathy names the most proper trait of our nature, it also names that which founds the possibility of family, of community, of civilization, of general sociality. One gives sympathy, but there is an immediate return on the debt that the other incurs, even if only in the self-approbation that returns to the sympathizing self. Sympathy therefore stabilizes a certain economy, a kind of human and humanizing exchange. Central to this humanizing exchange is a cognitive style that obsessively focuses all actions, decisions, and thoughts on their future effects.

And so a third aporia: Although sympathy is posited as being universally lodged in our nature, its operation founds (bourgeois) culture, society, civilization; its very representation in the discourse of moral philosophy functions as a pedagogy of Christian European civilizing.

The rule of sympathetic propriation

As a gift responds to the call of otherness but one that immediately yields a return of approbation to the giver, sympathy both appropriates and makes proper all forms of otherness: the other's body embodied in pity; the savagery of the racialized other both renarrativized and normalized in the story of the "social affections"; the effeminacy of sentiment made proper to the civilized, re-masculinized, universal human. Sympathy founds the being (proper) of the (social) subject—through sympathy the subject comes to know the mode of sociality proper to the moral order; sympathy renders the other an object of identification, and so the other seems to be knowable, accessible, and so appropriable.

A fourth aporia: As the call of the other, difference must be both produced and effaced in the sympathetic operation. Sympathy, thus, renders the subject both homologous with the other, and autotelic with regard to the self. It both affiliates and differentiates. Sympathy at once makes proper (through identification, knowledge, and sentiment) that other and dislocates the sympathetic self through that other. We are back, in some sense, to our first aporia.

Such are the rules of sympathy. Circular and tangential, awkward and unreliable, they seem hardly to be rules at all. Now, if these rules of possibility for the sympathetic operation are strictly speaking impossible, this does not mean that sympathy doesn't "exist," or that there is no true sympathy, or that for Burke, Smith, and Hume sympathy was a sham that we have now finally unmasked. Quite the opposite: Sympathy functions through the play of these aporias, in the very folds of these contradictions. But if it does function these aporias haunt its movement, and so, promise something else, some other possibility, perhaps something else altogether. I end with a word on another kind of possibility.

I will conclude, that is, with some speculations. Is there some remainder or uncontrollable overflow in the sympathetic relationship? I believe we have charted its effects—one of which is a kind of desire for propriation and abjection—in Burke, Hume, and Smith. But can this remainder also then be a resource or starting point in a counter-memory of sympathy? If the other of sympathy cannot be reduced to knowledge, cannot be made wholly proper to the (bourgeois, male) self or (European) civilization, could the circuit of force and desire be reversed, diverted, broken through this irreducibility? My sense is that, if listened to with another ear, the history of sympathy reverberates with an otherness that is no less essential to the constitution of European civilization. Isn't it this otherness that is legible in the terror of black femininity in Burke, or the insistent call of difference in Hume, or the relays between the savage and the spectator in Smith—and the lingering problem of justice in all these texts?

Reading Equiano and Cugoano with this tradition would be the beginning of such a counter-memory.[121]

Levinas writes, "Our relation with the other certainly consists in wanting to comprehend him, but this relation overflows comprehension. Not only because knowledge of the other requires, outside of all curiosity, also sympathy or love, ways of being distinct from impassible contemplation, but because in our relation with the other, he does not affect us in terms of a concept. He is a being and counts as such" ("Is Ontology Fundamental?," 6). On the one hand, what Levinas neglects here, and what I have sought to remember in my reading of Burke, Hume and Smith, is that the concept and practice of sympathy has always involved the other in relations of force or violence, knowledge or comprehension, representation, and so propriation.[122] As we have seen, multiple forms of difference are produced, denied, and appropriated in the discourse of sympathy. It is this relation between force, representation, sympathy, and the heterosexual family that provoked my critical re-reading of Foucault's theory of governmentality. At the same time, and on the other hand, I believe that this overflow heralds a new principle and practice of sociality. One that is born through relations of European sympathy but lives a kind of occult life beyond it, one that both promises and betrays the other, one that will have been named but never quite recognized in the practice and history of solidarity.[123]

Chapter Three

"Some Inscrutable Appeal"

Race, Gender, and the
Closure of Sentimentalism

How to Read the Man with the Piebald Hair

The sympathetic relation in British sentimental literature often seemed beyond the order of reason. A relation that almost could not be named, whose workings were part of the secret of humanity itself, as if an occult bond were underwriting the new social dispensation of industrial capitalism. Consider Ezra Jennings, the man with the piebald hair. In *The Moonstone* (1868), Wilkie Collins's masterpiece of suspense and colonial guilt, Ezra is that marginal figure who seemingly is hated by everyone, and yet is the very person who helps resolve the novel's central mystery. He himself remains a mystery throughout. First, there is the strangeness of Ezra's body: "speaking from a popular point of view," Ezra's appearance was against him. "His gipsy-complexion, his fleshless cheeks, his gaunt facial bones, his dreamy eyes, his extraordinary parti-colored hair, the puzzling contradiction between his face and figure which made him look old and young both together—were all more or less calculated to produce an unfavorable impression of him on a stranger's mind" (364). Ezra's appearance it seems produces an immediate and universal antipathy. "And yet," continues Blake, his only friend, "feeling this as I certainly did—it is not to be denied that Ezra Jennings made some inscrutable appeal to my sympathies, which I found it impossible to resist." The strange looking Ezra in fact produces an even stranger response in Blake: an inexplicable sympathy.

For eighteenth- and nineteenth-century writers, sympathies were strange things. One had to listen to them with another ear because they could be signs and presentiments of unconscious, divine, or natural bonds. Remember Jane Eyre's warning: She confessed, "Presentiments are strange things! and so are sympathies; and so are signs: and the three combined make one mystery to which humanity has not yet found the key. I never laughed at presentiments in my life, because I have had strange ones of my own. Sympathies, I believe exist: (for instance, between far-distant, long absent, wholly estranged relatives; asserting, notwithstanding their alienation, the unity of the source to which each traces his origin) whose workings baffle mortal comprehension. And signs, for aught we know, may be but the sympathies of Nature with man" (193).

This chapter focuses on these literary representations of "sympathies whose workings baffle mortal comprehension." I argue that sympathy, and the broader semantic field of sentiment, functioned as a fundamental force of what Foucault once termed the "police"—that far-flung apparatus of normalization which tied together as widely disparate phenomena as hygiene boards and evangelical missions. Another name for the strategies and technologies that constituted this process is, as we have seen, governmentality: new savoirs (absolute knowledge) of state, with statistics as their science and population as their target, incorporating policing techniques of discipline and security.[1] That sympathy and liberal sentiment emerged in the late eighteenth century at precisely the moment that Michel Foucault locates the rise of governmentality is not fortuitous or anomalous; indeed, discipline was enabled by, and security legitimized through sympathy for the other—the poor, the heathen, criminals, delinquents, deviants, prostitutes, slaves, colonial subjects, and the insane were to be sympathized with, and their condition ameliorated. In other words, sympathy was central in making the other proper to the self, and so a way of habituating the self to propriety. In what follows, I narrate the career of sympathy in sentimental and gothic literature, slave narratives, and colonial history, focusing on the relationship between specific genre conventions and the political and social fields of their operation. I argue that sympathy engenders subjects whose sovereignty is predicated on certain dynamics of racial and class abjection. The agents of sympathy, moreover, are invested with anxieties and desires of propriation that return to haunt their scenes of sovereignty. Teasing out the implications of this history of literary sentimentalism, I turn to three novels that seem to me to articulate the key aspects of this history: Richardson's *Pamela*, Brontë's *Jane Eyre*, and MacKenzie's *Man of Feeling*. Through a contrapuntal reading strategy[2] I put these canonical works in relationship to slave narratives and missionary discourses, as each text becomes an "entrance into a network with a thousand entrances; to take this entrance is to aim, ultimately, not at a legal structure of norms and departures, a narrative or poetic Law, but at a perspective (of fragments, of voices from other texts, other codes), whose vanishing point is nonetheless ceaselessly pushed back, mysteriously opened: each (single) text is the very theory (and not the mere example) of this vanishing, of this difference which indefinitely returns, insubmissive."[3]

The Codes of Sentiment

Let us turn first to the contexts of sentimentalism in eighteenth-century fiction. Sympathy was a central narrative device in the new genre of "sentimental fiction," a genre that was overwhelmingly associated with the "feminine" and the discourse of politeness. As literary historians have noted, the sentimental novel attracted an unprecedented audience to literature; this audience was not only numerically larger than before, it was also made up of a new social alliance; sentimental fiction was addressed to women as much to men, and to those who belonged to "the middle station of life."[4] Moreover, the eighteenth century saw the emergence of a "mass audience" that consumed newspapers, magazines, pamphlet controversies, and literature; this print culture expanded to wider audiences through institutions and practices such as public readings in taverns, coffee houses, private libraries, and circulating libraries. From its inception, this growing middle-class literary culture was rooted in an anxious discourse of politeness. Mary Poovey notes that

> one early response to the charge that the new system of credit had undermined civic humanism was that of Joseph Addison and Richard Steele. In the *Tatler* (1709 to January 1710–11), then the *Spectator* (March to December 1712, June to December 1714), Addison and Steele suggested that the practices associated with taste, sociability, sympathy, and honesty, among others, could form the basis for a new kind of virtue, which served national interests by promoting civility and, not incidentally, by strengthening Britain's commerce with the rest of the trading world. . . . [The *Spectator*] linked beneficial national government to effective *self*-government, through manners and civility.[5]

To make this connection palpable we could start by keeping in mind that Samuel Richardson's Pamela, perhaps the eighteenth century's most famous heroine of sympathy, was an avid reader of both Addison and Steele.[6] As we shall see, sentimental literature was yoked to the work of constructing a viable bourgeois civil society through the production of a particular kind of gendered, national, and racial subject. Initially, however, the novel of sentiment was suspected of being an overly feminine (if not feminized) genre. Indeed, works such as Richardson's *Pamela* (1740); *Clarissa* (1748), and *Charles*

Grandison (1754); Charlotte Lennox's *The Life of Harriot Stuart, Written by Herself* (1750) and *Female Quixote* (1752); Henry MacKenzie's *Man of Feeling* (1771); Sarah Fielding's *David Simple* (1744); or Frances Burney's *Evelina* (1778) popularized the novel of sentiment and offered a form of cultural autonomy and some psychological release to hundreds of female readers and authors.[7]

Simultaneously, a new kind of European bourgeois subject emerged in and through this fiction. As Moira Ferguson argues, sentimental literature emerged at the moment when the capitalist marketplace was restructuring the relationship between writer, reader, text and representation (92). Ian Watt, in his classic study of *The Rise of the Novel,* points out that the novel's popularity in the eighteenth century is indebted to increases in literacy, the changes in the writing profession that followed the shift from patronage to publishing houses, and the proliferation of bookshops and circulating libraries. For Watt, the novel rose under the mixed sign of Cartesian realism and Lockean individualism: As a form of literature, it put into practice that epistemological, spatial, and temporal framework that takes individual subjectivity as its optic, and a continuous identity sutured through (linear) memory and situated in a (demarcated) space as its "principle of individuation."[8] Drawing on more recent historians of the novel, Firdous Azim has remarked that there are subtle national, colonial, and gender contexts to this new literary form: thus, not only does the novel embody elements of a certain "family romance," which narrates the adventure of the domestic affections through the fantasy of bourgeois normality, but these norms (for instance, sexual, racial, social and national) are tied to the dual history of European expansionism and its civilizing mission.[9] For our purposes, we can locate the novel form at this intersection: the elaboration of apparatuses of civil society (tied, as they often were, to the printed book), the propulsive force of capitalist national integration and colonial expansion (with the requisite forms of subjectivity that those forces entailed) and the piecemeal fabrication of individualized yet well-integrated subjects of "domestic affection."[10]

In its ability to dramatize "moral sentiments," fiction was believed to be an indispensable tool in the production of such individuated subjects.[11] This production of moral sensibilities shifted the determination of meaning in a text to a highly subjective and interactive process of understanding "wherein meaning is produced through an act of sympathetic imagination on the part of the reader."[12] As we saw in the last chapter, this individualizing and intersubjective process was rooted in a certain aesthetic: the "pleasure we derive from someone else's pain."[13] In the literature of sensibility, both physical and emotional distress became pedagogical moments of sympathy. As Catherine Gallagher remarks, fiction was "thought to allow the exercise of sympathy, that process by which one feels the joys and sufferings of another and may thereby be motivated to perform benevolent actions" (166–167). Writing in 1785, Clara Reeve (1729–1807) argued that the novel "gives a familiar relation of such things, as pass every day before our eyes, such as may happen to our friend, or to ourselves." Markman Ellis comments that her "definition relied on an idea of credible sympathy, as 'the perfection of it, is to represent every scene, in so easy and natural a manner, and to make them appear so probable, as to deceive us into a persuasion (at least while we are reading) that all is real, until we are affected by the joys or distresses, of the persons in the story, as if they were our own.'" In Reeve's formulation, then, the novel reproduced the logic of Adam Smith's theory of sympathy.[14]

For this newly sensitized, specifically feminized (and often female) reader of fiction, the object of sympathy was usually an antihero, a protagonist whose passivity in an otherwise cruel and vicious world provided a subtle and mutlivalent social critique. G. A. Starr has argued that

> [t]he form of the sentimental novel is typically that of an anti-bildungsroman: instead of a progress toward maturity, it deals sympathetically with the character who cannot grow up and find an active place in society. Its ideal is stasis or regression, which makes for episodic, cyclical narratives that often go nowhere or back where they began. Owing to different social assumptions about masculinity and femininity, the sentimental heroine can figure in conventional romance plots that end with wedding bells, since her role conforms to the popular sense of what a young woman should be; the sentimental hero poses an implicit challenge to accepted notions of masculinity, and he cannot be assimilated into the world represented in the novels. As a consequence, sentimental novels tend to become satires on "the world," but satires in which the hero himself cannot usually take part because of his naïveté, good nature, and general childlikeness.[15]

Although lacking in irony or wit, and commonly represented as a passive victim, the sentimental hero, in his very victimization, embodies a certain hopeful vision of human nature. As such, sentimentalism draws on the English religio-literary technique for reviving the role of emotion in human conduct.[16] (It is no accident that the Book of Job, with its classic antihero, figured prominently in many sentimentalist texts.) Informed by the works of numerous Anglican Latitudinarians such as Isaac Barrow, John Tillotson, and Samuel Clarke, sentimentalist writers staged the connections between virtue, benevolence, charity, and philanthropy.[17]

This religious tradition was also implicitly a nostalgic pastoralism: In the sentimental world of these novels, "people are still capable of intense emotions; here they still care about each other; here they do not disregard one another's pain and suffering."[18] Sympathetic identification, then, also produces a certain desire for return (to childhood, to a simpler time, to the primitive, to a pure, "natural" world, etc.). Not surprisingly, sentimentalism is closely tied to eighteenth-century primitivism "insofar as it looks upon social institutions as thwarting or perverting human dignity." The sentimental hero is not on a voyage of discovery. Rather, s/he is on a mission of recovery, "trying to recapture a sense of fixity amid distressing flux, or to regain a long-lost haven of secure devotion."[19] In sentimental fiction, the adventure of sympathy would involve both reader and writer in a nostalgic, universalizing, Christianizing quest for the (lost) self. Consequently, there is always an irreducible element of fantasy in this aesthetic of sympathetic identification (I will return to this fantasy of recovery). Moreover, as I argued in the last chapter, sympathetic identification is rooted in a specific paradox: for identification to happen, sympathy must simultaneously posit and transcend a necessary space of difference. McCarthy puts it thus: Sympathy "is contingent on an apparent paradox: the gap, or separateness of the individual parts, is a *sine qua non* of the process; but equally important is the fact that the individual identities remain intact despite their co-operation in the whole, brought about by the reader's sympathetic act" (29).

Now if sentimental narratives are both nostalgic and at times primitivist, the sympathetic scenario itself can nonetheless be integrated into disciplinary pedagogies. If narrative is that which translates "knowing into telling," how does sympathy function in and through this translation?[20] There is much that could be said here, but let me elaborate on one aspect of the narrative function of sympathy that seems to be absolutely crucial, the temporality of sympathy. First, as narratologists have been pointing out for some time now, narratives have a dual temporal structure: story-time and discourse-time. As Seymour Chatman explains, "all narratives, in whatever medium, combine the time sequence of plot events, the time of the *histoire* ('story-time') with the time of the presentation of those events in the text, which we call 'discourse-time.'"[21] So, for instance, a narrative's plot line can give off a linear biography (birth-life-death) while the presentation of that biography in discourse could happen through a series of flashbacks. One way to understand scenes of sympathy, then, is as tableaux vivants, detached scenes, imagistic and evocative, interrupting or "freezing" the story-time. The sentimental scenario works "by being personalized, unique and discrete, so as to place the maximum pressure on the relation between the subject and the viewer, yet manage[s] or mystif[ies] that pressure so as not to threaten the position of the viewer."[22] So it would seem then that sympathetic scenes function to interrupt story-time. And yet readers will recall from the last chapter that part of the very structure of sympathy is a certain proleptic temporality. I suggested there that sympathy operates as a kind of market discipline through the production of a future-oriented, utility calculating sensibility. Sympathy is a pedagogy of bourgeois humanism in so far as it constructs and sutures (through identification) the subject as one who looks at the suffering of another and learns to benefit by it, and so perfects him- or herself through that suffering. Is it possible then that as sympathy halts the story time of sentimental narratives, it simultaneously retemporalizes the reading subject as subject for and of the future? That as narratives linger over sympathy, another temporality is simultaneously born? We will return to this question of narrative, time, and sympathy in the analyses that follow.

From the inception of sentimental fiction, the feminine and feminized body bore the burden of the sympathetic gaze, indicating what was in fact a genre convention: sentimental fiction works out sociopolitical questions and conflicts through a gendered body.[23] As Barnes argues for the American context, the aesthetic of sentimentalism helped produce "the heteroerotic body politic"; in other words, "both sentimental literature and political rhetoric constructs its reader-citizens as wives and daughters of a patriarchal system" (16–17). This sentimental interpolation also marks a historical opening that allowed for the exercise of a particular kind of female agency. Indeed, the history of sympathy intersects with the remarkable emergence of middle-class women's political and literary voices in the late eighteenth and early nineteenth century, specifically in the fields of sentimental and Gothic literature, and in projects to overthrow slavery and implement other social reforms (such as prison reform, missions, Magdalen societies, working-class education, etc.).[24] As Ellis notes, "the eighteenth century witnessed a profound increase in the number of women writers, especially in the second half of the century. In the early decades of the century, it remained the case that publication left the woman writer open to vicious personal assaults on her honour and virtue."[25]

The ideology of the "amiable sensibility of the female breast" enabling the contemplation of suffering others (such as enslaved Africans), "through the pure medium of virtuous pity, unmixed with those political, commercial and selfish considerations which operated in steeling the hearts of some men against the pleadings of humanity" structured middle-class British women's agency in various humanitarian struggles.[26] Elaborating on the key role of Evangelical "Clapham sect spokesperson" Hannah More, Moira Ferguson remarks that in "1788 More claimed the right to a collective political voice for women and a narrative strategy for constructing slaves that depended on a sentimental approach. An inventory of topoi, a refashioned paradigm had come into being in coherent form, accompanied by a certain female gaze born of Christian love for, and perhaps a repressed identification with, the collectivized, dominated other. The compassionate, though unitary voice that told these evildoings spoke unflinchingly to the audience" (153).

As I will argue, however, there was nothing "unitary" in these "voices": compassion, pity, sensibility, sympathy (all concept-metaphors on the terrain of sentimentality) were divided and dividing rhetorical devices. I want to insist on this fact: sympathy was a protean form of power whose axes of identification cut across sex, class, and race. To argue that sentimentalism is essentially tied to the female body can preclude a consideration of this proliferating network of references. My argument (as well as Ferguson's) draws on the pathbreaking work of Nancy Armstrong, whose *Desire and Domestic Fiction* charts the role of the novel in the rise of "a specifically modern form of desire, that, during the early eighteenth century, changed the criteria for determining what was most important in a female."[27] What I would simply add to this profound insight is that this new womanly subjectivity merged with other forces of political and economic domination; for at precisely the same historical moment, an insurgent colonial bourgeois order was locked in mortal combat with "aristocratic despotism" and with the "savages and barbarians" (a phrase that from Burke to Macaulay to Arnold and beyond tied race, nation and class together).[28] In other words, if we can say that the "modern individual was first and foremost a woman" (Armstrong 8), this *individual* was also always raced and classed in such a way that the feminization of the modern subject was less a matter of sex than of gender, more a matter of an overdetermined subject-formation than the supposed given-ness of sexual identity. Thus, to write a political history of sympathy is to interrogate how this paradoxical and protean form of identification eventually became the ideal for both men and women, for white and black, for middle and laboring classes.[29] We must, that is, begin to consider the relays of power, discourse, materiality, and fantasy that enabled the novel to assume a preeminence as the arbiter of a specifically European form of desire and domesticity.

Slavery and Sentimentalism

I turn now to texts that cause us to think at the limits of European literary sentimentalism. I would suggest that the scenario of racial sympathizing pushes the limits of the paradox of European sympathy. As Markman Ellis has argued in his insightful study of sentimental literature, "Depictions of slavery are also felicitous to the sentimentalist interest in pain and suffering. In this way, sentimentalist writers had a significant role in the formation of the moral conscience of the abolition movement. Furthermore, their humanitarian and benevolent intentions (albeit unrealized) both produced and reflected the emergent anti-slavery politics, providing ready-made examples for more polemical activists."[30] Thus narratives written by ex-slaves as well as the numerous pamphlets, petitions, letters, illustrations, paintings, histories, poems, and tracts generated by the abolition movement all crucially drew **on** the conventions of sentimental fiction. We can get a sense of this in the famous inscription on the Wedgwood medallion, in which an enchained

African asks, "Am I not a man and a brother?" Rather than presuppose familiarity, the sympathy of antislavery seeks to render the racially and culturally other familiar *through* sympathetic identification, incorporating the abject slave into the "family of man." Like the nostalgic fantasy that demarcates the agency of the sentimental heroine, the sympathetic slave (of both genders) will remain the disciplined inmate of social institutions (again linking marriage to slavery, and emancipation to economic "freedom," as many British women writers did in their critiques of both slavery and patriarchy).[31] Usually, African men and women in slavery were represented as sympathetic subjects through some combination of socialized, free-trade capital and evangelical Christianity: Thus, to alleviate and emancipate the slave was also to make her more useful as a worker and citizen (which again relates sympathy to a capitalist, utility-oriented temporality).

And yet, the horizontal bond across race would always remain a question, as if it were always a *potential* bond, in the face of actual bondage. Consequently, the "pitiful" slave would question and push the limits of the very notion of bourgeois, white personhood. Her supposed childlike nature, her horrid suffering, her scarred and ravished body renders the sentimental hero of antislavery discourse an apt object for *universal* sympathy. But if a black person can be sympathetic, doesn't the universalist but decidedly European norm of humanity itself have to be supplemented, extended, revised? So, for instance, when ex-slaves such as Cugoano wrote parts of their narratives in the idioms of Christian humanitarianism they were both contesting their exclusion from the category of the human and reinscribing it.

> But why think ye prayers in churches and chapels only will do ye good, if your charity do not extend to pity and regard your fellow creatures perishing through ignorance, under the heavy yoke of subjection and bondage, to the cruel and avaricious oppression of brutish profligate men; and when both the injured, and their oppressors, dwell in such a vicinity as equally to claim your regard?

As we shall see in Equiano's narrative also, the rhetorical strategy of humanitarian sympathy implicated the ex-slave's agency in structures of domination that enabled European expansion in the nineteenth century.

In bourgeois antislavery discourse, the paradox of sympathetic identification centers on the presupposition of an active agent and passive object. Indeed, as I will argue below, antislavery sympathy explicitly marks *and* reproduces the unequal relations of force that divide the slave and emancipator. For sympathy to be an effective pedagogy, a vertical gap of power must continually be made visible—hence the necessity of repeating the question: "Am I not a woman and a sister?" But if differentiation and identification are the paradoxical effects of the sympathetic relation in abolitionist discourse, then the subject of such sympathy is always also the subject of terror, horror, of brutal, monstrous violence. It is as if sympathy needs the trauma of murderous violence to give it life. Pursuing the mode of representing the many horrors of slavery returns us to questions of literary and aesthetic contexts. Consider this often, perhaps too often,[32] cited passage from Douglass's first *Narrative;* speaking of the sadism of the overseer and his master, Douglass writes, "Mr. Plummer was a miserable drunk, a profane swearer, and a savage monster. He always went armed with a cowskin and a heavy cudgel. I have known him to cut and slash the women's heads so horribly, that even master would be enraged at his cruelty, and would threaten to whip him if he did not mind himself. Master, however, was not a humane slaveholder. . . . I have often been awakened at the dawn of day by the most heart-rending shrieks of an own aunt of mine, whom he used to tie up to a joist, and whip upon her naked back till she was literally covered with blood."[33] Since at least the 1780s, such scenes had become common "currency," as it were, in abolitionist strategies in both England and America. The innocent black woman (later Uncle Tom would become the most famous man) becomes an object of savage violence, a spectacle of horror, and by virtue of her (supposed) helplessness, of sympathy. Such scenes, of course, are "primal" in the discourse of abolitionism; as Saidiya V. Hartman argues in *Scenes of Subjection: Terror, Slavery, and Self-Making,* the "terrible spectacle dramatizes the origin of the subject and demonstrates that to be a slave is to be under the brutal power and authority of another."[34] What is the genealogy of this drama?

I argue that the reticulation of sympathy and slavery in British (and American) abolitionism draws on idioms circulating in another literary and cultural movement.[35] As I argued above, in sentimental fiction the transformative, salvific effects of suffering induced in the reader a proper sentiment: pity for the victim whose body is in distress.[36] But through the course of the eighteenth century, the sentimentalist preoccupation with the pedagogical effect of another's suffering transformed into a preoccupation with the experience of pain in the self. As Bruhm argues,

> This shift in focus from mind to body characterizes a shift in gothic and Romantic fiction from contemplation of suffering to the experience of suffering. For Lord Byron, the "great object of life is Sensation, to feel we exist, even though in pain." . . . The idealistic optimism of Shelley is often defined to a great extent by falling upon the thorns of life and bleeding. Keats sees "mortal pains," the "worldly elements" that prey upon sensation, as necessary to the soul's formulation.[37]

As the experience of suffering became a privileged site for the emergence of humanity and the staging of the social affections, the aestheticization of pain articulated sympathy between pity and horror.

This shift in the pedagogy of suffering to the aesthetics of pain was marked by the rise of a new literary movement: the Gothic. In June of 1764, Horace Walpole, the third son of the famous Whig statesman Sir Robert Walpole, awoke from a dream.

> I waked one morning . . . from a dream, of which all I could recover was, that I had thought myself in an ancient castle (a very natural dream for a head filled like mine with gothic story) and that on the uppermost banister of a great staircase I saw a gigantic hand in armour. In the evening I sat down and began to write, without knowing in the least what I intended to say or relate.[38]

Although Walpole never wrote another novel again, this one slender volume blending the "imagination and improbability" of ancient romance and the "accurate imitation of nature" found in modern novels,[39] launched a genre of fiction that, in hybrid and diverse forms, would have an enormous hold on the Western imagination for over two centuries. Certainly by the 1790s, the Gothic novel, better known to contemporaries as the "modern romance," was taking the book market by storm.[40]

Gothic literature and culture can be seen partially as a reaction against the solemn obedience to reason, and firm commitment to order that characterize eighteenth-century neoclassicism. Indeed, from its initial connotations of "barbarism and wildness," evoking associations to Goths (Northern invaders who hastened the decline of the Roman Empire), by the end of the eighteenth century, "gothic" became an antonym for "classical."[41] But the term seems to have a much more complicated genealogy in European thought; indeed, its wide semantic range might explain how it came to exert such an enormous power. As in the sentimental novel, the hero of Gothic fiction also lacks irony or wit, representing an "artless" nature. But the Gothic extends, and exaggerates, the Puritan tradition of nostalgic pastoralism: in the hyper sentimentalized world of these novels, the heroine is not only trying to recover "a long-lost haven of secure devotion," but often trying to escape from psychic, cultural, and bodily dissolution. This dissolution was also always a trace of the other. According to the OED, next to its obvious association with the Goths, the term Gothic also named the church of those Spanish Christians who adopted certain aspects of Arabic culture under Muslim rule and practiced a modified form of Christian worship: the Mozarabic Christians (from the Spanish *Mozárabe,* which is itself from the Arabic, *musta'rib,* translated as "would-be Arab"). Although the Orient often insinuates itself in Gothic tales (for instance, in William Beckford's *Vathek* [1786] or Charlotte

Dacre's *Zofloya, or The Moor* [1806]), very little has been written on this specifically Arabic genealogy of the Gothic.[42]

In any case, what is crucial for our concerns is that the Gothic was filiated in essential ways to the cultural, sexual, and religious other, to barbarism and savagery, in short to all that England had left behind in its onward march of progress.[43] It is useful to keep Walpole's words in mind: *The Castle of Otranto*

> was an attempt to blend the two kinds of romance, the ancient and the modern. In the former all was imagination and improbability: in the latter, nature is always intended to be, and sometimes has been, copied with success. Invention had not been wanting; but the great resources of fancy have been dammed up, by a strict adherence to common life. But if in the latter species Nature has cramped imagination, she did but take her revenge, having been totally excluded from old romances. (9)

If "Nature" had taken her revenge on imagination, Walpole would give those "dammed up" powers of Imagination another turn at sovereignty. This blending and mixing of realism and the fantastic would be the hallmark of all Gothic fiction. As Brennan notes, the Gothic provided English culture with cautionary tales, bringing back, in horrifying forms, all those reminders of what classicism sought to repress: feeling, mystery, superstition, instinct, spontaneity, excess.[44] As such the Gothic performs that double work of culture: marking a primitive state from which culture emerges, and establishing a later or higher state where it risks the return of that which has been repressed.[45] In a sense, the Gothic sensibility was the return of the barbaric double of civilization. Not surprisingly, then, many commentators have read the Gothic as a crucial transgression of eighteenth-century literary and cultural norms.[46]

Revived in architecture, literature, and art, the Gothic exploited the new aesthetic of the sublime and a newfound interest in the interiority of the subject. As for the latter, Edward Young, one of the founders of the Graveyard movement in poetry, advised, "Dive deep into thy bosom; learn the depth, extent, bias and full fort of thy mind; contract full intimacy with the stranger within thee; excite and cherish every spark of intellectual light and heat, however smothered under former negligence."[47] Depth, height, fullness, expanse, and the intimate strangeness of nature were all central to contemporary ideas of the sublime (the term means "set or raised aloft, high up"). As Terry Castle notes, the eighteenth-century concept of sublimity "derives from the first or second century A.D. rhetorical treatise by Longinus, *Peri Hupsous*. . . . Longinus characterized the poetical sublime as 'greatness' or 'grandeur' of expression, that which transported the reader and induced feelings of awe or wonderment. . . . The sublime led the individual to contemplate the power of divinity." When, in 1674, Boileau translated Longinus into French, the sublime became a popular topic for intellectual discussion, particularly among English writers and aestheticians. Such writers as John Dennis, the Earl of Shaftesbury, and Joseph Addison all contributed commentaries on the sublime.

As I noted in the last chapter, an even more influential work in the literary history of the sublime, and one of the most celebrated philosophical treatises of the century, was Edmund Burke's *A Philosophical Enquiry into the Origin of our Ideas of the Sublime and the Beautiful* (1757). Burke attempted to show that anything that conveyed ideas of "pain or terror" to the mind yet brought with it no actual physical danger produced emotions of sublimity in the spectator. Vast, powerful, obscure, dark, towering, or irregular objects in nature were often sublime in the extreme: "When viewed from a safe distance, they produced pleasure because they excited 'the passions' without causing real danger."[48] A specific rhetorical strategy produces "pain or terror" in Gothic aesthetics: sublime pleasure arises from the necessary distance of the horrifying spectacle, and so elevates the "viewer." Gothic fiction, indeed, exploited the sensation of (observable) pain. For Burke, pain and danger, sickness and death are ideas that give rise to the strongest passions of which we are capable, and can be a source of pleasure leading to the sublime. But always with a little distance, just close enough for a good look. "The history of pain . . . is in many ways a history of looking; it is a narrative of watching a pained object while occupying a contradictory space both within and outside that object. And within that narrative is a multitude of discourses that mediate the way a culture, or indeed an individual, experiences pain at any given time or place."[49] This necessary distance, and the imaginative bridging of it through a kind of identification—the double movement of the gaze of sympathetic power—repeats and adapts the effective paradox of the sympathetic relation in both abolitionism and missionary discourse as well as the sentimental and Gothic novel.

Let us pursue, a bit more closely, the contexts and conventions of Gothic literature. As George Haggerty argues, the Gothic novel emerges at the "moment when the battle lines of cultural reorganization are being formed in the later eighteenth century." Anxieties over propriety and property recur throughout Gothic literature: While the realist novel may celebrate the codification of middle-class values, eighteenth-century "terrorist fiction"[50] records the terror implicit in the increasingly dictatorial reign of those values.[51] Clery argues that this terror marks a key overlap between sentimental and Gothic fiction: "The demands of property inheritance are inimical to human happiness: this is the message of numerous sentimental fictions of the period, beginning with Richardson's *Clarissa*. Far from being a problem restricted to the feudal past, or to the pages of romance, this was a live issue, bearing on the conflict between aristocratic and bourgeois ideals of social being" (xxxi). The defenders of oligarchic property relations hotly opposed the emerging bourgeois critique of primogeniture as an "artificial imposition, which militated against the rights and happiness of individuals." Indeed, Whig hegemony (in the wake of the Glorious Revolution of 1688) was legitimized through a kind of cult of landed wealth. By introducing laws of "strict settlement" that prevented heirs from selling off portions of their estate to suit their interests, every landed proprietor was able to "fetter his estate for ever; to tyrannize over his heirs." These anxieties animate the Gothic sensibility: Like Walpole's enormous armored hand blocking the passage up the staircase, the "dead hand of the past weighing on the present" would be "embodied" in the figures of spirits and supernatural forces who haunt the living.[52]

Almost from its inception with Walpole's *Castle of Otranto* (1764), the conventions of the Gothic quickly congealed around a few recurrent anxieties. Today, we recognize the Gothic in the "dysfunctional family" or "wrongful usurpation," the sexual apprehensions of a victimized female coupled with the incestuous desire of a libidinous, tyrannical male, the mad, haunting "double" and, of course, the use of the physical features of a massive, cavernous castle to represent political and sexual entrapment; "abandoned rooms may be haunted, locked closets may harbor dreadful secrets, tattered manuscripts may divulge horrifying transgressions"; "midnight trysts, threatened sexual violence, and mere physical brutality" combine to create an atmosphere of "unrelieved gloom."[53] Staging scenes of sympathy, the Gothic effect depends on vivid, static images, rather than a gradual buildup of suspense (crucial for abolitionist and missionary discourses as we shall see); the fragmentation of the narrative mirrors the dissolution of the subject: "The rhetorical gestures, the moulding of physiognomy into hieroglyphs of rage or despair, the mysterious interchangeability of individuals suggested by the frequent instances of mistaken identity, are all . . . signs of a gothic code of selfhood at odds with the 'three-dimensional' characters of realist fiction. In gothic . . . identity is . . . determined . . . from the outside in; it is a matter of public interpretation rather than private expression, and to this extent the horror mode tells an important truth about the role of social convention in constituting subjectivity."[54]

Like the sentimental novel, the Gothic was also integrated in broader pedagogical projects. Haggerty argues, for instance, that with the novels of Clara Reeve (*The Old English Baron* [1777]) and Charlotte Smith (*Emmeline* [1788], *Ethelinde* [1789] and *The Old Manor House* [1793]), the Gothic became a crucial element in female education, making it available for respectable female readers and writers.[55] This process began early; so even though Walpole in his first Preface to *Otranto* admitted he could find no "more useful moral than this; that the sins of the fathers are visited on their children to the third and fourth generation," Eleanor Finn, writing under the pseudonym "Mrs. Teachwell," argued in the *Female Guardian* that the "whole volume is replete with refined morality," and selected some passages from the novel to include in an anthology of improving literature for young women.[56]

The Gothic as a sensibility and a mode of representation resonates strongly with the struggles to end the enslavement of African peoples and the project to evangelize colonial populations. Through the discursive practice of sympathy, the Gothic provided a new language to represent the savagery of slavery. The pained body, the distanced, sympathizing observer, the archaism of the detached scene of horror, the moral uplift of sublime terror, the ambivalent, anxious demarcation of savagery and civilization, and finally, the relentless haunting of those millions of Africans murdered in the slave trade and in the slave colonies—these Gothic practices would find their way into both evangelical abolitionism and missionary representations of Africa and India through popular texts such as Anthony Benezet's *A Caution and Warning to Great Britain and Her Colonies; in A Short Representation of the Calamitous State of the Enslaved Negroes in the British Dominions; Collected from various Authors, and submitted to the Serious Consideration of all, more especially of those in Power* (Philadelphia, 1766) and John Wesley's *Considerations Upon Slavery* (London, 1774).

Benezet (1713–1784)[57] for instance represents the enslaved Africans's "calamitous state" in the following terms: "Reader bring the matter home, and consider whether any situation in life can be more completely miserable than that of those distressed captives. When we reflect, that each individual of this number had some tender attachment which was broken by this cruel separation, who had not an opportunity of mingling tears in a parting embrace . . ." (19); and: "Can any human heart, that retains a fellow-feeling for the sufferings of mankind, be unconcerned at relations of such grievous affliction, to which this oppressed part of our species are subjected . . ." (22). In these moving words, we encounter sympathy as an instrument of exhortation. But something more: Benezet is asking the reader to imagine what it might be like for her or himself to feel the horrors of slavery; he is asking the reader to *identify* with the "miserable" slave through sympathy. The horror and terror of enslavement was "brought home" (one is reminded here of Adam Smith's injunction of "bringing the other home") in such texts through the idioms of a racial Gothic.

John Wesley, the famous Methodist preacher, writes against slavery and the slave trade using strategies of reversal and displacement. I think readers today would be struck with Wesley's text, confronted as we are with his unremitting righteousness and sense of justice. He articulates a series of antislavery arguments that he associates with other forms of struggles against domination, such as anticapitalism and anticolonialism. Needless to say, this articulation is also a romanticization and homogenization of the "African." Thus, until having been "corrupted by an intercourse with the Europeans, and stimulated by the excessive use of spiritous liquors," Africans were an "easy, innocent, gentle" people (16). Consequently, the crime of slavery cannot but raise the question of justice.

> Who can reconcile this treatment of the negroes, first and last, with either mercy or justice. Where is the justice of inflicting the severest evils, on those that have done us no wrong? Of depriving those that never injured us in word or deed, of every comfort of life? Of tearing them from their native country, and depriving them of liberty itself? To which an Angolan, has the same natural right as an Englishman, and on which he sets as high a value? . . . I absolutely deny all slave-holding to be consistent with any degree of even natural justice. (34–35)

Stirring, moving words. But why would anyone, let alone a slaveholder, be moved by them? On what basis? Here, again, we return to the uses of sympathy and the discourse of humanity. Wesley asks, "Are you *a man?* Then you should have an *human* heart. But have you indeed? What is your heart made of? Is there no such principle as compassion there? Have you no sympathy? No sense of human woe? No pity for the miserable? When you saw the flowing eyes, the heaving breasts, or the bleeding sides and tortured limbs of your fellow-creatures, was you a stone, or a brute? . . . Do you feel no relenting now? If you do not, you must go on, till the measure of your iniquities is full. Then will the great GOD deal with *you,* as you have dealt with *them,* and require all their blood at your hands. . . . But if your heart does relent, though in a small degree, know it is a call from the GOD of love" (52–53). A damning, terrifying sentence passed in the name of (racial, moral) justice, but simultaneously a cry for sympathy, compassion, and (human, divine) love. The two, the sentence and the plea, form only two facets of that multiform discipline of racialized Gothic sympathy. As such, sympathy does not name a state of being, much less the essence of the human but, rather, a relation and specific working of power. It is only a subject who is in a strategic position to effect some change in a particular social relation who is called on to act sympathetically; that is precisely why the discourse of sympathy as it becomes an instrument of exhortation in abolitionist texts forcefully reorients, in the name of the sovereign subject of humanism, the (white, oppressing) self toward the (black, dominated) other. Precisely why also that sympathy, even as it reinscribes a certain relation of power, destabilizes that very relation.

It is clear, I think, from these passages that antislavery discourse drew on the discursive resources of Gothic aesthetics. But the irony here is that both abolitionist and missionary discourses were engaged in the Enlightenment project of bourgeois reason, in the great struggle against "old privilege" and crude superstition. In profound ways, they were anti-Gothic discourses: chastising or deriding the mysteries of "savage superstitions" of enslaved Africans or the mysticism of "conquered" Hindu ascetics, censoring the unbridled "instincts" of slaves and natives, and warning against the criminal excesses of non-Christian religions. So, for instance, the rising missionary movement toward the end of the eighteenth century legitimized its complicity with colonialism as benevolence through such passages as this from Mungo Park's *Travels in Africa* (1799): "It was not possible to me . . . [not to lament] that a country, so abundantly gifted and favoured by nature, should remain in its present savage and neglected state. Much more did I lament that people and disposition so gentle and benevolent, should . . . be left as they now are, immersed in the gross and uncomfortable blindness of pagan superstition."[58] As Jean and John Comaroff comment, such passages "reinforced the vision of the rising evangelical movement, for it saw the spiritual cultivation of Africa as a moral, almost sacred duty, an essential part of colonizing the land." India and the Orient generally were included in this sacred duty of bringing light into the blindness of pagan superstition. Consider this passage from perhaps one of India's most famous evangelical workers, Alexander Duff. Here he is exhorting members of the Church of Scotland, "back home," to join together in sympathy for the heathens in India:

At home, any project, the pettiest and most insignificant, is sure to find ready advocates and willing supporters; but the cause of hundred and thirty millions of perishing heathen finds no echo in the breasts of the many, and but a feeble and languid response in the breasts of the few. And yet, this is a cause of such vast and overwhelming importance, that, in comparison with it, all the questions and interests of ordinary partizanship fade into utter nothingness! . . . Let me, therefore, however unworthy, become the representative and advocate of the famishing millions of India; and with single purpose of heart, let me strive to awaken general sympathy in behalf of those vast multitudes that have no tongue to proclaim their own woe-begone necessities. Maintaining an attitude of strict neutrality towards all belligerent parties at home, let me strive to turn their eyes toward the melting spectacle of a mighty but crushed and prostrated people, knit to them at once by the ties of a common humanity, and a common citizenship. And who can tell, but the fixed and concentrated gaze at a common object of such depth and intensity of woe, may have the effect of reacting on the observers, and fusing their own mutual antipathies in the glowing stream of a diffusive benevolence.[59]

We have here all the elements of a classic scene of sympathy: spectacle, gaze, suffering, representation, and call. But something more: sympathy in missionary discourse would also be a strategy of population: unlike sentimentalist and Gothic sympathy, where the individual is isolated through scenes of terror, in missionary discourse the suffering native would usually be pluralized into a homogenous mass of misery. As these innumerable scenes of horror were integrated into broader narratives of civilizational and moral progress, sympathy reconstituted Gothic horror through the discursive practice of evangelical colonialism. I will return to this argument in the next chapter.

Let us summarize the argument thus far. I have suggested that the practice of sympathy in the eighteenth century enables an interrogation of the reticulated network of power that made reading literature a gendered, raced, and classed act. The idea and practice of sympathy was central to the creation of a specific kind of subject in and through sentimental and Gothic fiction. These genres were closely tied to new ideologies of the "feminine," and, in different ways, associated to the new practices of middle-class politeness. Sympathy was yoked to the work of constructing a viable bourgeois civil society through the production of a particular kind of gendered, national, and racial subject. This humanized subject, whose experience of pain elicits a certain response in the observer, was also moored to specific religious traditions of Puritan, latitudinarian, and, later in the century, Evangelical benevolence and charity. Using sentimentalist and Gothic idioms, tropes, figurations and imaginings, antislavery and missionary discourses articulated practices of governing racialized populations and producing sympathetic selves. It would be through this particular prism of religious, gender, racial, and national identity that the career of sympathy would find a new life in the tropics of domination.

Pamela, Slavery, and the Police

I turn now to three literary texts that crucially elaborated this network of power and sentiment. As I see it, *Pamela, Jane Eyre,* and *The Man of Feeling* dramatize some fundamental aspects of the sympathetic relation. All three highlight the crucial relationship between representation and sentimentalism; the scenes of sympathy, embedded in narratives as if they were detachable tableaux, have a specific rhetoric, as well as a specific rhetorical function. Further, all three texts pose the question of the relationship between sympathy, justice, and otherness: in different ways, and with different effects, these texts register the history of Europe's other. Finally, each text shows how religious and domestic concerns articulate with discourses of usefulness, benevolence, and economy—in short with strategies of governmentality. In my reading of these texts, I trace the reticulation of these issues, but always with an eye toward the question of agency. I ask, how does the sympathetic relation enable a certain agency for the object of pity? What are the limits and possibilities of this form of agency? And, finally, through what processes of otherizing does this agent assume a certain power? These questions take us into the more general textuality of antislavery and missionary discourses and histories. And so I read these three European novels through a contrapuntal relation with texts written by ex-slaves (Mary Prince, Cuguano, Equiano), abolitionist evangelicals, and colonial missionaries.

As is well known, Richardson's *Pamela* was one of the most popular texts published in the eighteenth century; the travails of the "poor domestic girl" fascinated the newly emerging reading public throughout England and Western Europe. In what follows, I tie Pamela's narrative to specific relations of sympathy that seem to bridge the impossible divide between nature and culture. Throughout the text, nature is tied to piety, truth, godliness, religion, poverty, the home, and birthing; culture (or civilization) is linked to artfulness, coquetry, rakishness, education, adultery, vice, aristocracy, and, oddly, to barbarism. Although Pamela seems to embody all that is good in nature, by the end of the novel she becomes something of an educational reformer, with her own program for inculcating the best of nature's lessons. I aim to follow this strange movement in the figuration of Pamela. But, as an orienting gesture, I want to place my reading of this epistolary novel in terms of some of the "rules" of the sympathetic procedure with which I closed my consideration of eighteenth-century moral philosophy.

Recall the rule of agent/object: Although in the sympathetic relation an active sympathizer exerts power over the (mostly) passive object, in the case of the sentimental novels, the object is authorized with a certain agency through and limited by this relation. Indeed, the circuit of sympathy, if one can use that term in such a scenario, would demarcate the object's subjectivity. It is this overdetermined agency that comes to punctuate Pamela's negotiation of the structures of power she is forcibly drawn in to. As hostage to sexual terror, and then as domesticated wife, Pamela not only exercises a form of subjectivity that both reproduces but also undermines gender, racial, and class inequality; and like sentimental heroines throughout the century, hers is a static, fixed identity. This circuit is bodied forth through a liminal art, that is, through Pamela's sentimental, "natural" epistles (the rule of representation). Third, I argued that although sympathy is posited as being universally lodged in our nature the representation of sympathy in the discourse of moral philosophy functions as a pedagogy of Christian European civilizing. As we shall see, perhaps Pamela's principal role, especially after her marriage, will be the domestic pedagogue of benevolent nature, what I will tie to a certain "police" function. Oddly, by resisting B's drive for (sexual) possession, by not being appropriated sexually, Pamela is able to inhabit a sympathetic subjectivity that becomes a new model of propriation: the polite subject-citizen of sentiment (the rule of propriation). In what follows, I will attempt to tease out the subtle distinctions in the sympathetic function between the domain of moral philosophy and the sentimental novel. I turn now to the elaboration of Pamela as sympathetic subject.

Richardson has Pamela write her own story. And it is through her letters that a growing network of others (and eventually, her assailant and would-be rapist, Mr. B) comes to pity her, and through their pity they are "reclaimed." After all, an alternative subtitle of the text could just as easily be "The Rake Reformed." As the unreclaimed rake, the "barbaric" Mr. B (I: 53, 194)[60] at first bristles at Pamela's letter writing. Informing Mrs. Jervis that Pamela must "not write the affairs of my family purely for an exercise to her pen and her invention. I tell you, she is a subtle, artful gipsey, and time will shew it you" (I: 17). This "artful gipsey," "artful young baggage" (I: 16), "little hypocrite" (I: 24), "young sorceress" (I: 162), is a "mighty letter-writer" (I: 24), and B's self-image suffers much under her truthful and righteous pen. But despite all of his assertions to the contrary, B cannot help pitying this abject figure of piety. And his pity sets him on the virtuous path of truth, that is, domesticity.

As with all truth, Pamela's does not emerge: it merely is. Like nature. This is of course a genre convention of sentimental literature: Unlike the typical protagonist of the bildungsroman, Pamela does not develop but is, rather, linked again and again to a static nature. The haughty Lady Davers is thoroughly won over by Pamela's "noble simplicity," her "unaffected, sincere, free, and easy" conversation (I: 413); her letters give the "pleasure of sentiments flowing with that artless ease, which so much affects us when we read your letters" (II: 32); Pamela has "more prudence, by nature, as it were, than the best of us get in a course of the genteelest educations and with fifty advantages" (II: 33). Pamela herself wishes to show through her letters "how plain nature operates in honest minds, who have hardly any thing else for their guide" (II: 65). One of the techniques that enables her to claim a sympathetic nature as her own is the repeated assertions of her lowly, humble origins; indeed, she seeks always to remember and in some sense to resume her identity as poor obliged servant (II: 35) or the "pretty rustic" (I: 254): after B has declared his love and made known his intentions to marry, Pamela confesses her unworthiness: "O, Sir . . . expect not words from your poor servant, equal to these most generous professions. Both the means, and the will, I now see, are given to you, to lay me under an everlasting obligation" (I: 236). What is striking is that with each assertion of her humble origins, Pamela simultaneously declares her obligation to her sympathizers and claims a kind of agency *through* pity. Again, sympathy is the gift that necessitates an immediate return. But this very obligation, the return itself, enables her to speak as the natural, simple, and grateful rustic. The sympathetic debt is a form of agency. In fact, the effectivity of her voice could be charted in this play between an assertion of difference (humble servant, oppressed woman, pious wife), the pitying response or sympathetic gesture, and the obligation that maintains Pamela's new social and economic status.

But there is a form of agency that seems to be ex-centric to this circuit of exchange, and here, too, sympathy will have its role. I would suggest that the sympathetic appeal to nature names another kind of agency through which the subject of pity negotiates "mastery." Let us try to delimit the modality of this other agency. In a letter, she pleads with her would-be rapist, "For God's sake, good Sir, pity my lowly condition, and my present great misery; and let me join with all the rest of your servants to bless that goodness, which you have extended to every one, but the poor afflicted, heart-broken Pamela" (I: 101). None of this seems to have much of an effect on the lecherous B. It is only on reading some parts of her "prison-journal" that B is finally overcome with his "affection" for Pamela (I: 222) when he realizes that she wishes him well even though her own bodily and spiritual "interests" are against him. Moreover, that he is *reading* her journal is of the utmost importance: it is as if her journal representations, since they have no rhetorical purpose, no suasive intent, are themselves disinterested. Nothing, perhaps, could have been more convincing.

The narrative of sympathy inaugurates B's progress toward the sympathetic human. Although Pamela attributes this shift to a "blessed turn of Providence" (I: 309), divine nature can be read in her own exemplary behavior, that is, if one *reads* her journals and letters. The reclamation of barbarity through pity needs the mighty letter writer; as with Smith, natural pity needs some kind of representation. Certainly, the reformation of B and Lady Davers would be impossible without the agency of her exemplary letters. Pamela's agency, then, consists in persuading others by example, virtue might even become the fashion. Simon Darnford laments, "But what must I do? I'd be glad at any rate to stand in your lady's graces, that I would; nor would I be the last rake libertine unreformed by her example, which I suppose will make virtue the fashion, if she goes on as she does" (II: 78). Indeed, as Polly Darnford proclaims: "What a happy lady are you, that persuasion dwells upon your tongue, and reformation follows your example!" (II: 46).

In this way, the artless, naturally simple Pamela becomes a reformer of all whom she knows and an improver of everything she touches. Such training produces natural citizen-subjects. Consider for instance, Pamela's extended disquisition on Locke's *Treatise on Education,* written as a series of letters to her husband. Following Locke's injunction to "instill sentiments of humanity" in "young folks," the young mother and former servant proposes the following program of maintaining and deepening the bonds of distinctions of rank:

> I will . . . teach the little dear courteousness and affability, from the properest motives I am able to think of; and will instruct him in only one piece of pride, that of being above doing a mean or low action. I will caution him not to behave in a lordly or insolent manner, even to the lowest servants. I will tell him that that superiority is the most commendable, and will be the best maintained, which is owing to humanity and kindness, and grounded on the perfections of the mind rather than on the accidental advantage of fortune and condition: that if his conduct be such as it ought to be, there will be no occasion to tell a servant, that he will be observed and respected: that humility . . . [is] most conspicuously charming in persons of distinction; for that the poor, who are humbled by their condition, cannot glory in it, as the rich may; and that it makes the lower ranks of people love and admire the high-born, who can so condescend. . . . Thus will the doctrine of benevolence and affability, implanted early in the mind of a young gentleman, and duly cultivated as he grows up, inspire him with the requisite conduct to command respect from proper motives. (II: 396)

This adherence to a more humane propriety affords all of Pamela's correspondents with her "properest" example. And nowhere more so that in the regulation of the passions: as B puts it, she inspires in him a more "regular and uniform desire" (I: 320). Pamela becomes, in effect, an administrator of (a more proper) nature. And her administration extends well beyond the home. But certainly, as wife and mother, it should begin there.

Indeed, Pamela's first project of reform would be her "master's domestic economy." But that is only an initial target of improvement. Pamela gives a kind of program for wives' "useful employments":

> In the first place, Sir, if you will give me leave, I will myself look into such parts of the family economy as may not be beneath the rank to which I shall have the honour of being exalted. . . . Then, Sir, I will ease you of as much of your family accounts, as I possibly can. . . . Then, Sir, . . . I will visit . . . the sick poor in the neighborhood around you; and administer to their wants and necessities, in such matters as may not be hurtful to your estate, but comfortable to them, and entail upon you their blessings, and their prayers for your health and welfare. Then I will assist your housekeeper . . . in making jellies, comfits, sweetmeats, marmalades, and cordials; and to pot, candy, and preserve, for the uses of the family; and to make myself all the fine linen of it for yourself and me. . . . But one thing, Sir, I ought not to forget, because it is the chief: my duty to God will, I hope always employ some good portion of my time. . . . With all this, Sir, can you think I shall be at a loss to pass my time? (I: 234–235)

Family economy, note, entails not only the smooth, orderly management of the home but also accounts, expenditures, and, by extension, good works, that is, acts of benevolence and charity—a whole program of governmentality we might say. As we see in other sections of the text, Pamela regularly makes "benevolent rounds" to the "industrious poor," especially those who are "blind, lame or sickly" (I: 427); directing the local apothecary and surgeon to attend to her "poor sick" neighbors (II: 73, 182–183); and, of course, the very sight of her heals the ailing B (I: 227): She is a dynamism of health. This may at first seem like a rather old notion of what virtuous, condescending wives of the gentry should do. But Richardson's text introduces some signal nuances. Pamela, as a "common" woman of "humble" origins, sets an example of domestic bliss that becomes the principle of a nonaristocratic femininity; her polite behavior is in fact a not so subtle censure of, and, eventually, antidote to, the overweening arrogance of the well-born.

As such Pamela represents something new, a new principle of sociality that first began to take hold in the eighteenth century. In moral philosophy, the principle of sociality that was to found a new, bourgeois civil society was sympathy; in *Pamela* the sympathetic subject turns out to be in fact an agent of the "police." Foucault remarks that

> in the eighteenth century we find a . . . function emerging, that of the disposition of society as a milieu of physical well-being, health and optimum longevity. The exercise of these three latter functions—order, enrichment and health—is assured less through a single apparatus than by an ensemble of multiple regulations and institutions which in the eighteenth century take the generic name of "police." Down to the end of the *ancien régime,* the term "police" does not signify, at least not exclusively, the institution of police in the modern sense; "police" is the ensemble of mechanisms serving to ensure order, the properly channelled growth of wealth and the conditions of preservation of health in general.[61]

Elaborating on this suggestive analysis, Jacques Donzelot argues that the history of the "police" is marked by "the proliferation of political technologies that invested the body, health, modes of subsistence and lodging—the entire space of existence in European countries from the eighteenth century onward." Policing "encompassed all the methods for developing the quality of the population and the strength of the nation."[62] What I am suggesting is that, at a specific juncture, the history of sympathy fuses with the apparatuses of "police" in the eighteenth century. In other words, as a technology of subjectivation, sympathy at strategic moments becomes unevenly integrated into the "ensemble of multiple regulations and institutions" known as the police. I insist on this unevenness since, as is clear from Pamela's example, traces of a moral or religious ground of sociality are legible in the history of sympathy. But we can go even further: what we see is that from the end of the eighteenth and throughout the nineteenth century, sympathy would be the Christian element that ties together new projects of social and domestic reform, emerging police regulations and institutions, and the evangelicalization of British governmentality. That this connection is legible more clearly in Richardson's novel than in Smith's moral philosophy should not obscure the broader point that a certain project was common to both. And that was the fabrication of a principle of sociality—tied to both the family and religion—that would produce a well-, indeed, self-policed citizenry.

The extent of such policing did not end with the nation, but spilled beyond it, into a variety of colonial contexts that were represented through the idioms of sentimentalism. So the police could also name the operations of colonial expansion. For evangelical imperialists of the Clapham Sect, whose members included a former governor of Sierra Leone (Zachary Macaulay) and a former governor-general of India (John Shore, Lord Teignmouth), it was precisely the question of how to forge enduring links between colonizer and colonized that exercised their imaginations. But in the end the answer was obvious: evangelization. And of course, for the evangelicals explicit use of force was not the answer. According to Charles Grant, one of the sect's chief propagandists, for the British, having won an empire and established a rule that was intended to be permanent, the best way to secure power was to use every prudent method of spreading a knowledge of "Christian truth."[63] As he had stated it in his influential tract *Observations on the State of Society among the Asiatic Subjects of Great Britain, particularly with respect to Morals and on the means of Improving it* (1792),[64] the only "cementing principle" conceivable was that of "common religious sanctions shared by the government with the people."[65] If it were possible, said Grant, by "calm reason and affectionate persuasion" to make "any large portion of our Indian subjects Christian, it is clear that they would then have strong common principle with us, and render our government more secure."[66] (I return to Grant's *Observations* in my analysis of Wilberforce in the next chapter.) This is crucial: First, the spreading of Christianity is good colonial policy, and, second, it could be the means of creating a bond of sympathy between rulers and ruled in India; it is for this reason that the question of the affections, tastes, habits, and customs of the natives become central to the argument for evangelizing colonial populations. What is at stake, finally, is the creation of a sympathetic population.

And yet this crucial connection between sympathy and the police is legible also in abolitionist slave narratives. Consider, for instance, Equiano's *Interesting Narrative* (1789).[67] The first and arguably the most influential autobiography written by an ex-slave, Equiano's *Narrative* represents an important moment in thinking about the emergence of a racialized discourse on sympathy. As we know, he was an Ibo from the northern Ika Ibo district (in present day Benin, Nigeria).[68] In the style of contemporary travel narratives, Equiano gives a detailed account of the manners, customs, government, culture, economy, religion (which he terms superstition—an intimation of the evangelical discourse to come). He goes on to narrate his birth, parentage (making it quite clear that his father owned other African slaves—apparently spoils of war), his own kidnapping, his harrowing journey through the middle passage (describing in graphic detail the horrors and degradations of the slave trade). He is taken to Barbados and eventually sold, ending up in Virginia; from there he is resold to a Captain in the British Navy. After years as a sailor, Equiano is again sold to a Quaker merchant, Robert King residing at Montserrat; he is trained in a variety of occupations, starts trading goods for himself, saves a sum of money, and eventually buys his own freedom and returns to "Old England."

It is toward the end of his narrative that Equiano articulates most clearly the particular ways in which sympathy brings together considerations of both "justice and policy" (readers will keep in mind that another translation of *Polizeiwissenschaft* is in fact policy). Just as Pamela is a force of civility, health, and economy, abolitionist sympathy draws once benighted Africans into the circuits of civilization and commerce. And Equiano was clear about this connection:

> May the time come—at least the speculation to me is pleasing—when the sable people shall gratefully commemorate the auspicious aera of extensive freedom: then shall those persons particularly be named with praise and honour, who generously proposed and stood forth in the cause of humanity, liberty, and good policy; and brought to the ear of the legislature designs of royal patronage and adoption. . . . May the blessings of the Lord be upon the heads of all those who commiserated the cases of the oppressed negroes. . . . As the inhuman traffic of slavery is not taken into the consideration of the British legislature, I doubt not, if a system of commerce was established in Africa, the demand for manufactures would most rapidly augment, as the native inhabitants would insensibly adopt the British fashions, manners, customs, &c. . . . Population, the bowels and surface of Africa, abound in valuable and useful returns; the hidden treasures of centuries will be brought to light and into circulation. Industry, enterprise, and mining, will have their full scope, proportionably as they civilize. . . . The abolition of slavery would be in reality an universal good.[69]

What one must affirm, it seems to me, is the complicity between Equiano's deployment of abolitionist sympathy as resistant humanism and sympathy as good colonial policy. The one is not the exclusion of the other. Far from it: the one enables the other precisely because sympathy needs to produce interminably an object on which to act. As it is integrated in to overall strategies of governmentality, sympathy both produces good subjects and leads to a "universal good."

In sentimental narratives, the colonies are the home of monsters and fallen angels. Let us end our consideration of Richardson's text with the bad example—the improper subject, Pamela's colonial, abjected double, "poor Miss Sally Godfrey." As B tells the story, while at Oxford he was "tricked" into seducing Sally by her own mother. She gives birth to a girl, and out of shame gives up the child to B's care, and goes off to Jamaica, where she eventually marries, and raises a family (I: 436–437). There are a number of striking aspects to this episode. The first, as we shall see shortly, is the structural filiation to the deployment of the West Indies in *Jane Eyre*. How does Jamaica function in *Pamela?* There is no mention of slavery in relationship to Sally; and there is only the occasional reference to coffee and chocolate. All that we do read of actually enslaved Africans in the West Indies, is that little Miss Goodwin (Sally's daughter) receives a present of "a little black boy," who dies of illness soon after his arrival in England (I: 440). Rather, as if through a circuitous projection, the question of slavery enters into the dual languages of rape, and domesticity and the marriage contract. This is also a genre convention. As Markman Ellis notes, "The theme of slavery in the sentimental novel celebrates the rhetorical slipperiness of the figure of slavery. The figure of slavery is often deployed transferentially, to discuss something else—for example notions of national identity, incarcerative punishment or even existential melancholy. However, the most significant relation in the theme of slavery is the conjunction of race and gender: where slavery is made to figure gender relations such as the 'bonds' of love or marriage."[70] This link between racial slavery and domestic bondage would become a standard trope in protofeminist arguments, for instance in Mary Wollstonecraft's *Vindication of the Rights of Woman* (1792) and, later, in John Stuart Mill's *The Subjection of Women* (1859).

In Pamela's case, the bonds in question result from the violence of rape. Querying her jailor, Mrs. Jewkes, Pamela asks, "Do you think [B] intends to make proposals to me as a kept mistress, or rather a kept slave?" (I: 118); in a letter to her "Honoured Sir," the captive writes, "Whatever you have to propose, whatever you intend by me, let my assent be that of a free person, and not of a sordid slave, who is to be threatened and frightened into a compliance with measures, which your conduct seems to imply" (I: 121); and, in her letter to her fumbling rescuer, Mr. William, she declares woman's equality, founded upon the purity of the soul, or rather the sacredness of female chastity, "Were my life in question, instead of my honesty, I would not wish to involve you . . . in the least difficulty, for so worthless a creature.

But, O Sir! My soul is of equal importance with the soul of a princess, though my quality is inferior to that of the meanest slave" (I: 137). For his part, B, arguing against mothers' nursing their children, writes,

> . . . consider . . . the station you are raised to does not require you to be a domestic animal. You are lifted up to the rank of a lady, and you must act up to it, and not think of setting such an example, as will draw upon you the ill-will and censure of other ladies. For will any of our sex visit one who is continually employing herself in such works as either must be a reproach to herself, or to them? You'll have nothing to do but to give orders. You will consider yourself as the task-mistress, and the common herd of female servants as so many negroes directing themselves by your nod. (II: 25)

What are we to make of these evocations of the figure of the slave? Of so many enslaved "negroes"? The text circles around a certain ambivalence on the question of slavery. Certainly, Pamela nowhere takes exception to Sally's choice of exile; nor does she make any comment on the probability of her owning slaves; and yet she does make a clear statement against the slavery of women, against the servitude of (her) sex. But, further, what is the relationship between what I have argued is Pamela's sympathetic agency, a Janus whose two faces bear the names police and pity, and the figuration of the enslaved African or, for that matter, "the domestic animal"? Does the animalized African participate in the agency of the subject of sympathy? It would seem that the sovereignty of the sympathetic subject is in fact predicated on the abjected figuration of animalized, collectivized African subjects. This is then the framework through which the sympathetic subject would exercise her peculiar agency: at once resisting violence, and on another register reproducing it, and being enabled by it. This agency, this very model of subjectivity, moreover, is what will tie race to class to gender in the career of sympathy. Is it possible that through this relation of sympathy we could consider the agency, the history, the very lives of "so many negroes"?

The Black Spectre of Sympathy:
Jane Eyre and *Mary Prince*

> "What have you heard? What do you see?" asked St. John. I saw nothing: but I heard a voice somewhere cry—"Jane! Jane! Jane!"—nothing more. . . ."I am coming!" I cried. "Wait for me! Oh, I will come!" I flew to the door, and looked into the passage: it was dark. I ran out in to the garden: it was void. "Where are you?" I exclaimed. . . ."Down superstition!" I commented, as that spectre rose up black by the black yew at the gate. "This is not thy deception, nor thy witchcraft: it is the work of nature. She was roused, and did—no miracle—but her best."[71]

Jane Eyre hears a voice call to her from hundreds of miles away. She cannot help but respond—"it spoke in pain and woe, wildly, eerily, urgently" (369). Readers will recall the moment: St. John, the would-be missionary, at his most sublime, is on the verge of subduing and ruling Jane, claiming her for the work of Christ in India. For Jane it is her second great temptation.

> He had spoken earnestly, mildly: his look was not, indeed, that of a lover beholding his mistress; but it was that of a pastor recalling his wandering sheep—or better, of a guardian angel watching the soul for which he is responsible. All men of talent, whether they be men of feeling or not; whether they be zealots, or aspirants, or despots—provided they only be sincere—have their sublime moments: when they subdue and rule. . . . I was tempted to cease struggling with him—to rush down the torrent of his will into the gulf of his existence, and there lose my own. I was almost as hard beset by him now as I have been once before, in a different way, by another. I was a fool both times. (368)

St. John, taking on the "look" of the pastor, or angel, watching over the struggles of the wayward soul, is about to triumph over the reluctant Jane: If she had stayed only a moment longer, she would have laid her hand "on the Christian cross and the angel's crown" (370). But another call intervenes, she feels a presentiment of another future, the chords of her heart vibrate with other sympathies, she reads the signs and acts. This is not the "black spectre" of "superstition" Jane insists, and yet, earlier she has also told the reader that presentiments, sympathies, and signs are all part of a fundamental human mystery. "Presentiments are strange things! and so are sympathies; and so are signs: and the three combined make one mystery to which humanity has not yet found the key. I never laughed at presentiments in my life, because I have had strange ones of my own. Sympathies, I believe exist: (for instance, between far-distant, long absent, wholly estranged relatives; asserting, notwithstanding their alienation, the unity of the source to which each traces his origin) whose workings baffle mortal comprehension. And signs, for aught we know, may be but the sympathies of Nature with man" (193). Moved by Rochester's call, beyond all reason and comprehension, Jane acts: she breaks with St. John, and decides to return to the scene of her first temptation. She goes back to Rochester. And everything changes. "It was *my* time to assume ascendancy. *My* powers were in play, and in force." It is the moment of Jane's sovereignty. Was she right? "The reader shall judge."[72]

Of course, Charlotte Brontë's famous novel is a narrative of a female subject's rise to a certain power: social, psychological, moral, class, domestic, national, and racial power. This is a story whose elements—both Gothic and sentimental—have been analyzed with brilliance over the past 30 years in different strands of feminist, cultural studies, psychoanalytic, postcolonial, Marxist, and deconstructive criticism.[73] For a number of complex reasons, *Jane Eyre* has become canonical to different kinds of literary criticisms; certainly, its historical moment is central to the story of the novel as a literary form. No doubt the text repeats and displaces some of the fundamental genre conventions of both Gothic and sentimental literature: a female narrative, the return to home and the domestic, the impulse of Christian benevolence, the ghostly, savage double, the "explained supernatural," the persecution and suffering of a wronged woman, and so on. There are also signal differences: for instance, unlike Walpole's fantastic Gothic novel, all "supernatural" events are explained through a realist logic; also, unlike the sentimental novel, Jane does progress and develop as subject. Jane's narrative poses the question of power: the power of poverty or wealth, the power of love or desire, the power of sin or redemption, the power of hope or despair, the power of race or humanity. I, too, will pose this question of the agent's power, but through the agency of sympathy. If, as I argued in the last chapter, sympathy is that paradoxical mode of power that writes itself on the body, that reinscribes inequality at the very moment it seems to obliterate it, it is also an effect of a certain call of otherness, of an irreducible difference. In *Jane Eyre,* Jane's ascendancy is enabled by her assumption of a certain sympathy—as a force of police; however, sympathy also names a fundamental mystery that cannot be integrated into the realist, rationalist logic of the text. There is an interminable relay, a necessary complicity between these two modes of sympathy, as, for instance, in the scene of the blind Rochester's calling forth Jane's pity. It is as if the violence of propriation and abjection that enables the integration of sympathy with the police returns as "a perspective (of fragments, of voices from other texts, other codes), whose vanishing point is nonetheless ceaselessly pushed back, mysteriously opened" to a certain "difference which indefinitely returns, insubmissive." This sympathetic call is the fundamental mystery that the narrative grapples with: not race (Bertha and the heathen Hindu), not ghosts (the hideous laughter that terrifies Jane), not sexual abandon (Rochester's temptation), not the colonies (Jamaica, India, Madeira)—all these are finally explained, reintegrated through a rigorous, one might even say colonizing realism. No, what remains beyond all explanation is, precisely, sympathy. It is this mystery that must be situated in terms of a certain displacement of (racial and cultural) difference, and its final assimilation in Jane's vision of companionate love and domestic bliss. I argue in what follows that the two colonial contexts that seemingly frame plain Jane's narrative function as a kind of relay of sympathy: between Bertha Mason, the Creole madwoman, and St. John Rivers, the impassioned missionary, an entire history of colonial sympathy is legible in its displacements and torsions in one woman's assumption of power.

Let us narrate this assumption in terms of sympathy. Jane comes to Lowood with a particular, even peculiar kind of identity. Under the Reeds's tyranny she had been brought to the point of mutiny and rebellion, she was an antipathetic, "heterogeneous thing" (12), a savage (32), a rebel slave (9), who longed for freedom and "worthier objects of affection" (24). This language of difference and enslavement—one that is thoroughly racialized, of course—both establishes and threatens the identity of Jane as object of pity. Yet Lowood is hardly the land of milk and honey. Under the new tyranny of that evangelical terror, Mr. Brocklehurst, Jane and her fellow inmates struggle against hunger (burnt porridge, indifferent potatoes, shreds of rusty meat, etc.), cold ("the water in the pitchers was frozen"), and general privation. But it is here that Jane first breaks with her "nature and habits" (42) and forms new ones. The agent is Helen Burns, and she is reading. Jane asks her what her book is about, but "I hardly know where I found the hardihood thus to open a conversation with a stranger; the step was contrary to my nature and habits: but I think her occupation touched a chord of sympathy somewhere; for I too liked reading, though of a frivolous and childish kind; I could not digest or comprehend the serious or substantial" (42–43).

Helen, and then Maria Temple, strikes this chord of sympathy again and again in Jane, till her very nature and habits are transformed through the reverberation. Sympathy with her betters lifts Jane from the frivolous and childish to the serious and substantial. From holding doctrines more common to "heathens and savage tribes" (significantly around ideas of justice), Jane becomes a "Christian member of a civilized nation." Or does she? I will return to this question shortly. In any case, this transformation does not come about only through the sympathy she shares with Helen and Miss Temple; for sympathy works through discipline: "it comprised an irksome struggle with difficulties in habituating myself to new rules and unwonted tasks" (51). Much could be said about the regime of discipline at Lowood under Brocklehurst: ascetic, rigid, and clock-governed, the orphan's home is a space of normalization through punishment and incitation. But how is the relationship between sympathy and this regime of discipline staged in *Jane Eyre?* It would seem that they belong to separate realities of Victorian life: the utilitarian-evangelical (Brocklehurst, St. John) as opposed to the genuinely humanitarian (Jane, Helen, Ms Temple).

Consider the pivotal scene of Jane's humiliation. The "dread judge," Brocklehurst, in one of his routine disciplinary tirades, seeks to expose Jane's character. She responds, at first, with anything but Christian humility: "an impulse of fury against Reed, Brocklehurst, and Co. bounded in my pulses. . . . I was no Helen Burns" (57). Let us mark Brocklehurst's language, his tone, his diction; it is the entrance into another textuality.

"My dear children," pursued the black marble clergyman, with pathos, "this is a sad, melancholy occasion; for it becomes my duty to warn you, that this girl, who might be one of God's own lambs, is a little castaway: not a member of the true flock, but evidently an interloper and an alien . . . you must shun her example: if necessary, avoid her company, exclude her from your sports. . . . Teachers, you must watch her: keep your eyes on her movements, weigh well her words, scrutinise her actions, punish her body to save her soul: if, indeed, such salvation be possible, for (my tongue falters while I tell it) this girl, this child, the native of a Christian land, worse than many a little heathen who says its prayers to Brahma and kneels before Juggernaut—this girl is—a liar!" (57–58)

Duty mixed with pathos, a Gothic horror blended with sympathetic righteousness: In Brocklehurst's discourse, the play of these elements serve to legitimize the radical exclusion of the "alien." And it is not the first nor the last time Jane is filiated to heathenism and infidelity, nor is it the last time that the colonial Gothic is invoked. Indeed, her peculiar racialization, which places her somehow beyond the pale of Christian humanity, continues to haunt her, as we shall see.[74] But let us mark first of all that Brocklehurst's rhetoric is in fact an incisive parody of evangelical missionary discourses.

As the Comaroffs note, missions and missionaries were not unknown terrain to Charlotte Brontë.[75] Brontë's father, Patrick, had been the curate of one John Buckworth, at Dewsbury, Yorkshire, from December 1809 to March 1811, and as curate probably gave religious instruction to some young members of Buckworth's congregation who were destined for the Indian and African mission field. The Comaroffs write, "A 'Low Church Evangelical' with increasingly conservative political and religious views, Patrick Brontë had come from Irish peasant stock and, by turns an artisan and a teacher, had entered the ministry by way of Cambridge. He raised his children in the vicarage at Haworth where their small circle was made up largely of clergy and their families. . . . Even more significantly, Haworth was in the West Riding, one of the regions of England most affected by the industrial revolution. It was also an area in which Christian revivalism gained a firm hold and from which many Protestants departed for Africa to extend the Empire of Christ, and, no less, of Great Britain."[76]

A further source of information on the subject of missionary motives was the other man in Charlotte's life. Jane Eyre was first published in 1847 under the pseudonym of Currer Bell. In 1845, Arthur Bell Nicholls, graduate of Trinity College, Dublin, had become Brontë's curate at Haworth, and, in June 1854, he married Charlotte. It is not known if he had entertained ideas of becoming a missionary before Jane Eyre was written. But it is possible that, like many other graduates of Trinity College, Dublin, whose opportunities for preferment in the church were few, he had thoughts of emigrating,

and he may have mentioned this to Charlotte. In December 1852, he proposed to her. Her father would not hear of it: His celebrated daughter could
do better than marry an impoverished, Puseyite Irishman, who was less than
a gentleman. Distraught, Nicholls threatened to emigrate, and in January
1853, he actually applied to the Society for Propagating the Gospel to be
sent to Sydney, Melbourne, or Adelaide. He gave as his only motive: "I have
for some time felt a strong inclination to assist in ministering to the thousands of . . . our fellow Countrymen, who by Emigration have been in a
great measure deprived of the means of grace."[77] Two months later he with-
drew his application.

 The Comaroffs argue that missionary discourse at the turn of the century
was articulated within a complex class and national context. Of course, the
idea and practice of missions had a much longer genealogy in British social
history. The Society for the Propagation of the Gospel in Foreign Parts had
been founded in 1701 and throughout the century was active among North
American settlers and Native American populations. Moravian missionaries
had been sent to Greenland, the West Indies, and the Cape of Good Hope.
John Wesley's disciple, Thomas Cook, had published his *Plan of the Society for
the Establishment of Missions among the Heathens* in 1783 (Wesley had had his
own missionary fiasco in Georgia in the late 1730s);[78] from 1786 Methodist
missionaries were working in the West Indies. In India, the Danish settlement
of Tranquebar had been the scene of Protestant missionary activity since
1706, mainly by Lutheran pietists from Halle, although from 1728 the mission had been the responsibility of the Anglican Church, through the Society
for Promoting Christian Knowledge (SPCK; established in 1699). But the industrial transformation of English social life from 1780 onward radically
shifted the landscape of power for missionary endeavor. Drawing on Pierre
Bourdieu's work on class fragmentation, the Comaroffs argue that Nonconformist missionaries to the colonies in early nineteenth century overwhelmingly came from the "dominated fraction of a dominant class": "Low
churchmen were not merely the lowest-paid members of the privileged orders; many of them, especially in rural northern parishes, were former arti-
sans who had climbed rather unsteadily into the ranks of the middle class. . . .
Their biographies, built on an unremitting commitment to rational self-im-
provement, were the very embodiment of the spirit of capitalism, a living tes-
timonial to its moral and material workings. To the degree that they sought
to evangelize and civilize by personal example (itself an expression of bourgeois ideology), the pathway along which they were to lead the heathen was
to retrace their own journey through contemporary British society—or,
rather, toward an image of that society as they wished to see it."[79] So, for instance, in his *Statement of Reasons for Accepting a Call to go to India as a Missionary* (Glasgow, 1839), John Macdonald argued that the "Church of Christ

is essentially and constitutionally *Evangelistic* or Missionary . . . her unceasing duty is evangelical aggression, and perpetual expansion . . . the evangelisation of the world being the will of her Head, is the law of her being."[80] This colonization of souls, this expansionism of the spirit, precisely because it is unceasing ran up against the romantic conservatism of British colonialism in the early decades of the nineteenth century, leading to sometimes quite explosive confrontations between missionaries and colonial authorities.

And yet almost all missionaries were clear about one thing: Colonial order enables missionary endeavor, linking Western civilization to evangelization. As the Serampore Baptist missionaries (in Bengal) put it in an 1807 Memorial to Governor General Minto, the "British Government is the greatest national blessing vouchsafed by Divine Providence to India for many ages; and that the safety of themselves and their families, and of their native converts, depends in a peculiar manner on the permanent prosperity of the British Government," which all inclines to the conclusion that judicious missionary activity should duly promote "the peace, tranquility, and prosperity of the British Empire in India."[81] Acknowledging this enabling colonial order became a conscious part of missionary discourse in India as well as in Africa; as a rhetorical device, in fact, it set up the argument for colonial evangelical "improvement."

And for improvement to go on, colonial power, and the missionary's gaze over it, could never be relaxed. Hence, the government must be coaxed as it were, to join fully the widening current of Christian, European civilization, that onward flow of progress and sympathy. This would be in keeping with "justice and policy." Thus: Hindu women "may endure continual agony under the apprehension of the dreadful doom which they know awaits them on the first fatal attack of disease on their husbands,—they may feel their anguish renewed at the sight of every female neighbour they behold led forth to the flames—they may tremble at every touch of disease which affects their husband, and weep at every recollection of their hapless children;—but can they leave the scene of suffering? can they make *known* their sorrows? dare they betray even in the slightest degree the anguish which preys on their vitals? They lie bound as sheep for the slaughter;—and thus they must remain, suffering in silence, till *British feeling and sympathy shall duly realize* their hitherto unknown, unpitied misery."[82]

The sympathetic figuration of the abject sati-suicide in missionary discourse brings us back to *Jane Eyre*—or, rather, Bertha Mason. It is as if by identifying Jane with the heathen other that Brontë can fracture the iconography, discourse, even the very identity of missionary sympathy. Jane performs in fact what the text argues is genuinely humane sympathy—as opposed to the patent hypocrisy of Brocklehurst. But Jane, whose agency is demarcated by the flow of sympathy, is also implicated in the project of improvement—not of heathens or barbarians, but of rude rustics, rakes, and French girls. Let us chart her ascendancy into a force of national sympathy from the moment of her abasement.

Something breaks the true horror of Jane's humiliation and its force is redirected, and in that movement the enraged heathen is called back to humanity. Again, the agent is Helen Burns:

> What my sensations were, no language can describe: but just as they all rose, stifling my breath and constricting my throat, a girl came up and passed me: in passing, she lifted her eyes. What a strange light inspired them! What an extraordinary sensation that ray sent through me! How the new feeling bore me up! It was as if a martyr, a hero, had passed a slave or victim, and imparted strength in the transit. I mastered the rising hysteria, lifted up my head, and took a firm stand on the stool. . . . [Helen Burns] returned to her place, and smiled at me as she again went by. What a smile! I remember it now, and I know that was the effluence of fine intellect, of true courage; it lit up her marked lineaments, her thin face, her sunken grey eye, like a reflection from the aspect of an angel. (59)

What is this new feeling that bears up the slave, the victim? It is a gift (it gives strength), but not one that could be returned through a calculus of exchange (Jane cannot simply return the feeling).[83] It gives the gift of self-mastery, of firmness, of subjectivity itself—Jane subdues her rising passions, as she is penetrated by that extraordinary ray, an encouraging look, and so buoyed by the flow of a fine intellect (thus inaugurating reasonable Jane's war with passion). And the giver cannot but be hero, martyr, angel. This scene stages the doubleness of sympathy. If this gift of genuine sympathy and "true courage" (contrasted sharply with Brocklehurst's hypocritical rhetoric and perverse cruelty) imparts strength to the slave/victim, and so establishes a relationship of empowerment, at the same time, and through the same movement, sympathy, as that which uplifts the oppressed, renders visible a certain gap between giver and victim. But is it a gap of power?

I shall argue that it is, or at least can be, but this should not blind us from seeing that sympathy can also be a horizontal bond between relational subjects. A relation that would draw sympathy into something like solidarity. A relation that operates both within and beyond language, and not entirely within reason—its proxy could be the strange light of a look or an echo transmitted from the soul of someone hundreds of miles away. Its hauntings could leave the soul a touch mad. It is here, in this strange bonding, I think, that we must locate Jane's specific relationship to religion and spirituality. Up to this moment of humiliation, Jane is only a nominal Christian; indeed, if we go by the language of the text itself, she is more a savage, heathen, even "Hindoo" than a good Anglican girl.[84] But it is Helen Burns who introduces

Jane to higher thoughts, directed to God, and so lifts Jane's pained gaze above and beyond the suffering self. "Seek justice above," Helen seems to be saying. Yet Helen's religion is itself a strange amalgam. It seems to fly in the face of Brocklehurst's sin-obsessed evangelicalism, but really forms a kind of counter-discourse to it. Speaking as much to the death that begins to grip her as to Jane, Helen asserts that "the time will soon come when . . . we shall put [our faults] off in putting off our corruptible bodies; when debasement and sin will fall from us with this cumbrous frame and flesh, and only the spark of the spirit will remain,—the impalpable principle of life and thought pure as when it left the Creator to inspire the creature: whence it came it will return; perhaps again to be communicated to some being higher than man—perhaps to pass through gradations of glory, from the pale human soul to brighten to the seraph! Surely it will never . . . be suffered to degenerate from man to fiend? No; I cannot believe that: I hold another creed; which no one ever taught me, and which I seldom mention; but in which I delight, and to which I cling: for it extends hope to all: it makes Eternity a rest—a mighty home—not a terror and an abyss" (51). Later, in urging Jane to forgiveness and mildness, Helen speaks of an invisible world, a kingdom of spirits that is a resource in our struggles with injustice; those spirits watch and guard us, says Helen (60). Although she mentions the teachings of Christ, it is significant that, unlike in evangelical discourse in this period, Jesus does not function as mediator between God and the repentant sinner (on her death bed, Helen states with moving simplicity, "God is my father; God is my friend: I love him; I believe he loves me" [71]). Instead, an original spiritual spark returns home, transmigrating upward from human to angel. And perhaps these angels come back to rule the invisible kingdom of guardian spirits.

At key moments in the subsequent narrative, Jane will be visited by these spirits, she will even join their fairy empire—and will deny it. Rochester recognizes not only a kindred spirit in Jane but also a spirit somehow not of this world; to him she is a "nonnette" with "the look of another world," reminding him of tales of fairies and witches. When she is tottering on the brink of a moral abyss during her first temptation by Rochester, she is visited by an angelic mother who whispers, "My daughter, flee temptation!" (281). One of those strange presentiments, no doubt, but notice how Jane later narrates this struggle of duty over desire: "Which is better? To have surrendered to temptation; listened to passion; made no painful effort, no struggle;—but to have sunk down in the silken snare. . . . Yes; I feel now that I was right when I adhered to principle and law, and scorned and crushed the insane promptings of a frenzied moment. God directed me to a correct choice. I thank His providence for the guidance" (316). The angelic, mystical visitation of the Mother is assimilated to principle, reason, law, and God the Father and his Providence. Finally, after her second temptation (when desire, articulated as compassion and pity, triumphs over duty without human affection), Jane comes back to the partially blind and lame Rochester precisely in the form of an "invisible" spirit sent to minister and guard over him. But through this very return, Jane has transferred her ministry from the savage Hindu (for whom she has no sympathy) to her soulmate, the "brownie"[85] Rochester, and in the transference she reconstitutes herself as both desiring subject and dutiful wife. What Brontë stages, then, in *Jane Eyre* is a struggle between a kind of pagan spirituality, whose occult agency is a certain sympathy, and evangelical Christianity, or those narrow projects of benevolence that would be founded on it (Orphan Homes or Missions to the Heathens): the two demarcate different duties, different relationships to the body, to love, to utility, to humanity. And yet, the two converge in Jane's relationship to Rochester. But not without a certain, abjected excess: Helen is dead, as is Bertha, and St. John is on his death bed.

What I am suggesting is that the two forms of spirituality are complicitous but irreducible. This non-reducible complicity ties Jane's spirituality to that process which I marked in my analysis of *Pamela,* and which Foucault named the "police." We can trace this complicity back again to the moment of Jane's humiliation. Miss Temple's inquiries prove Brocklehurst's charges to be false, Jane is vindicated, and

> [t]hus relieved of a grievous load, I from that hour set to work afresh, resolved to pioneer my way through every difficulty: I toiled hard, and my success was proportionate to my efforts; my memory, not naturally tenacious, improved with practice: exercise sharpened my wits; in a few weeks I was promoted to a higher class; in less than two months I was allowed to commence French and drawing. (65)

From this point onward in the narrative, in various ways, the (at-times murderous) struggle between duty, work, utility, masculinity, Christianity, and reason, on the one hand, and passion, desire, femininity, nonreason, and the savage, on the other, will be staged again and again. We can follow its staging in the physical, moral, and psychic struggle between Bertha and Rochester, in the subsequent fight Jane has with her own desires, in the temptation of St. John, and even in Jane's rather more subdued "silent revolts" against her "absolute stagnation" (96). It will be a certain sympathy that mediates and synthesizes these two poles in the direction of humanity and humanization. After Brocklehurst's tyranny is ended by "gentlemen of rather more enlarged and sympathizing minds" who knew how to "combine reason with strictness, comfort with economy, compassion with uprightness," Jane becomes a teacher in this "truly useful and noble institution"

(72–73)—she becomes, that is, a more sympathetic agent of discipline and, thus, a kind of "police" agent. Which only means she is a more effective agent of that technology of subject formation. In this way, the memory of Helen's transgressive sympathy is normalized through a narrative that ties Jane's progress to the compulsions of bourgeois and national utility. Speaking of Adèle, Jane remarks, "My pupil was a lively child, who had been spoilt and indulged, and therefore was sometimes wayward; but as she was committed entirely to my care, and no injudicious interference from any quarter ever thwarted my plans for her improvement, she soon forgot her little freaks, and became obedient and teachable" (94–95). That she only draws closer to Adèle after she learns of her history further sutures improvement to humanity—by mutual affection. Or consider Jane's relationship to her "rustic" scholars after her inheritance. She feels with pleasure that many of her students liked her, that she really had a place in "their unsophisticated hearts." In a few short months, under her sympathetic tutoring they were converted into "as decent, respectable, modest, and well-informed young women as can be found in the ranks of the British peasantry. And that is saying a great deal; for after all the British peasantry are the best taught, best mannered, most self-respecting of any in Europe: since those days I have seen paysannes and Bauerinnen: and the best of them seemed to me ignorant, coarse, and besotted, compared to my Morton girls" (343). Here, a kind of euphoric nationalist sympathy, a very strained horizontal bond, masks those processes of discipline that transform rural girls (whose families are most likely tied to the local wage economy on farms and in the factories) into the best mannered peasants in Europe. What this suggests, I think, is that like much of liberal thought during midcentury, the arguments around sympathy in *Jane Eyre* reinscribe the proper object of sympathy within the borders of the nation and the home.[86]

But precisely because this inscription entails both the use of idioms of race (of slavery, oriental despotism, of sati) and a kind of national abjection (the deaths of Bertha, St. John), this cannot be a closed circuit. Indeed, the memory of slavery, of class privation, of Helen's martyrdom, of Bertha's "sati," of a non-Christian spirituality, and the "temptation" of the colonies all haunt the merging of compassion and utility that forms Jane-as-subject. This national(ist) sympathy explains why, for instance, there is no sympathy between Jane and Bertha, or between Jane and the Hindu. Through this structure of abjection and language of racialized oppression (slavery, despotism) a series of displacements is effected: so Jane is Bertha displaced (as Bertha is Sally displaced!), Rochester is a Hindu (or a pagan heathen) displaced. This structure of displacement is crucial to the narrative energy of the text; it helps us to see complicities where essential affinities are disavowed and elided. But by reducing colonial and racial difference to elements of the "same" subject (Jane,

Rochester), we also risk forgetting precisely that it is the racial other that enables Jane's ascendancy. Another memory must interrupt this assimilative displacement. Let us not forget that Jane is given a new social life by the death of her rich colonial uncle in Madeira. In multiple ways, Jane's ascendancy is tied to the colonies, to the history of slavery in the West Indies and colonialism in India, not to mention class struggle. But these kinships are denied again and again. For Jane, Bertha inspires horror and dread rather than pity and sympathy; certainly, any fellow-feeling seems, as it were, beyond the realm of possibility (for his part, Rochester, in rejecting the "embruted" Bertha and embracing fairy Jane, seeks "sympathy with something at least human" [257]). And this seems to be because Jane has no sympathy for what is alien, or different. Uncannily repeating Brocklehurst's language of the alien, the broken hearted Jane rejects the option of marriage, declaring simply, "I do not want a stranger—unsympathising alien, different from me; I want my kindred: those with whom I have full fellow-feeling" (341). As for St. John, Jane remarks again and again that he wants "no sympathy," and, just as damning in her eyes, he himself cannot sympathize as he lacks all "domestic affections":

> "This parlour is not his sphere," I reflected; "the Himalayan ridge, or Caffre bush, even the plague-cursed Guinea Coast swamp, would suit him better. Well may he eschew the calm of domestic life; it is not his element: there his faculties stagnate—they cannot develop or appear to advantage. It is in scenes of strife and danger, where courage is proved, and energy exercised, and fortitude tasked, that he will speak and move, the leader and superior." (346)

In rejecting St. John, Jane does not reject the project of missionizing, per se. What she rejects is the keen, cold, unsocial, merciless "enslaver" of her mind and the blighter of her affections. He is her "iron shroud," who knows "neither mercy nor remorse" (354–355). In rejecting such a living death, Jane embraces another kind of Christianity, one that ties femininity to (English) domesticity, and domesticity to the regenerative social, even national affections. Rochester becomes her mission; the grizzled brownie accepts her "soft ministry," and she is content to serve "both for his prop and guide" (395). And so, Reader, she married him. I have tried to show how *Jane Eyre* plays on many of the concepts that in fact occupied Smith and Hume and the moral sense philosophers: nature, utility, domestic affections, the call of the other, and the mystery of sympathetic kinship. As the initial quote shows, sympathy is tied to nature at key moments of the text, seemingly taking its operation beyond the realm of reason and comprehension. But in the same movement its occult, even pagan genealogy, that "black spectre," is abjected again and again as Jane travels the straight path of the proper Christian—or at least tries to. In this double movement of sympathy, we are obliged to pose again the question of the other, of the colonies, or those happy rustic girls. If Jane embodies the mechanisms of discipline, health, morality, and domesticity that are central to the civilizing mission of sympathy, what are we to make of the occult mystery that finally seems to punctuate the text with a question mark?

> "In spirit, I believe, we must have met. You no doubt were . . . in unconscious sleep, Jane: perhaps your soul wandered from its cell to comfort mine; for those were your accents—as certain as I live—they were yours!" "Reader, it was on Monday night—near midnight—that I too had received the mysterious summons: those were the very words by which I replied to it. . . . The coincidence struck me as too awful and inexplicable to be communicated or discussed. . . . I kept these things, then, and pondered them in my heart." (394)

True love? Perhaps. But something else besides. Keep in mind that this moment the two lovers are recalling is the moment of Jane's "ascendancy." It is as if in the circuit of sympathy the very moment of so-called agency is simply too "inexplicable to be communicated." Indeed, it is the ascendancy of the spirit. Recall, also, the OED definition of sympathy that I cited in the last chapter: a "(real or supposed) affinity between certain things, by virtue of which they are similarly or correspondingly affected by the same influence, affect or influence one another (*esp. in some occult way*), or attract or tend towards each other." I return again to the parenthetical comment, which now can be seen in a new light, and I repeat some questions I posed in the last chapter: What if through sympathy a kind of premodern occultism, even mysticism, came to be adapted by modern modes of power? What if, in sympathy, a principle, at once non-rational and non-secular, is operative, at least in terms of a certain haunting, and yet without being irrational or properly Christian? Posing these questions entails I think following a kind of analysis that would bring to life the haunting of difference, and so another memory of sympathy.

Once again, this abjected, disavowed history leads on to another indomitable textuality. If one considers the narrative of Jane's assumption of a sympathetic police-agency that I have offered here what we must see is that certain exclusions (racial, class, and spiritual) are constitutive of this European woman's subjectivity: Through racialized language she constitutes herself as sympathetic subject, and then fashions that very sympathy into a force of national and domestic pedagogy. Sympathy indeed turns out to be good policy for Jane. Yet, as I have shown, Jane's sympathetic subjectivity is a relationship with the unrepresentable. The moment of her agency is simply too awful and inexplicable to be communicated or discussed. A sense of sympathy calls the subject into being, but the experience is beyond comprehension.

A black spectre that refuses "a prior disclosure of being," of reason, of even possibly a certain governmentality.

This racial genealogy of subjectivity in *Jane Eyre* suggests another trajectory of female subjectivity informing, even prefiguring Jane's—that of the enslaved black woman. Now, a long tradition of black feminist criticism has elaborated the politics of this process of European subject formation through the abjected black slave woman—the classic "self-consolidating other." But there is another lesson to be learned I think by contextualizing plane Jane's progress in the field of slavery. And that lesson has to do with how sympathetic humanism functions through certain unrepresentable silences to fashion an agency for itself. Let us consider, in this regard, the *History of Mary Prince*. As a slave, and then a free woman, Mary Prince literally embodies the violence, struggle, and contestation that goes into making an entire apparatus of racial, economic, and sexual domination. Born on a farm in Brakish Pond, Devonshire Parish, Bermuda, in 1788,[87] Mary was the first black British woman to escape from slavery. After a life lived amid horrifying brutality, she was able to gain her freedom with the help of British abolitionists in 1830. Through her history, this ex-slave never lets us forget that as much as anything else, slavery was an economic system of superexploitation: "Sick or well, it was work—work—work!" (73).[88] And through her narrative, we hear the strategic plea for sympathy: "Oh the horrors of slavery!" Mary says. "How the thought of it pains my heart! But the truth ought to be told of it; and what my eyes have seen I think it is my duty to relate; for few people in England know what slavery is. I have been a slave—I have felt what a slave feels, and I know what a slave knows; and I would have all the good people in England to know it too, that they may break our chains, and set us free" (74). Mary Prince's testimony was the first narrative of a black slave woman published in England. In it, she speaks the tortured "truth" of slavery with a voice that is mediated and double (a British woman "transcribed" and no doubt translated her history), and asserts an ambivalent agency that negotiates sexual and racial exploitation through the idioms of sentimentality and the norms of evangelical propriety. This negotiation at times takes the form of a forcible, even radical refusal of the violence of slavery. "Sir," she says to her brutal master who is about to beat her yet again, "this is not Turk's Island" (77); or speaking out against her mistress, the "hard-hearted" Mrs. Wood, she says powerfully, "To be free is very sweet" (85). Mary Prince speaks within the idioms of European sympathy, but through that sentimental language she testifies to the horrors of slavery and asserts her solidarity with others. Mary is clear that the history of her sufferings is also an occasion to remember all those others who continue to slave and suffer. "In telling my own sorrows, I cannot pass by those of my fellow-slaves—for when I think of my own griefs, I remember theirs" (75).

But what of those things Mary doesn't say, or says only partially, or even lies about? How do we remember Mary Prince's silences? Finally, I think Mary Prince's testimony poses for us today a fundamental problem of interpretation: How do we read with solidarity the sentimentalized life of the slave woman?

We have recently been given two different responses to this question: Moira Ferguson's Introduction to her edition of *The History of Mary Prince,* and Jenny Sharpe's "Something Akin to Freedom." Both these feminist critics are concerned to get at the "truth" of Mary Prince's life (but for both critics, that truth is a relational one); both want to show that the black woman was much more than a laboring and reproducing machine that slave masters tried to reduce her to (both want to foreground the question of agency); and both read Mary's life in solidarity with her struggles to be free (what Sharpe calls reading "in the interests of"). But there are profound differences between the two thinkers. Although for Ferguson, Mary Prince "comprehended her authentic situation at the time" (3), she also argues that there is a "pattern of omissions" that structure her narrative, making it a double-voiced text. This structure of omissions names also the representational strategies that Mary uses to obfuscate, counter, or deflect both the stereotype of the black women in proslavery propaganda as well as the image of female slaves as "pure, Christlike victims and martyrs" in abolitionist literature.[89] What are we to make of the whole "pattern of omissions" that structure this black woman's "truth"? Attending to these omissions takes us beyond proslavery stereotypes, it takes us beyond abolitionist moralizing, and beyond also feminist heroizations.[90] It takes us to that obscure region of resistance and struggle that is in excess of any received script of what the black slave woman should be.

For Jenny Sharpe, if we go by Mary Prince's narrative alone, her life seems to "reaffirm the political mission of the antislavery campaign" (31).[91] Her narrative both creates "sympathy for the Negro race by showing slavery form the perspective of its victims" and also presents Prince "as a socioethical being who is active in obtaining her freedom" (31). The narrative gives us a picture of a black woman who moves from "ignorance to enlightenment and from slavery to freedom" (32); "The slave woman acts, then, only inasmuch as she exhibits the moral agency of a free individual." Sharpe wants to "complicate an academic recovery of [Mary's] voice" (36) by contesting this image of the slave as moral agent. Not because she wants to defend racist stereotypes but because she wants us to consider aspects of slave life that would complicate the "Protestant ideals of obedience, self-discipline, hard work, and moderation" (33). She focuses, therefore, on the question of Prince's sexuality and the "narrative restraints" that this slave woman had to negotiate in representing herself as a sexual being. For Sharpe, power is multiple and so are strategies, which implies we must begin to think of Mary's truth as situational and context-bound, constituted as much by her silences as her voice (in other words, an analysis of Mary Prince's agency must consider her silences, which would oblige us to consider texts, memories, histories outside of her narrative and the norms that structure it).

Sharpe argues that remembering is always haunted by a resistance, by the possibility of a forgetting. That is why any act of resistance is never singular, since it functions in multiple contexts at the same time, and has differing effects in each of them. An act of resistance in one context could be the trace of a silence in another context. Consider, in this regard, Sharpe's notion of residual knowledges—knowledges that seemingly get written out of slave narratives: she gives the example of the magic root in Douglass's autobiography that must be disavowed as pagan superstition (34). As I have been arguing throughout this study, such silences, if we are to remember them, can have effects that enable us to trace out another history from inside a certain European enlightenment.

What are some of these silences in Mary Prince's narrative? First, consider how Susan Strickland, the transcriber of Mary's narrative, "pruned" Mary's speech and language through the editing process. Since Mary Prince probably spoke a combination of English, Spanish, French, and West African languages, the fact that this language was deemed inappropriate for a slave narrative suggests that there is a crucial shift in authority "from slave woman to text" through the editing process. Other silences happen around Mary's religious conversion: It seems that she started seeing one of her white lovers and stopped attending church *after* she had espoused Moravianism.[92] But this is excised from the history in the interests of representing Mary as a proper object of evangelical sympathy. Other silences (significantly around the body and sexuality) go into remaking this ex-slave as the proper subject of abolitionism: her work as a prostitute, her swearing, her experience of sexual violence, her lovers. Finally, in arguing for a "more complicated agency" for Mary Prince, Sharpe analyzes texts beyond the narrative, like court testimony and proslavery propaganda; in doing so, she wants to render visible the complex negotiations of "a black female subjectivity [that] cuts across seemingly incompatible documents" (50). For Sharpe, a "simple and linear plotting of the slave's quest for emancipation is inadequate for explaining such negotiations. . . . If we are to read *The History of Mary Prince* in the interest of the slave rather than the ex-slave, then we must acknowledge the limitations of a model of subjectivity based on notions of self-autonomy and/or free will" (53).

Can we read *Jane Eyre* in the interests of the black slave woman rather than the domesticated agent of the police? What would it mean to read "in the interests of" in any case? Do we identify with those interests? Are we in sympathy with them? Now, as I have argued, the trajectory of Jane's assumption of power gives off a certain haunting; to commune with these others, to hear them without reduction, and equally without romanticization, with, that is, a certain responsibility is to engage critically the textuality of other histories. Which means that we must always think at the limits of such discourses as European sympathy and humanitarianism—Mary's silences take us to that limit. What one learns, I think, from Mary's complex negotiations of power under slavery is that the disclosure of Jane's sympathetic subjectivity, as it is haunted by its own silences, by Mary's testimony, by Mary's own silences, opens the possibility that the subject is after all a relation with the unrepresentable. That is why, I think, Mary's text poses questions that cannot simply be resolved through recourse to a presentist intentionality—her text poses the problem of the subject's relationship to the unrepresentable itself. And that is why the sympathetic call, that black spectre of superstition, as that which is also in some profound sense unrepresentable, punctuates Brontë's text with, precisely, a question mark.

Emmanuel Levinas once said that in all of Western thought from Aristotle to Heidegger, "Every meaning and every psychism, all spirituality, lead back to *dis-covery*, gathering together, synchronous appearing, even if intentional correlation does not remain the ultimate structure."[93] One can see this gathering together in the anxious iteration of abjection in Jane's assumption of power, but also in the rendering proper of Mary's slave narrative. And this violent gathering together is also a kind of fencing in within the confines of a certain being. Levinas continues: "Every confession of truths comes back to a prior disclosure of being, that is to say, situates within the limits of being every sensible thought, and *subordinates sense to being*. Language either refers to this previous discovery or contributes to it, receiving, in this case, transcendental status; but language in no way would know how to signify beyond being." In my readings of *Jane Eyre* and the *History of Mary Prince* one can, again, discern this subordination of sense (or the body) to being (or the law, the proper, even a certain "spirit") in the repeated elisions of sexuality in Mary's mediated narratives of slavery, or in Jane's disavowal of that "black spectre" of another spirituality outside normative Christianity. But Levinas suggests other possibilities. "Testimony—the confession of some knowledge or of an experience by a subject—can be conceived only in relation to the disclosed being which remains the norm; it brings about only indirect truths about being, or about the relations man has with being. These truths are evidently inferior, secondhand, and uncontrollable, distorted by the very fact of their transmission: 'self-effacing subjectivity,' by circulating information, is capable of bad faith and lying." We come face to face with these subaltern, uncontrollable truths in the experience of that occult sympathy that questions Jane's narrative, or in Mary's "lies" that bring about those indirect truths that tie slavery to sexual violence. If these "testimonies" are a structural part of both narratives, as I have argued they are, they signal the possibility of another relationship between subjectivity, sympathy and spirituality. Even another soul: " . . . the notion of the soul has been purified over the course of the history of philosophy of any connotation other than that which evokes consciousness or thematizing contemplation. The importance that the concept *intentionality* has taken on in recent times marks the culmination of this trend. Is not calling into question such a structure of the psychism to hint at a role for testimony. . . . Far from being subordinated to the disclosure of being, are they not the source of a meaning signifying otherwise? Do they not allow a glimpse of a sensible adventure that would not be played out within the limits of being? An intrigue from beyond being?" What we see in these novels of sentiment and slave narratives is that this intrigue beyond being is at least as old as the history of normalization in the West. It would be the starting point, too, of thinking a sympathy beyond the police. I will return to the implications of Levinas's crucial insight in my conclusion to this chapter.

What I have argued here is that, at a specific juncture, the history of sympathy fuses with the history of "police," and in this way sympathy becomes unevenly integrated into mobile strategies of governmentality, such as charities, social improvement, class-based education, the cult of domesticity, national integration, and other utilitarian and evangelical reforms. Both *Pamela* and *Jane Eyre* stage this uneven integration; both texts confront, and finally appropriate colonial, racial, and class otherness through the narrative of a British woman's assumption of class, racial, and national sovereignty, even as this power is thoroughly circumscribed by patriarchal domesticity. The power of domestic affections is precisely what is at stake in both narratives. But what, finally, do we make of this call of the other? This occult compulsion that inexplicably pulls souls from their bodily cells to wander the earth? I ask again, is there some remainder or uncontrollable overflow in the sympathetic relationship? Again, I have tried to chart its effects in the figuration of the sympathetic agent in both *Pamela* and *Jane Eyre,* and in the desire to remember with solidarity in my reading of the *History of Mary Prince.* My sense is that this call, which I read as the call of justice as well, requires another critical optic altogether, a kind of reading strategy that begins to reconstruct a counter-memory of sympathy.

Sympathy into Solidarity:
Slavery, Colonialism, and Memory

As readers we are obliged to pose today our own relationship to this pedagogy of sympathy staged so fantastically in eighteenth- and nineteenth-century literature. Do we read with sympathy? And if so, what kind of sympathy is it? Can we fracture the imbrications between sympathy and the police? Do scenes of sympathy thrill us with horror, move us with pity, and so humanize us, as was once thought they would? I would venture "no" as an initial answer, but as I have tried to make clear, we are certainly not free or beyond these violent pedagogies. And yet there are other ways of reading these texts of sentiment, strategies that take us into the general textuality of the world and its histories of domination and resistance. In sentimental fiction there are moments when sympathy take the reader beyond the pale of humanity and civilization, and so pose the naturalness or givenness not only of the sympathetic relation but of the proper boundary of the proper human itself. For within this tradition, from inside a discourse that seems to abject relentlessly the racial other, we also come across those scenes where a man or woman will sympathize with those who seem to be savages and barbarians, or even Indians.

I end this chapter with a brief consideration of Henry Mackenzie's *Man of Feeling* (1771)[94] and Quobna Cugoano's *Thoughts and Sentiments on the Evil of Slavery*. Mackenzie's fragmentary novel is in some senses paradigmatic in the literature of sentiment: an antihero whose adventures pose a certain social critique through poignant scenes of suffering. In this narrative, we can also discern a certain distrust of "deduction." Writing to his cousin in the course of composing *The Man of Feeling* in July 1769, Mackenzie remarked that he had avoided mere "argument or moral reasoning," and had instead focused on introducing "observations of men and manners": "In this way I was somehow led to think of introducing a man of sensibility into different scenes where his feelings might be seen in their effects, and his sentiments occasionally delivered without the stiffness of regular deduction."[95] We shall return to this order of representation outside of mere deduction, but we should first recall that Mackenzie's Harley has come to stand for all of (European) humanity and the subsequent history of "aid to the underprivileged"; as one critic put it, "The world was learning humanity. In this respect the novel of sentiment is closely related to the social consciousness inherent in the romantic movement. The eighteenth-century men and women who literally wept over the world's distresses began fumblingly to try to alleviate them. The Victorians, only a little less obviously sentimental, organized charitable societies. Today, aid to the underprivileged is international in scope; but among its progenitors is Harley, who gave tears and alms to the distressed."[96] It is this genealogy that I would want simultaneously to trace and contest. I argue that the social consciousness that Harley in some sense stands in for takes us actually to the limit of what it meant to be human in the eighteenth and nineteenth centuries.

For Harley, a "blush, a phrase or affability to an inferior, a tear at a moving tale, were to him like the Cestus of Cytharea, unequalled in conferring beauty" (19). Harley, as a man of feeling in an unsentimental world, fosters "every nobler feeling" in those around him (268), so much so that even in death he inspires those who knew him to something higher: By his grave, says the editor, "there is such an air of gentleness around it, that I can hate nothing; but, as to the world, I pity the men of it" (268). Harley's strange observations of the world voice a particular social critique, as well as a gender reversal: as Starr remarks, "the sentimental hero poses an implicit challenge to accepted notions of masculinity, and he cannot be assimilated into the world represented in the novels. As a consequence, sentimental novels tend to become satires on 'the world,' but satires in which the hero himself cannot usually take part because of his naïveté, good nature, and general childlikeness." Such men as Harley problematize the association of sentiment with femininity, even as they question the possibility of acting in the world when weighed down with such an excess of sentiment. Harley, through his tears, is always grappling with an excess of emotion (the phrase "transport of excess" was common in sentimental literature) where others would merely shrug and walk on; what seems everyday and normal will suddenly seem strange and inexplicable through his eyes. For Harley, Bedlam[97] seems to name not a mental asylum in London but the true state of the world of rational beings: "the world may be said to be a large madhouse." Fashion, wealth, and selfishness make worldly people monsters in Harley's estimation. It is in considering the other of reason, of power, and of culture that Harley is led to avow a certain madness that haunts British civilization. And so Harley withdraws from the world. In pitying the people of the world, he can take an ironic distance from it; part of the work that social critique does in the text is to suture the identity of the man of sentiment through sympathy—it is almost as if, by sympathizing, Harley is able to tower over the world, and so dominate it by rejecting it. But the world he takes distance from is in fact a very specific one: London in the late eighteenth century. As his refined sentiment seems to withdraw him from civilized London, and so sutures a sense of anti-urban, farmer-yeoman superiority, Harley also opens the possibility of a strange sympathy with the racial other.[98]

I am thinking of a particular scene of sympathy. The destitute Edwards becomes an object of Harley's "active sympathy," not just his tears. He sets the elderly farmer, and his surviving grandchildren, up on a small piece of property on the Harley estate. But Edwards is interesting for another reason. He narrates his time as a forced conscript in India, "where I was soon made a serjeant, and might have picked up some money, if my heart had been as hard as some others were; but my nature was never of that kind, that could think of getting rich at the expense of my conscience" (189). Notice already that for men of conscience like Edwards and Harley using India as a means to mend or make their own fortune was out of the question. Edwards continues, and I will quote at length:

> Amongst our prisoners was an old Indian, whom some of our officers supposed to have a treasure hidden somewhere. . . . They pressed him to discover it. He declared he had none; but that would not satisfy them: so they ordered him to be tied to a stake, and suffer fifty lashes every morning, till he should learn to speak out as they said. Oh! Mr. Harley, had you seen him, as I did, with his hands bound behind him, suffering in silence, while the big drops trickled down his shrivelled cheeks and wet his grey beard, which some of the inhuman soldiers plucked in scorn! I could not bear it, I could not for my soul; and one morning, when the rest of the guard were out of the way, I found means to let him escape. I was tried by a court-martial for negligence of my post, and ordered, in compassion of my age, and having got this wound in my arm, and that in my leg, in the service, only to suffer 300 lashes, and be turned out of the regiment. . . . I set out however, resolved to walk as far as I could, and then to lay myself down and die. But I had scarce gone a mile, when I was met by the Indian whom I had delivered. He pressed me in his arms, and kissed the marks of the lashes on my back a thousand times: he led me to a little hut, where some friend of his dwelt, and after I was recovered of my wounds, conducted me so far on my journey himself, and sent another Indian to guide me through the rest. When we parted, he pulled out a purse with two hundred pieces of gold in it: "Take this, said he, my dear preserver, it is all I have been able to procure." . . . He embraced me: "You are an Englishman, said he, but the Great Spirit has given thee an Indian heart; may he bear up the weight of your old age, and blunt the arrow that brings it rest!" (190–192)

What difference does it make that Mackenzie is probably confusing cultural stereotypes of Native Americans with South Asian natives? A great deal no doubt, but how are we to read this passage today? The scene is by now familiar: a suffering object of pity, freed and rescued, by a sympathizing agent. But the relations of power are slightly skewed: Both the Indian and Edwards are relatively disempowered in different ways. The object of pity returns the act of sympathy—an act that earns Edwards three hundred lashes from his fellow Englishmen. The (nameless) Indian and Edwards then actually switch places. I think that even though it is related in the language of sympathy, and even considering that there is a gross misrepresentation of "actual Indian culture," we can discern another operation in this scene. There is a return, an exchange, but nothing was expected. It is not simply or only a circuit of sympathetic civility that is voiced here: Neither the Indian nor Edwards attempt to convert, improve, or enlighten the other. Propriation does not seem to be part of this scene, or it seems to frame the possibility of something else. Each maintains and even honors the difference of the other, even as they relate, communicate, and act for the other.

This performs, I believe, the underground crossing of sympathy into solidarity. For keep in mind that Harley takes a very particular lesson away from Edwards's narrative. Again, I quote at length:

> Edwards . . . I have a proper regard for the prosperity of my country: every native of it appropriates to himself some share of the power, or the fame, which as a nation, it acquires; but I cannot throw off the man so much, as to rejoice at our conquests in India. You tell me of immense territories subject to the English: I cannot think of their possessions, without being led to enquire, by what right they possess them. They came there as traders, bartering the commodities they brought for others which their purchases could spare; and however great their profits were, they were then equitable. But what title have the subjects of another kingdom to establish an empire in India? to give laws to a country where the inhabitants received them on the terms of friendly commerce? You say they are happier under our regulations than the tyranny of their own petty princes. I must doubt it, from the conduct of those by whom these regulations have been made. They have drained the treasuries of the Nabobs, who must fill them by oppressing the industry of their objects. Nor is this to be wondered at, when we consider the motive upon which these gentlemen do not deny their going to India. The fame of conquest, barbarous as that motive is, is but a secondary consideration: there are certain stations in wealth to which the warriors of the East aspire. It is there indeed where the wishes of their friends assign them eminence, where the question of their country is pointed at their return. When shall I see a commander return from India in the pride of honourable poverty? You describe the victories they have gained; they are sullied by the cause in which they fought: you enumerate the spoils of these victories; they are covered with the blood of the vanquished! Could you tell me of some conqueror giving peace and happiness to the conquered? . . . did he endear the British name by examples of generosity, which the most depraved are rarely able to resist? did he return with the consciousness of duty discharged to his country, and humanity to his fellow-creatures? (209–12)

As if anticipating the sharp criticisms of the British East India Company that would devastate company officials, directors, and shareholders in the coming years, Mackenzie's Harley makes plain the charges of corruption and cruelty that mar, or better, found British rule. The moment of British ascendancy in Bengal (ca. 1765) was the culmination of a complex process of internal fragmentation in South Asia (linked to the fate of the Muslim empires in the eighteenth century) and of European expansionism. Let us consider this history briefly. As is well known, during the sixteenth and seventeenth century three great Muslim empires flourished in Asia and north Africa: the Ottoman, Safavid, and Mughal dynasties. These three empires dominated the population and wealth of a huge territory between Algeria and the borders of Burma. Uneven economic growth and political instability within the Muslim empires and the seaboard fringes of Asia also created pressures and opportunities that encouraged European nations and trading companies to seize political power in key regions before 1800 (Bayly, *Imperial Meridian,* 16).

In India, the death of the Emperor Aurangzeb (1707) was followed by two decades of fighting between factions of Indian-born notables from the localities and great imperial nobles from Iran and central Asia. During this time, the office of vazir (or chief minister) became more autonomous. Provincial governors, basing themselves on the entrenched commercial and landholding elites that had grown up over the previous century, were gradually to assert de facto autonomy of Delhi. In the eighteenth century, powerful but unstable coalitions of Afghan, Persian, or central Asian warlords overthrew or dispersed the old nobilities. Nadir Shah, who built his power on Iranian and Turkish men, sacked Delhi in 1739. North India was again invaded by Afghans in 1747 and between 1759 and 1761 (Bayly, 36–37). The consequences for Indian politics and the Indian economy were momentous. The process of state-building and "decentralization" was speeded up. In time, the Afghan invasion of the 1750s allowed the Marathas, Sikhs and Jats, who activated seemingly old animosities of the Mughal empire, to recoup a position that was still quite vulnerable in 1720. The invasions also had profound consequences for the political economy of the empires. The Persian invasion of Delhi made it impossible for the nobles of Delhi and Agra to buy the rich produce of Bengal. This in turn made difficulties for the regular remittance of revenue from Bengal to the center and encouraged the growing independence of the Nawabs of Bengal (38–39). Between 1720 and 1740, the imperial notables in Awadh, Bengal, and Hyderabad, began slowly to amalgamate together fiscal, military, and judicial powers, which the Mughals emperors had tried to keep separate. They transformed their offices into hereditary holdings, gradually took control of the enfeebled *jagir* (or state-bestowed salary) system and patronized both Hindu and Muslim landholding groups that might act as the intermediaries between and the fractious countryside. These political and economic realignments, in turn, encouraged the British in Bengal to contemplate more aggressive schemes of military and commercial expansion.

The servants of the various trading companies (French, British, Dutch) as well as private merchants or military officers began to play a more openly political role in these various regions torn by internal strife. Seizing control of monopolies of agricultural or artisan products which had been created by local rulers, Britons, Frenchmen, and Dutchmen became linchpins in farms of revenue and local structures of power in the coastal regions, commanding movements of capital and peoples. The European military presence became more pressing as Europe's dynastic wars became more desperate. The War of Austrian

Succession (1744–1748) intensified English and French attempts to find Indian clients, and led to damaging local conflicts in Persian and eastern Mediterranean waters between the armed traders of the two nations. Such conflicts became sharper during the Seven Years' War and the War of American Independence. Global warfare increased the military resources that the Europeans had in readiness in their colonial enclaves and also encouraged them to use force to resolve their trade disputes with Asian and African powers.

It is this complex history that Harley is referencing—without knowing it. Indeed, he goes even further than referencing this history of colonizing—he poses the more radical question of the legitimacy of that rule in India. Of course, this figure of the generous British colonizer would become the model and norm for the Indian civil servant in the nineteenth century. And we can discern that later history here as a structural possibility of sympathy. That future anterior possibility should give pause to any desire for romanticization. But there are also some basic presuppositions of colonial rule that Harley contests in this passage that would take us beyond the sympathetic relation. He founds at least part of his judgments on the basis of equality and justice, on the basis that is of a kind of solidarity with the colonized.

To gauge the effectivity of Harley's words, we must have a sense of the contours of the British debate around colonialism and in particular Indian affairs that underwent such a profound crisis and transformation from 1770 to 1813. I will delineate the trajectory of this debate in the next chapter, but we should keep in mind that by the time of the contentious East India Company Charter renewal debates in 1813, the argument for commercial colonialism and company monopoly needed a very particular representation of "native culture," one that would combat the pernicious effects of a whole generation of company nabobs, Orientalists, and romantic colonial administrators. Men such as Warren Hastings, Edmund Burke, Williams Jones, Thomas Munro, Charles Metcalfe, John Malcolm, and Mountstuart Elphinstone had argued for a personal, human, and, precisely, sympathetic, *ma-baap* (mother-father) or paternalistic rule rooted in the right of the peasant to the fruits of his labor.[99] They fought—vainly—the "innovations" of the rising generation of utilitarian and evangelical imperialists—innovations that were themselves also couched in the discourse of sympathy.

We can situate Harley's critique of company venality within the romantic tradition of British colonial administration. By 1813, the era of romanticism was already on the decline. Yet, residual voices would be heard during the parliamentary debates of 1813, voices that would remind people of another orientation toward the Orient. Consider the testimony before parliament of one of the most prominent and articulate romantic imperialists, Colonel Thomas Munro. When asked of his opinion of the "civilization" of the Hindus, Munro responded cautiously, as if with perplexity:

I do not exactly understand what is meant by the civilization of the Hindoos; in the higher branches of science, in the knowledge of the theory and practice of good government, and in an education, which, by banishing prejudice and superstition, opens the mind to receive instruction of every kind, from every quarter, they are much inferior to Europeans: but if a good system of agriculture, unrivaled manufacturing skill, a capacity to produce whatever can contribute to convenience or luxury; schools established in every village, for teaching reading, writing and arithmetic; the general practice of hospitality and charity amongst each other; and above all, a treatment of the female sex, full of confidence, respect and delicacy, are among the signs which denote a civilized people, then the Hindoos are not inferior to the nations of Europe; and if civilization is to become an article of trade between the two countries, I am convinced that this country will gain by the import cargo. (*Hansard's Parliamentary Debates*, XXV, 786)

One is reminded here of Harley's words. That Munro returned to India in 1814 as head of the commission to reorganize the judicial and police system of the Madras presidency—or that Mackenzie distanced himself from calls for black emancipation in the colonies as bad policy—should again warn us of the dangers of our own postcolonial romanticizations.[100] The work of propriation does not stop with the rupture of difference. Indeed, there is nothing that would immunize, as it were, these moments of what seem to be solidarity from being infected by such violent colonialist discourse, history, and practice.[101] And one cannot simply escape this complicity.

But one might do other things with it. It is because of this complex, contradictory, and overlapping history that I believe that another principle of sociality is both heralded and betrayed in these strange moments when the force of difference, of power, and of justice erupts onto the landscape of sentiment. We must develop critical tools, even another memory, to reorient the possibility of solidarity toward another future, a principle of sociality that can think difference outside of propriation. That is why every tradition, every institution of Western literature must be rememorized through voices that speak with the doubleness, even prophetic wisdom, of the slave, the colonized. This premise has guided my readings of sentimental literature in this chapter, and I end with another example of such rememorization. Cuguano's *Thoughts and Sentiments on the Evils of Slavery* (1787) was written collaboratively with Equiano (which complicates the all too neat dichotomy between the two as radical vs. accomodationist).[102] As if echoing Mackenzie, both Cugoano and Equiano, in their respective narratives, refer to slaves as "men of feeling."[103] But Cugoano seems rather more marginal to the tradition of sentimentalism than Equiano. And this for specific reasons.

Written in the vein of a radical jeremiad against slavery and slave owners, Cugoano's *Thoughts* poses the question of justice through a biblical idiom that prophesizes sure doom to the "iniquitous nations." As such his text performs a series of reversals that repeatedly threatens to engulf the association of abolitionism and sentimentality. Cugoano argues that the enslavement of African peoples contravenes every imaginable law—both secular and sacred: thus, slavery goes against common reason: "But what the light of nature, and the dictates of reason, when rightly considered, teach is, that no man ought to enslave another; and some, who have been rightly guided thereby, have made noble defences for the universal natural rights and privileges of all men" (28). And, of course, slavery transgresses the law of God, whether Christian or heathen: "Or can the slave-holders think that the Universal Father and Sovereign of Mankind will be well pleased with them, for the brutal transgression of his law, in bowing down the necks of those to the yoke of their cruel bondage? . . . I cannot but wish, for the honor of Christianity, that the bramble grown up amongst them, was known to the heathen nations by a different name, for sure the depredators, robbers and ensnarers of men can never be Christians, but ought to held as the abhorrence of all men, and the abomination of all mankind, whether Christians or heathens" (25).

Indeed, for this ex-slave, any enslaver or oppressor of men should rightly be called the "Antichrist" (67). Rereading Revelations 13:10 and 18:2–3,[104] Cugoano damns the European slaveholding powers: "That grand umbrageous shadow and image of evil and wickedness, has spread its malignant influence over all the nations of the earth, and has, by its power of delusion, given countenance and support to all the power of evil and wickedness done among men; and all the adherents and supporters of that delusion, and all the carriers on of wickedness, are fitly called Antichrist" (67). And such anti-Christianity, through colonialism, has spread its withering tentacles the world over:

> It may be said with confidence as a certain general fact, that all their foreign settlements and colonies were founded on murders and devastations, and that they have continued their depredations in cruel slavery and oppression to this day: for where such predominant wickedness as the African slave-trade, and the West Indian slavery is admitted, tolerated and supported by them, and carried on in their colonies, the nations and people who are supporters and encouragers thereof must be not only guilty themselves of that shameful and abandoned evil and wickedness. (62)

> At last when the wars subside, or other business calls them home, laden with the spoils of the East or elsewhere, they have then the grand part of their business to negotiate, in buying up bank stock, and lodging their plunder and ill-got wealth in the British or other funds. Thus the nation is loaded with more debt, and with an annual addition of more interest to pay, to the further advantage of those who often occasioned it by their villainy; who, if they had

their deserts, like the Popish inquisitors, are almost the only people in the world who deserve to be hung on the rack. (70)

And just as all those who profit, even indirectly, from iniquity participate in the guilt of the guilty, justice demands that none of us are free until all of us are free. "In such a vast extended, hideous and predominant slavery, as the Europeans carry on in their Colonies, some indeed may fall into better hands, and meet with some commiseration and better treatment than others . . . but what are these to the whole, even hundreds of thousands, held in perpetuity in all the prevalent and intolerable calamities of that state of bondage and exile. The emancipation of a few, while ever that evil and predominant business of slavery is continued, cannot make that horrible traffic one bit the less criminal" (75). Just as Mary Prince "cannot pass by" the suffering of those of her "fellow-slaves—for when I think of my own griefs, I remember theirs"—just so Cugoano remembers all those others who went before, all those who continue to suffer and to struggle. In so many ways, such solidarity always also performs a certain work of mourning: Cugoano knows that "blessed are those who mourn for they will be comforted." And so his first proposal for a "general reformation" of British society, even before "a total abolition of slavery" (his second proposal), would establish days of mourning and fasting so that the people of England might "seek grace and repentance, and find mercy and forgiveness before God Omnipotent" (98).

Like Prince's history, Cugoano's *Thoughts* is a mixed discourse, one that cannot but participate in the dominant frame of reference that tied justice to a certain propriative structure of sympathy,[105] but simultaneously and through that very structure his text gestures to an agency beyond European sentimentality. And so I will end with Cugoano's "plea" for sympathy:

> And we that are particularly concerned would humbly join with all the rest of our brethren and countrymen in complexion, who have been grievously injured, and who jointly and separately, in all the language of grief and woe, are humbly imploring and earnestly entreating the most respectful and generous people of Great Britain, that they would consider us, and have mercy and compassion on us, and to take away that evil . . . and . . . desist from their evil treatment of the poor and despised Africans, before it is too late; and to restore that justice and liberty which is our natural rights, that we have been unlawfully deprived and cruelly wronged of. . . . But if the people and legislature of Great-Britain altogether hold their peace at such a time as this, and even laugh at our calamity as heretofore they have been wont to do . . . : we sit like the mourning Mordecai's at their gates cloathed in sackcloth; and, in this advanced aera, we hope God in his Providence will rise up a deliverance for us some other way; and we have great reason to hope that the time of our deliverance is fast drawing nigh, and when the great Babylon of iniquity will fall. (96)

Note how a "plea" for compassion very quickly turns into the threat of a coming armageddon. More, black emancipation is a revelation of scripture, progress, and the advent of modernity—the passivity of Christian sympathy erupts into the possibility of a certain agency rooted in revelation. For this ex-slave, the universal law of God guarantees the natural rights of enslaved peoples. And so like Mordecai, "who had been carried away from Jerusalem among the captives" (Esther 2:6; see also 4:1–3), Cugoano prepares the way for this revelation with a hope.

In Conclusion

Do we today have a responsibility toward this hope? There is a specific discursive structure, which I have analyzed under the sign of propriation, that mark texts such as *Jane Eyre, Pamela,* but also legible in the narratives of Mary Prince, Equiano, and Cugoano. The propriative energy of these narratives assimilates and domesticates difference as a prior stage of the sympathizing, civilized Self. As such, sympathy integrates the other into overall strategies of governmentality. And yet I have also annotated the ways in which this propriation of difference gives birth to something else altogether. What I have tried to show is that these "sympathies whose workings baffle mortal comprehension," even as they betray that other outside of reason, draw us to another history outside of Europe as well, and inspire another spirituality beyond evangelical missionizing. It is the call of the other, all these others that I have tried to bring to a certain voice in my analysis of the sympathetic relation. A call heard I think in Harley's anticolonial lament, or in Sally's narrative, in the (displaced) mystery of wandering souls in *Jane Eyre,* in Cugoano's hope of justice, in the silences that structure Mary's history. This call interrupts and displaces propriation. It is the call of a counter-memory of sympathy.

If sympathy is to take us into what Levinas calls an intrigue beyond being we must break radically and *repeatedly* with all structures that would tie its practice to propriation and the police—always keeping in mind that even what is dead wields a specific force. A sympathy beyond sympathy through a different kind of responsibility toward the other. A sociality with and through difference. "Initially approached from responsibility for the other human—beginning from human solidarity or fraternity—the subject would be alienated in the depths of its identity—an alienation that would not empty the Same of its identity, but which would constrain it in the unimpugnable summons of me by the other, where no one could stand in for me. The soul is the other within me, a sickness of identity, its being out of phase, its diachrony, gasping, shuddering. But is not the one-for-the-other meaning itself?"[106] This soul is "already a touch mad" in its hauntings by the other, in its responsibility and solidarity with the other. Now, let us recall the OED definition of solidarity: "Solidarity: 1. a. The fact or quality, on the part of communities, etc., *of being perfectly united or at one in some respect, esp. in interests, sympathies, or aspirations;* spec. with reference to the aspirations or actions of trade-union members. b. Const. of (mankind, a race, etc.). c. Const. between or with (others). 2. Community or perfect coincidence of (or between) interests. 3. Civil Law. *A form of obligation involving joint and several responsibilities or rights.*" We can now, I think, understand the ruptural effect of slashing solidarity into this history of sympathy. But only if we come to terms with the profound insight that these texts of sentiment and humanitarianism offer us: if to be in solidarity with another is to be perfectly united or in sympathy with her then what is demanded is that "every meaning and every psychism, all spirituality, lead back to *dis-covery,* gathering together." But if we can experience an intrigue beyond being, a certain, perhaps unnamable other, irreducibly different and even slightly mad, must always stand guard over our relationship to each other. And to the hope that a sympathy beyond the police could give birth to a solidarity with (a) difference.

Chapter Four

Theaters of Horror

By the start of the nineteenth century, projects governed by sympathetic humanitarianism dominated the social agenda of Britain's oligarchic elites. Nearly every project of reform—abolitionism, Indian government, prison reform, hygiene, poor relief, the redeeming of fallen women, to mention only a few—was in some ways tied to an emergent sensibility that reticulated sympathy with a fundamentally new vision of the human. I have argued throughout this study that sympathy was a paradoxical, even protean form of power, both bridging and reproducing inequalities through an acrobatics of identification and differentiation. Its ambitions at the level of the everyday can be gauged in the proliferation of humanitarian institutions that sought to transform the social landscape of both metropole and colony. This transformation is indissociable from the rise of a new, increasingly rigid ideology of racial superiority in Britain: the ideal human, sympathetic and ever improving, was also the self-same agent of a specifically European form of racism.[1] That sympathy, humanitarianism, and a new racism emerged at nearly the same moment in British history seems rather less anomalous when we consider the crucial role that evangelization played in (re)producing, circulating, and bolstering the civilizing mission of the British empire. And yet what I have also insisted on throughout this study is that sympathy enabled a form of agency that at least partly broke with its axioms and so left opened the possibility of a counter-memory of sympathy.

In this chapter I aim to reconstruct this reticulated field of discourse, institutional practice, and resistance. I trace the specific strategies deployed by parliamentarians in two crucial debates, the abolition of the slave trade (1804–1807) and the renewal of the British East India Charter (1812–1813). In different ways, the West and East Indies became for the

British theaters of horror—a particular kind of aesthetic of sympathy figured both colonies as apt stages for the humanitarian imperialist. In the first section, I look at the debates around abolition and the use of sympathy as a strategy of assimilation and appropriation; humanitarian sympathy in these discourses renders the untutored, brutalized slave economically and politically proper to the regime of Western liberal discipline. By contrast, in the section concerning the debates around the charter, I show how sympathy produces another figure: the despotic, murderous, antihuman Hindu, whose abjection from the signifying economy of evangelicalism was the condition of possibility for the appropriation of India for the empire of Christ.

Humanity and the Strategies of Sympathy: The Abolition of the Slave Trade

On May 30, 1804, William Wilberforce rose to submit a "motion relative to the slave trade." It would be another three years before parliament would actually pass legislation banning the forcible importation of African peoples in to the colonies, and another 34 years before emancipation. Since the beginning of the British slave trade in 1562, more than 11 million African women, men and children had been sent into slavery in the Americas; huge numbers had never reached the colonies, as millions died en route to the African coast and on the slave ships in mid-ocean; the 11 million who arrived were the survivors of perhaps more than 24 million people enslaved in Africa.[2] By 1804, the struggle to end the trade was entering its final stage. Still, Wilberforce knew what he was up against. It had after all already been nearly a 30-year struggle, and various mass mobilizations (abolitionist and slave revolts) had greatly contributed to finally shifting the balance of power in the debate. Let us first reconstitute this field of power.

No doubt, the overthrow of colonial slavery was "one of the turning points in the history of the world," as George Macaulay Trevelyan was to put it in his *British History in the Nineteenth Century* (1930).[3] Although Trevelyan was decidedly speaking from the vantage point of British imperial security, we can begin to displace this narrow vision by considering the actual arguments of the parliamentary supporters of slavery and the trade in African peoples. These men marshaled their "evidence" (siting various "authorities," such as Mungo Park, Edward Long, Bryan Edwards, and even Thomas Malthus), defending "this country, . . . our revenues, and even . . . our existence as a nation" against the "sentimentalism" and "philosophy" of the abolitionists.[4] First, there was the concern for the future of the planters, the economic stability of the colonies, and eventually the future of the empire. As William Young put it, "The article of sugar alone amounted to 10 million, and the whole was between 16 and 17 millions. The whole of this

property is, by these discussions, put in the greatest hazard from an insurrection among the negroes, on account of the inseparable connection in the
minds of the negroes between abolition and emancipation. Under these circumstances then, is it not equally impolitic and unjust to allow a measure of
this nature to pass?"[5] Young's sense of the far-flung network of sometimes
conflictual interests that had developed along with slavery and empire was
of course absolutely right.[6]

Merely 32 years after the founding of the British Royal African Company, in 1695, the Bristol sugar merchant, John Carey, wrote that the slave
trade was "the best Traffick the Kingdom hath . . . as it doth occasionally
give so vast an Employment to our People both by Sea and Land."[7] From
the 1780s, when the abolition movement gathered momentum, until the
Abolition Act in 1807, the commercial and political elites of Bristol and Liverpool (both cities were literally created from the slave trade) predicted
doom and depression following the ending of the slave trade; MPs, leading
merchants, and local politicians were as one for the better part of 20 years in
believing that the slave trade was vital to the economic interests of those
cities and the nation at large.[8]

Let us schematically outline this "Traffick." By the first decade of the
nineteenth century, there is no question that the slave trade was vital to the
British West Indies; given the brutality of West Indian slavery, without regular supplies of African peoples the plantations's human stock of forced
labor would decline.[9] Between 1650 and 1800 British tastes were transformed by slave labor. Luxury goods that would have seemed beyond their
means and desires a generation earlier seemed, by the end of the eighteenth
century, absolutely essential to the British: " . . . foodstuffs, clothing, exotic
drinks, tobacco, coffee, sugar, books, toys and a range of leisure activities.
There was, quite simply, an amazing rise in consumer demand in Britain itself, and a great deal of that demand was for tropical produce, most of which
was the fruit of slave labour. As the British consumed ever more sugar and
tobacco, those products created further opportunities for export of British
goods to the Americas and Africa." In short, by the dawn of the nineteenth
century, the British were consuming gallons of tea and coffee sweetened with
pounds of sugar (sugar consumption was especially pronounced in the newly
industrial regions which enjoyed a rise in material prosperity during these
same years). These changes in consumption and production, underwritten
by the slave trade and enslaved African labor, fueled British industrial development and global expansion. Thus, West Riding woolen goods, copper,
brass, and wrought iron were exported to Africa and the Americas; by the
end of eighteenth century, some 40 percent of all British exports went to
those two regions, both linked to slavery and the slave trade. By the 1770s,
in fact, the average annual value of goods exported from Britain to the

Caribbean was in excess of £1.33 million (around $168,000,000 in today's currency); nearly a third of the growth in British exports in the 30 years before American independence, and perhaps a half of all the increase in British goods produced for export went to satisfy demand in the West Indies—without a doubt, from about midcentury onward, the Caribbean stimulated an enormous growth in British industrial output.[10] But, and this is the crucial point, these trading networks ranged far beyond the "Black Atlantic." As Walvin notes, "The increase in West Indian purchasing power stimulated other areas of British overseas trade. For example, the trade to Africa (for slaves destined for the Caribbean) did not consist solely of goods from Britain itself. About one-quarter of all the goods shipped from Britain to Africa were in fact of East Indian origin; the rise of the export trade to West Africa served to increase British trade to and from India" (314). This reticulation of consumption, production, exchange, and enslaved and colonial labor drew together Kingston and Calcutta, Lancashire and Sierra Leone in a conflictual weave of interests, profits, sentiments, and imaginings.

The sanctity of property was central to the stability of this network. For the parliamentary supporters of planter interests like Charles Ellis, the enslaved peoples of Africa were essentially property (Speech on June 13, 1804; II, 653), and under British law property was inviolable. Again, the idea that enslaved African peoples were the inviolable property of their white masters was as old as the debate on abolition itself—long before the infamous "Zong" trial, planters, slavers, and their parliamentary backers had been insisting on the fundamental connection between slavery and (white) property rights.[11] Put in such terms, the planter interests attempted to secure the equation of African peoples with property; like any other commodity, African slaves were defined by their fungibility.

But by the beginning of the nineteenth century the relationship between property, humanity, and slavery had to be reconstellated. Threatened with the ending of the slave trade, the plantocracy was now arguing that since British laws were far more humane than those of any other nation in the world, slaves were better off in the British West Indies than they would be even in Africa. Thus, all the Saints's[12] talk of "humanity" and "justice" was misguided at best, hypocritical at worst. In a direct attack against evangelicalism, and Wilberforce in particular, John Fuller lashed out:

> The situation of the negroes has been the subject of complaint. Is not the situation of the poor in this country in many instances worse than that of the negroes? Without meaning to boast, I have given permission to my own negroes to cultivate considerable spots of ground for themselves, and ample time for this purpose. I have lodged and clothed, and have engaged a physician to attend and prescribe to them. I have done everything for their comfort. Can

the hon. gent. [Wilberforce] say that he has done so much, with all his talk and noise about humanity, for the peasantry of Yorkshire? I do not want to impute any unworthy motives to the supporters of the bill, but I am convinced, that as the man who pretends to more courage than another has generally less, so he who pretends to more religion than others is often the greater cheat. (February 28, 1805; III, 657)

We mark a discourse in the moment of its emergence into dominance: the practice associated with evangelical humanity had become the index for the proper treatment of enslaved (and, at around the same time, colonized) populations such that even the planters had to fashion their discourse around humanity. My argument here is that this human would be the ideal object of sympathy; conversely, to sympathize with such humanity also was a means to normalize difference: racial, cultural, civilizational difference would come to be the horrific signs of a static savagery or barbarism. As we shall see, to sympathize and to colonize would come to be directly filiated in evangelical thought.

But let us contextualize another aspect of Fuller's attack on the evangelical abolitionists: the contrast between oppressed African slaves and proletarianized Yorkshire peasants (William Wilberforce, the leading evangelical abolitionist in parliament, was a member for Yorkshire, and his family had been settled in the area since the twelfth century).[13] As was well known, African slaves could save for their freedom and some in fact had already manumitted themselves—which was not something that English wage slaves could do: One supporter of the trade remarked "that the situation of the negroes in the West India colonies was equal, nay, superior to the condition of the labouring poor of this country. They were better fed and more comfortably accommodated" (II: 459; speech by John Fuller, May 30, 1804).[14] This "look at home" critique of evangelical and utilitarian "improvement" projects (made famous some years later by Dickens's brilliant caricature of Mrs. Jelleybee's "telescopic philanthropy" in *Bleak House*) would be a recurrent theme in much anti-abolitionist discourse, and it would provide the impetus and idiom for the elaboration of the radical and Chartist critique of "white slavery" in England.[15] I suggest that these later radical strategies both drew on and repudiated the history of African slavery; the very idea of "wage-slavery" took hold and had such a profound rhetorical effect precisely because of this prior racial history. If this is so, what we must consider is how specifically arguments around "uplifting" the enslaved African reached their limit when sympathetic humanitarianism had to deal with wage slaves breaking the chains of property at home: if justice and humanity are tied to the practice of sympathy, who is to say where sympathy should stop? (I return to this question in my concluding chapter.)

According to the plantocracy and their parliamentary advocates, the very future of British colonialism was at stake in the West Indies. If the British were to give up this trade, they affirmed, the Spaniards or Portuguese would inevitably take it over, and with disastrous results for both the enslaved peoples and Britain. European competition, and continental struggles for dominance in the shadow of Napoleon, were never far from these colonial debates. What could be the effect, asked another planter ally "of our abolishing the trade, but only to throw it into the hands of other nations."[16] Abolition of the trade was not a mere abstract question, opined General Isaac Gascoyne, since "everyone must see . . . that its ultimate object was emancipation, and nothing could be more dangerous to our colonial system, than a discussion which involved such a question. . . . Was it upon the speculations of a few individuals that we were to give up our colonial system, or was this the time, at the moment when we were engaged in an expensive war, which was likely to be of no ordinary duration; was this the time to move such a question when we had seen the effect which had been produced by similar opinions in a neighbouring isle to our colonies, and when it must be evident to every one what extreme danger would be produced by the spreading of such a spirit in the West Indies? Was not the West Indies a favourite object of Bonaparte, and would he not eagerly seize the advantage which our agreeing to the abolition of the slave trade would throw into his hands?"[17]

Looming over these arguments around colonialism, empire, and national greatness was always the horror of black revolt, Haiti having declared independence in 1804. Thus, if anyone needed further proof of the "train of mischief" that abolition would lead to (II: 653), one need only look toward "the late atrocities at St. Domingo" (II: 653, 661). This shows, ranted the slavery lobby, that abolition, emancipation, national decline, and bloody insurrection were absolutely tied together. Without doubt, the revolution in Haiti was the touchstone for all anti-abolition arguments, and Dessalines and the "Black Jacobins" would reappear time and again in all these discussions. "During the phrenzy of the revolution in France, the slave trade was abolished, and that measure led to all the horrors which had since occurred in St. Domingo" (Speech of Charles Brooke, February 28, 1805; III: 645); and so the abolitionists were a bunch of Jacobins: "I was . . . told that a diploma of Jacobinism was . . . sent to [Wilberforce]. I am convinced that the principles of Jacobinism are those upon which this measure is founded."[18] In many ways, "bloody insurrection" was the final, frenzied alarm that slavers put forth. " . . . if 3 or 400 negroes were to fly from their masters and get into the woods, the whole military force of the island would not be able to subdue them. It was therefore necessary the house should be cautious in what they did in that respect, for he believed, in his conscience, that if the act should pass, there would not, in the space of three years, be a white person left alive in any of the islands."[19]

The anti-abolitionist position during this last phase of the struggle, then, consisted of a chain of contradictory arguments. First, slavery was good for empire; this far-flung network of colonial interests would be jeopardized by abolishing the trade: Abolition was bad policy. Second, abolition would lead to insurrection and the extermination of the white planters; the revolution in Haiti would be reproduced in every West Indian colony if the trade in Africans was abolished: Only the continuance of the trade and of slavery as a whole could ensure the dominance of whites in the colonies. Third, humanity would be best furthered by keeping African peoples enslaved, because it was only under British slavery that one could ensure the steady improvement of the "savage mind": True religion, as well as true justice, consisted in maintaining and bettering the institution of slavery. Fourth, slaves were essentially property, and no amount of humanitarian palaver could alter that basic fact: slavery and the trade was rooted in the sanctity of property. Fifth, the condition of enslaved Africans was in fact much better than the "labouring poor" in some of the home parishes of the saintly members of parliament; if the saints were going to be consistent in their sympathy, the nation's poor must first be redeemed. These divergent arguments delimited the terrain of anti-abolition. As we shall see, the parliamentary evangelicals maneuvered and transformed this discursive field through the deployment of sympathetic horror, but we must always also understand these discursive shifts in the contexts of a new overall historical conjuncture: the French Revolution, the rise of Napoleon, the liberation of Haiti, the slow consolidation of evangelical hegemony, the transformation of property relations, and the emergence of middle class social agitations (ranging from Corn Laws, East India monopolies, protofeminism, and of course abolition)—all these massive changes came together in a very specific historical conjuncture that enabled the elaboration of sympathetic governmentality.

When William Wilberforce rose in the House of Commons in 1804 to move for the Abolition Bill he reminded his listeners of the "very long and serious investigation" that had generated "a mass of evidence" against the slave trade in 1792. But the resolutions that were passed at that time "had never been followed up, and the trade, with a few alterations that were then made, was still continued as formerly" (441). Although he hopes that parliament will finally bring this "abominable traffic to a termination," Wilberforce seems to be speaking with the sense that the parliamentary struggle against the trade will have to begin from the beginning: since 1796, he notes, "300,000 additional negroes had been imported into the West Indies: thus consigning 300,000 of our fellow-creatures and their posterity to perpetual bondage" (454). He then starts by arguing that the "pernicious tendencies" of the slave trade (II: 441) vitiate the happiness of Africa, the West Indies, and even Britain. Indeed, he "was sure that it was impossible for a feeling mind to survey the picture without indignation, sympathy, and disgust" (457). Wilberforce goes on to outline the evil effects of the trade on the coast of Africa.

> Such is the infatuation of those ignorant and unfortunate princes that in order to procure slaves for sale they engage in wars with each other, either on frivolous pretenses, or, should these not occur, without any pretense but the arm of power. To augment this evil, and to render the passion still stronger, we tempt them with spirituous liquors, their attachment to which becomes so strong, that they will not hesitate to perpetrate any injustice to gratify the passion. In pursuance of this abominable trade . . . we go still farther, and, when other means fail, we set fire to their villages, that we may catch the wretched fugitives in their attempts to escape from that dangerous element. . . . We thus violate the most sacred rights of mankind, and introduce violence and injustice, by our incitements and example, into those unfortunate countries, which, from their ignorance, become a prey to our avarice. (II, 442)

This particular argument would have a great deal of effectivity and force in evangelical representations of slavery and Africa. That slavery was contributing to the overall disintegration of social relations in West Africa shows, says Wilberforce, that in Africa at least the British were agents of savagery. This reversal was a crucial device in evangelical abolitionism; through such tracts as Anthony Benezet's *A Caution and Warning to Great Britain and Her Colonies; in A Short Representation of the Calamitous State of the Enslaved Negroes in the British Dominions; Collected from various Authors, and submitted to the Serious Consideration of all, more especially of those in Power* (1766) and *Some Historical Account of Guinea; Its Situation, Produce, and the General Disposition of its Inhabitants with An Inquiry into the Rise and Progress of the Slave Trade; Its Nature, and Lamentable Effects* (1762), Equiano's *Interesting Narrative,* and John Wesley's *Considerations Upon Slavery* (1774), the abolitionist movement sought to reverse the assumed relationship between African slavery and European civilization. John Wesley, for one, argued in his *Considerations* that instead of the shining light of civilization leading Africa and its natives out of darkness, the once reasonable and good-natured people of Africa are a reminder of the degradation of Europe. Thus,

> Upon the whole . . . the negroes who inhabit the coast of Africa . . . are so far from being the stupid, senseless, brutish, lazy barbarians, the fierce, cruel, per-

fidious savages they have been described, that on the contrary, they are represented by them who have no motive to flatter them, as remarkably sensible, considering the few advantages they have for improving their understanding:—As
very industrious, perhaps more so than any other natives of so warm a climate.—As fair, just and honest in their dealings, unless where white men have
taught them to be otherwise:—And as far more mild, friendly and kind to
strangers, than any of our forefathers were. Our forefathers! Where shall we find
at this day, among the fair-faced natives of Europe, a nation generally practicing
the justice, mercy, and truth, which are related of these poor black Africans?
Suppose the preceding accounts are true, (which I see no reason or pretense to
doubt of) and we may leave England and France, to seek genuine honesty in
Benin, Congo, or Angola. (14–15)

Wilberforce knew Wesley's text thoroughly, and so did most of his audience.
In his speeches, and those of his evangelical allies, a propriative sympathy integrates this reversal according to a narrative of civilizational and moral
progress. For Wilberforce the behavior of the British slaver is the "disgrace"
of "civilized" nations, and through the British connection with Africa "the
general progress of civilization has been reversed . . . even where any sparks of
civilization have appeared, our traders have taken care to extinguish them"
(442). If we direct our gaze inland, says Wilberforce, we see where civilization
in Africa has taken refuge; but on the western coast "we shall find neither arts
nor commerce, nor any vestige of civilization; but on the contrary, wretchedness, ignorance, and superstition." Moreover, the British, in order to ensure a
constant supply of slaves, withheld the saving light of Christianity from the
Africans, and were thus retarding their moral improvement. "Even their superstition, in order to be consistent in our wickedness, we attempt to en-
courage, and notwithstanding our professions of Christianity, endeavour to
confirm and even increase their absurd ideas of witchcraft, and their other
prejudices. . . . If there are any corruptions of Christianity, we scruple not to
communicate them to them; but, whatever can enlighten or improve them,
we carefully withhold" (443). Slavery was blocking, in other words, missionary colonialism.[20] This movement is crucial: The reversal of civilized (England) and barbaric (African) has effectivity only in so far as sympathy can
assimilate African cultural difference ("superstition," "witchcraft") in an overall narrative of progress, enlightenment, and christianization.

But that is not all. The treatment of enslaved Africans is "unworthy [of]
the character of men" (II: 443). Wilberforce argues against the slave masters's
own representations of Africans as "no better that a species of brutes" or
"Ourang Outangs" (444). As is well known, this "theory" of the animality
of African people was by no means an uncommon idea; it is safe to say that
for many in parliament this idea formed part of their common sense.[21] Citing the "historian of Jamaica," Edward Long, Wilberforce condemns these

ideas in no uncertain terms: "They had been compared to the Ourang Out-ang in the desert; but nobody who had attended to their mode of acting, or who would attend for a moment to the operations of their feelings, could maintain a proposition of this preposterous nature. . . . He would allow that they were very deficient indeed in the arts of life, and in many respects in-sensible to the finer feelings of our nature. . . . At the same time, he could by no means think they were destitute of those qualities. . . . In the West In-dies they have shewn themselves to be something more than brutes. They displayed the highest degree of courage and resolution. They have discovered astonishing perseverance in the pursuit of their purpose. They have shewn they are capable of steady resistance; that not any number of men, however small, is sufficient to oppose them, but that they can resist and even prevail" (444–445). This subtle allusion to slave insurrection also did not escape his audience.

For Wilberforce and his allies the enslaved Africans were an "unfortunate people" (445), enslaved through a traffic that "outraged every principle of humanity." The language of sentiment and Gothic horror became essential to abolitionist rhetorical strategy as they strove to appeal to all those "who were susceptible of a sentiment of humanity."[22] One of the crucial differ-ences, however, between this form of aesthetic sympathy and that found in sentimental novels is that where literary sentimentalism individuates and separates out sympathetic subjects and scenes, the scenes of horror reiterated in parliamentary debates incorporates an entire people ("Africans") into sympathetic narratives. Sympathy is part of the "massification" of racialized populations; it gathers together heterogenous peoples into a single, objecti-fied category: an "unfortunate people." We will return to this aspect of so-cial sympathy shortly.

According to Wilberforce the responsibility for their wretched condi-tion and depraved character rested chiefly on the shoulders of the British: " . . . we must not forget . . . what share we have in fixing the uniformity of their character. We must not forget what share we have had in convert-ing them into an ignorant, low, peevish, and bloody, and thievish race. Our conduct to that unfortunate people has certainly had that tendency. Our cruelty also must have made them ferocious. It is very customary in-deed to excuse cruelty, by saying it is necessary, and that its victims deserve it. We therefore wish to make these men every thing that is bad, in order to serve as an excuse for our own conduct" (445). (It is no accident that we hear echoes of the famous, if ambivalent words of Montesquieu: "We must suppose them not to be men, or a suspicion would follow that we ourselves are not Christians.") Let us mark the structure of this thought on civilization and race. First, all humans have a character that is shaped in some way and to a certain extent by outward factors, factors that "convert" people from one state into another. Cruelty begets ferocity. The importance of this argument will be seen shortly, and, as is already probably obvious, the word "conversion" is not fortuitous or innocent in this context. Second, the representations of the "sub-human African" was itself a strategy of legitimating "our own conduct"—in this case the enslavement of the people of Africa. The irony here is that Wilberforce will use almost exactly the same kind of self-legitimating representations to justify the evangelicalization of India—sub-human natives legitimate missionizing. How can we explain this radical difference in the deployment of sympathy? The crux of the matter, it seems, is difference itself.

One can say, I think, that the victory of the Clapham Saints in the struggle for abolition lay in a series of discursive displacements that integrated civilizational and racial difference into specific narratives of humanitarian sympathy. They were able to convince parliament that all possible considerations of the slave trade would lead to the same troubling conclusion: that Britain was not a civilized nation and that certainly British slavers in their savage injustice to the peoples of Africa were not quite human, and certainly not Christian. Abolition would reverse this connection and so restore Britain to its rightful place in the hierarchy of nations.

And this opened up the possibility for other kinds of displacement. First, by linking civilization to humanity and benevolence, evangelical abolitionists were able to identify the cause of civilization with good government, that is better policy, and thus with justice and humanity.[23] For Wilberforce "the arguments of the abolitionists are founded in the justest views of policy, as well as the most enlarged ideas of introducing knowledge, humanity, and religion into that vast continent" (Speech on June 12, 1804; II: 658). Obviously, such views of good policy had to include the economic and political interests of the West Indian plantation owners. "Those who advocated the abolition, had frequently been accused of being indifferent to the interests of the West India proprietors. This was a charge that, he begged leave to say, was utterly unfounded. But although the friends of the abolition were not indifferent to these interests, they had higher calls to attend to, and these were the calls of humanity and of justice. What he had now stated, however, as to the possibility of keeping of the numbers of our negroes in the West India islands, sufficiently proved that, even on the score of policy, the abolition of the trade was not liable to the objections which were urged against it. It was satisfactory to find, that the West India proprietors would sustain no material loss by the immediate abolition of this inhuman and unchristian traffic" (II, 452). The "however" of the fourth sentence is the crucial suture that seems to leave humanity and justice dangling between interest and policy ("numbers of our negroes") and the call of "something higher." But the very success of the abolition struggle in parliament lay in such crucial back and forth (thus, Wilberforce spends much of his time noting the dangers of vesting too much capital in the West Indies given the rise of Napoleon and the liberation of Haiti.[24] But the situation in Haiti, according to Wilberforce, provided another, even more compelling reason for abolishing the trade: "Was it wise . . . to increase the number of new negroes in our West India islands, under the present circumstances of the colonies? During two years, the number of negroes imported into Jamaica was not less than 27,000 or 28,000 and it was perfectly well ascertained that newly imported negroes were the most ready to join insurrection. . . . Was it forgotten that St. Domingo was almost in sight of Jamaica, and that Gaudaloupe [sic] was in the centre of our Leeward islands? The abolition of the slave trade appeared to be called for by every consideration of justice, of policy, and of humanity" (455). As we have seen, the threat of violence was never far from the minds of these parliamentarians—the acknowledgment that insurrection and bloody reprisals were part of the very workings of slavery. Wilberforce subtly invokes this spectre of violence but in the name of a higher aim: justice, policy, and humanity stood forth and called imperatively for abolition. This is a key figure and trope of social sympathy: a figure placed above the combatants, higher up, calling for some action or remedy. But, although Wilberforce was quite willing to ventriloquize the voice of justice, apparently its call only went so far. Answering the charge that the agitation for ending the slave trade would lead to more insurrections, Wilberforce flatly denies the possibility, arguing "whatever danger might be supposed to exist, arose not from the question of abolition, but of emancipation. After the question of abolition was disposed of, any subsequent measures must be left to the colonial assemblies . . . and with them would rest how far the condition of the negroes was capable of greater improvement. It was not fair in those who opposed the abolition, to confound it with the question of emancipation, which in the first instance, it has no immediate connexion" (456). This might at first seem like a remarkable concession to the slave interests from one who had just spent hours cataloging the horrors not just of the trade but of slavery itself; certainly such moments of disavowal suggest, I think, how the vacillations between slave interests and human justice insistently prompt the discourse of social sympathy into a strategic negotiation with political and economic exigencies.[25] But in fact Wilberforce defended his gradualist position on emancipation on other grounds. (We should also note here Wilberforce's near total silence on the question of the exploitation and repression of the working classes in England.)

And this was another kind of displacement: The slave trade was good policy in light of the onward march of civilization. If the British slave trade was impeding the march of civilization in Africa, choking the forces of humanity, and sabotaging all improvement, abolishing the trade would open Africa to British colonization—and it is precisely here we can see once again the close linkage between civilization, sympathy, and colonization. Human sympathy seemed to be at odds with the radical dehumanization that enabled slavery; conversely, as humanity, civilization, knowledge, and European identity were reticulated together in colonial discourse, to sympathize and to colonize would never entirely be dissociated in Western thought. Henry Thornton, another Clapham evangelical, reflected on what probable effects the abolition of the slave trade would have on "civilizing" Africa, declaring that he "did sanguinely look forward to the influence of the [abolition of the slave trade] as laying the surest foundation for civilizing the inhabitants of Africa. Till the abominable trade . . . was abolished, it was impossible for any exertions, however benevolent, wholly to succeed in accomplishing this most desirable object. He was convinced that it was a measure equally founded on the most enlarged views of policy, humanity, and justice."[26] Some two years later, Lord Grenville in the House of Lords outlined the shape of things to come: "The narrowing of this trade or even its abolition, would not shut us out of Africa. We might visit there in another shape, and not as robbers and pirates, carrying off the helpless inhabitants. If they were so rude and savage as represented, let us rather endeavour to civilize them, and by a just and equitable traffic for their minds to the pursuits of civilized life."[27] Thornton here outlines the shape of an anticipated empire; Wilberforce[28] voiced it with his characteristic mixture of vision and strategy in his defense of his gradualist position on emancipation:

> And here he did not wish to avoid that part of the subject on which the opponents of the abolition dwelt so much; he meant the eventual emancipation of the negroes in the West Indies. He had never concealed that his hope was, that such might be the ultimate effect of the abolition of the African importation, but that was a period, the distance of which he had never attempted to calculate, although his opponents accused him of having it immediately in view. Had that been his object, or even his hope, he should deserve the word humane to be added to his views; but a shorter one, and that was the word man, ought to be applied to his object; but although he felt that the immediate emancipation of the negroes in the West Indies could not be expected, for that before they could be fit to receive freedom it would be madness to attempt to give it to them, yet he owned he looked forward . . . to the time when the negroes . . . should have the full enjoyment of a free, moral, industrious, and happy peasantry.[29]

How does one transform an enslaved people, supposedly degraded by their condition and brutalized by the whip, into a "free, moral, industrious, and happy peasantry" (one hears the proleptic echo of Jane Eyre's project of transforming her pupils into the "happiest peasantry in Europe")? No one in parliament doubted that Christian education was the chief means by which

Wilberforce would choose to bring about this transformation.[30] For Wilberforce, abolition would open the doors more fully to the beneficial effects of Christianity. "It would make it the obvious interest of the master that the slave should be kept with as much care as possible, because his place could not be supplied; that after this, means would of course be adopted to take care of the health of every negro, and also of his moral improvement; encouragement would be given to marriage, and other legitimate objects would be pursued, by which they would become populous, industrious, intelligent, moral and happy; by which we should have a powerful, though laborious and obedient peasantry" (672). That Wilberforce's domestic and capitalist agrarian fantasy proved woefully myopic in the West Indies should not obscure the power of his sympathetic vision for Christianizing Africa and African slaves.[31]

Sympathy in these evangelical arguments follows a consistent narrative movement. Linking together questions of justice, policy, progress, civilization, and humanity, abolitionist discourse rendered the slave an apt object of humanitarian sympathy. Racial and civilizational difference would be integrated in this narrative through the propriative power of evangelical progressivism. We also see the kinds of concessions and struggles that went into the final passage of the abolition of the trade in African peoples: British justice was in fact a gradual experiment into the safe limits of social change. In such a context, humanitarian sympathy could be rather dangerous: In societies structured in dominance, injustice is endemic, and so who is to say that sympathy must stop at a particular object of pity? As we have seen, it was precisely the Saint's use of sympathy that allowed anti-abolitionists to push the class contradictions within abolitionist discourse. I would suggest that this danger of transference is a structural possibility of sympathy. Throughout the long nineteenth century, this possibility of transferring sympathy to other subjects—which is also the interminable call of justice—was managed through a utilitarian calculus that tried to organize and normalize an increasingly heterogeneous society. Perhaps today we can hear in it something else besides.

The Sympathy of Evangelization:
The British East India Company Charter Debates

As I turn to the 1812–1813 parliamentary debates on the evangelization of India, the reader would do well to keep certain things foremost in mind. By the first decade of the nineteenth century, the British were already acknowledged rulers of vast expanses in South Asia. As I remarked in my historicization of Harley's anticolonial sentimentalism in the last chapter, by force of arms, political strategy, and sometimes outright deception, the British at times almost haphazardly insinuated themselves into the sinews of a crumbling empire. Such was the historical conjuncture that led to British dominance in South Asia. It was a very different history from the wholesale development of the plantation system of the West Indies, or the centuries-old transformation of property relations in Britain. Let us also keep in mind then another context: the crucial material and discursive differences that characterize these three modes of political and economic domination within the British empire. Perhaps the defining feature of slavery as a form of economic and racial subjugation is that its mode of power was pain and terror. Developing an elaborate machinery of pain and enjoyment for the production of subjects of slavery (which included such cultural forms as minstrelsy, black Christianity, the pastoral, slave "holidays," etc.), the "consent" of enslaved Africans in their own abjection was always part of the grotesque fantasy of the master.[32] No doubt, the practices and institutions of class domination, as they were elaborated throughout the eighteenth and nineteenth century, also depended on their own machinery of pain—we should never forget that the frequent reading of the riot act in the first half of the nineteenth century was almost always the prelude to the brutal reassertion of the rights of property.[33] But the project of constructing a viable hegemony relied, in a fundamental way, on other modes of domination in England than in the West or East Indies. Or should we say modes of domination that had other histories, other genealogies from the ones developed under slavery and colonialism? In England, patriotism and imperialism (retailed through such oft-repeated catchphrases as "Free Britons!" and "White Slaves"), worker discipline, family surveillance, education, religion, and the development of varieties of mass culture—all these led to different kinds of subjugation as well as different avenues for resistance. As for India under colonial rule, massive widespread violence and daily terror were not the usual modes of colonial power. Which is not to say that during certain periods, and at times for extended numbers of years, the British did not unleash their own colonial reign of terror—the military's notorious "movable column" that desolated whole swathes of north India in the wake of the 1857 Rebellion should also never be forgotten. But again, when the British, as merchant conquerors, took over the reigns of power from the Mughals and the native princes, or when they insinuated themselves in existing patterns of trade and networks of (sometimes indentured) labor, they also had to negotiate with existing structures of sociality in ways that were fundamentally different from emergent slave communities or residual agrarian relations in the British countryside. Violence was never far from these procedures of colonization in South Asia, but it was also never their defining feature. That by 1820 the British were seeking to transform these patterns of sociality in order to produce a more moral, more docile, more sympathetic subject population; or that in parliament, Indians were routinely referred to as "our fellow oriental subjects" (the famous Hindu reformer Rammohun Roy actually considered contesting a parliamentary seat—something inconceivable for Denmark Vessey or Nat Turner): these filiations show perhaps the closer connection between forms of colonial domination and strategies of class domination. Slavery would always haunt these forms of power, however: materially, in the rise of indentured servants throughout the colonies after 1840; discursively, in the anxious construction of a British "democratic" nationalism predicated on the disavowal of wage slavery, an erasure of colonial slavery, and the displacement of oriental despotism (colonial despotism)—all throughout a century that saw the rise of an increasingly rigid form of racial hierarchy.

It is in this context that we must consider the debates on the renewal of the East India Company Charter. In fact, "John Company" was under serious attack: It had to contend with a well-organized demand that the trading monopoly be abolished and that all British ports be allowed to trade freely with India.[34] According to its most outspoken advocate, the evangelical Charles Grant, the Charter Act of 1793 had conceded that the company had certain "property rights" in India, which were not essentially different from any other such rights, and which it had acquired "through a long course of dangers and vicissitudes and at the expense and hazard of the Company themselves."[35] By invoking the claims of property rights, the defenders of the monopoly were appealing to a principle that was central to a recently consolidated bourgeois order; as we have seen in the case of slavery, property had become a "natural right," seemingly not dependent on the will of the state.[36] Of course, by 1813, to a generation that was beginning to regard the teaching of Adam Smith as almost self-evident truth, the defense of the company's monopoly seemed to be founded on a mass of absurdities. (Smith had himself argued[37] against the strange supposition of the East India Company that "the clerks of a great counting house could rule justly over a great Empire.")[38]

In 1813, the opponents of the company's monopoly had Smith's notion of unfettered "real wealth and revenue" in mind when they turned to India. Just as production was increasing in England, Napoleon's successes were closing European markets to British goods; with the closing of the Mediterranean and the Portuguese ports in 1800 and 1801 respectively, India seemed to many the perfect solution.[39] The attacks on the company's monopoly came mainly from the cotton manufacturers and the Liverpool shipping interests.[40] The economic situation in much of England at the time was decidedly not conducive to monopolists, as the opening of the charter debates (roughly around 1810) coincided with a severe depression affecting North England and the Midlands, the areas most dependent on foreign trade; the situation worsened dramatically in 1811 when the American Non-Intercourse Act came into force as the value of exports fell from

£11,217,685 to £1,847,917 (in contemporary currency). The hundreds of petitions that poured into parliament from these troubled regions dwelt on the iniquity of the company's monopoly, "which seemed to rob the British people of a rightful market for their surplus goods."[41] Not surprisingly, the overwhelming majority of the debates during these years centered not on the new "pious clauses" (Resolution 13—those clauses that were to set up an Anglican ecclesiastical establishment and enable missionaries from any denomination to enter British India) but, rather, on questions of the company's expenditures, profits, the continuation of the monopoly, and economic forecasts on commodities (the principal commodities being spices, pepper, opium, sugar, coffee, raw silk, saltpeter, indigo, and raw cotton).[42]

In keeping with the growing consciousness on the part of the Board of Directors and the Indian Council of the political "duties" of governing "60 millions" of Indian subjects, the debates as well as the testimonies of the numerous witnesses always returned to the best means of possessing, consolidating, and managing the company's extensive territorial acquisitions; from one end of the political spectrum to the other, the common frame of reference was how to maintain the empire now that "the British nation is sovereign in India." There is a subtle linkage between these overtly political considerations, the "commercial" concerns, and the sympathetic function in the pious clauses; as we shall see, the evangelical members had recourse to the practicality of nurturing the affections and attachments of the colonized population in order to ensure markets for British commodities. Indeed, what was at stake was the religious and aesthetic "education" of the native Indian even as a new British subject was being formed. As I will argue, this was the moment of a profound transition in the regime of race and empire that tied Britain, the Caribbean and India together. The idea and practice of sympathy was crucial to this transition.

In the charter debates on evangelization, sympathy is deployed in specific ways. First, Hindu (and less often Islamic) heathenism is shown to produce monstrous subjects: intransigent, slavish, unruly, immoral, despotic, and irrational. Second, evangelicalization is shown not only to save these subjects for the greater glory of Christ's empire, but in fact Christianity turns out to be good colonial policy. It is in this movement that sympathy would function to secure an abjected native other, even as religious and cultural difference would be erased through the propriative power of what should now be a familiar narrative: Western progress, civilization, and the good word—all in the name of sympathy. Third, after the abolition of the slave trade new vistas of sympathy seemed to open up before the wondering gaze of the imperial evangelical subject, almost as if the good work in the West Indies had been accomplished and a new theatre of engagement was needed. Certainly, a new human was born, an abstract, ideal fantasy of colonial power that became the object (as telos) and instrument (as norm) of all these projects of benevolence. But it is by attending to the multiple contradictions, vacillations, concessions, and, perhaps most significant, silences cutting across these debates that one can see the odd, piecemeal, tactical processes through which such ideals become dominant.

The charter debates show us how the ideal human of sympathy is haunted by its abjected other(s). One such other was the (usually Hindu male)[43] Native. Through literally hundreds of hours of evidence given before the committee of the whole House of Commons,[44] witness after witness presented testimony on "native character." Usually retired or currently employed company servants who had spent some time in India, these men were in a sense the first "native informants." Having come back to England as rich "nabobs," many of these former employees still had considerable economic and political ties to India in the form of trading concerns or relations in the service. And they spoke of India with "first-hand" knowledge, authenticated by experience, and reinforced by the published accounts of the Orient in histories, travel narratives, political and missionary tracts, and memoirs. As I have already remarked above, the aim of the company's advocates in eliciting this testimony was to establish beyond any doubt the unsuitability of India for free trade and large-scale European settlements (what was termed the threat of "colonization"). And this argument in turn needed a particular representation of "native culture." Native culture was to be represented, first, as the logical outcome of a grinding despotism[45]—which produced an enslaved populace; second, native character was fixed and stationary—thus, native "tastes" were unlikely to change in the near future, and so increasing European imports was pointless; and, third, native religious sensibility was peculiarly, even morbidly sensitive. "Are you of the opinion that they are a people peculiarly unchangeable in their manners, habits and opinions?" was usually the first question asked by the examiners.[46]

The actual testimony of the respondents, however, was varied and the effects contradictory. Let us compare, for instance, some of the testimony of some key company servants. On the matter of the tastes of the natives, what emerged from just about all sides was an image of a fixed native character slowly being transformed by colonial government and European trade. Consider this typical series of question and answer. The respondent is John Shore (Lord Teignmouth), former governor-general of India from 1793 to 1798 and a member of the Clapham Saints.

> Does your lordship know of any wants . . . that have not been most amply supplied by the existing system of commerce in India, with regard to European articles for the consumption of the natives . . . ?—I am not aware of any.

> Does your lordship conclude that any material increased consumption of European articles upon the part of the natives is wholly unlikely?—I think very improbable. (XXV, 433)

Simple assertions taken as authoritative testimony. In much of this testimony, the impoverished natives are represented as in fact having no wants, and so the question of tastes was rather irrelevant. But there were other, sometimes dissenting voices; many former administrators argued that the only thing keeping the natives from buying European goods was the high prices—better their economic condition and an increase in consumption would necessarily follow (XXV, 628–30).[47] Between these various positions what emerged was a complex field of contradictory claims about native character, their wants, and patterns of consumption. The evangelical parliamentarians, for instance, generally held a position that was roundly criticized by the free traders and conservative romantics as being untenable; they were monopolists in trade and free traders in religion.

I will turn to this contradiction in the evangelical project below; for now let us turn to the representation of native society. Warren Hastings, the famous former governor-general of India, was a firm adversary of missions and an advocate of company monopoly; he opines that if Europeans "were permitted to sojourn in India, according to their own pleasure, and without any restraint" the effect would be "hurtful and most ruinous, both to the Company's interest, to the government, and to the peace of the country" (XXV, 415). Hastings represented the prereform era (roughly prior to 1790) of company servants, men who romanticized and often profoundly identified with the "Orient." Thus, before the House of Lords, Hastings spoke out as a staunch defender of the "native Indians," taking aim at the evangelicals and their allies: "Great pains have been taken to inculcate into the public mind an opinion that the native Indians are in a state of complete moral turpitude, and live in the constant and unrestrained commission of every vice and crime that disgrace human nature. I affirm . . . that this description is untrue and wholly unfounded. . . . Gross as the modes of their worship are, the precepts of their religion are wonderfully fitted to promote the best ends of society, its peace and good order; and even from their theology, arguments may be drawn to illustrate and support the most refined mysteries of our own . . . they themselves possess in a very high degree the principles of gratitude, affection, honour, and justice."[48] For Hastings, speaking with all the bitterness of his famous trial still very much on his mind, the greater danger was that a free and open trade with India would flood the country with "adventurers" who would "insult, plunder, and oppress the natives because they can do it with impunity."[49] This would "inevitably lead to the ruin of the country," since "[n]othing can be more opposite than the characters of Europeans and that of the natives of India":

> The native Indian is weak in body and timid in spirit; he is not unsusceptible
> to resentment, but without that feeling of shame, which, under the appella-
> tion of honour, in the breast of an European, makes resentment a species of
> law, and which over-rules the fear of law, pain, danger and death. This is not
> the absolute character of the people taken in the mass; the native Indian is in-
> dividually such as I have described him; but there are cases in which a provo-
> cation of general grievances would excite a whole people, and even a detached
> number of them to all the ferocities of insurrection.[50]

Mark first of all the ever-present anxiety of insurgency. Yet what perhaps first
strikes us today is the obvious contradictions between the absolute opposition of European and Indian and the denial of any absolute character. But
such contradictions didn't seem to bother either his audience or Hastings
himself. Indeed he goes on to make a great many assertions on the basis of
his notion of native character. For Hastings, it would seem that if the characters of the Indian and the European were mutually exclusive, then an "unrestrained intercourse" between England and India could prove fatal to
empire because, although individually timid, the native when taken in a
mass could be pushed to resentment, and thus to insurrection. And like
Haiti during the 1807 debates on the slave trade, insurrection was on the
minds of everyone concerned with India at the time.

In 1807, at the military outpost in Vellore, native Indian soldiers revolted
supposedly in defense of caste and religion. This "mutiny" had convinced
certain observers that "native character" was particularly sensitive when in
came to religion. Consequently, religion and native custom became trouble-
some issues for the company, the colonial government, and the evangelicals
hoping to transform that government. Vellore was the fortress in the "Eastern Ghats," about ninety miles from present day Chennai. As part of the
peace settlement after the fall of Seringapatam in 1799, Governor-General
Wellesley banished the family of Tipu Sultan to Vellore. There, on July 6,
1806, the company's Indian troops rose against the British officers and soldiers and killed nearly a hundred of them. The sepoys (from the Hindi *sep-
ahi*) gained complete control of the fort; elsewhere, notably in Hyderabad,
there were signs of unrest among the native soldiers. "The uprising," as Embree tells us, "did not last long, however, and the fort at Vellore was quickly
recaptured by a relief force from nearby Arcot. Nevertheless, the Vellore
Mutiny was the most profound shock British power in India had received
since the fall of Calcutta in 1756. . . . Both in India and England there was
a sudden awareness of how lightly-based dominion in India might really
be."[51] If the consolidation of empire through sympathy was one edge of the
frame around the debates, the possibility of an insurgent native solidarity
marked its outer limits. For Hastings, as for many of his colleagues, this pos-

sibility was a clear warning sign that the "peculiarities of native character" should be respected.[52]

For the evangelicals, however, this religious sensitivity indicated very different things. Since Charles Grant had become Deputy Chairman of the East India Company in the spring of 1807, the question of the causes of the Vellore Mutiny became an intensely important issue.[53] As Grant noted, in 1793 the opposition to the pious clauses centered around the fear that through Christian teaching and Western learning the natives would learn democratic, Enlightenment ideas that would inspire them to overthrow British dominance; but in 1813, "with the Vellore Mutiny a very potent memory, it was argued that missionaries would antagonize the people through attacks on the old religions."[54] In countering this argument, the evangelicals tried to show that there was not the slightest evidence that missionaries had caused the Mutiny; Grant, in fact, argued that the Mutiny, far from providing evidence that there had been interference in the customs and religion of the people, was the clearest proof that "no enduring links" had been forged between colonizer and native.[55]

It was precisely the question of how to forge these enduring links that exercised the imaginations of the evangelicals. Force was not the answer. According to Charles Grant, for the British, having won an empire and established a rule that was intended to be permanent, the best way to secure power was to use every prudent method of spreading a knowledge of "Christian truth";[56] as he had stated it in his influential tract *Observations on the State of Society among the Asiatic Subjects of Great Britain, particularly with respect to Morals and on the means of Improving it* (1792),[57] the only "cementing principle" conceivable was that of "common religious sanctions shared by the government with the people."[58] If it were possible, said Grant, by "calm reason and affectionate persuasion" to make "any large portion of our Indian subjects Christian, it is clear that they would then have strong common principle with us, and render our government more secure."[59] (I return to Grant's *Observations* below.) This is crucial: What is being argued here is that, first, the spreading of Christianity is good colonial policy, and, second, that it could be the means of creating a bond of sympathy between rulers and ruled in India; it is for this reason that the question of the affections, tastes, habits, and customs of the natives become central to the argument for evangelization. What is at stake, finally, is the creation of a sympathetic, if not exactly Christian population.

The evangelical solution, then, was at once more simple than forcible conversion and yet much more complicated: transform native character. Consider the testimony of John Shore (Lord Teignmouth), another former governor-general, and a close friend of Charles Grant and an ally of William Wilberforce. When asked, "In reference to your lordship's personal acquaintance with the Gentoo natives of Hindostan, what is the general standard of their moral character, in comparison with the inhabitants of Christian countries in general?" he declared simply,

> My estimate of their moral character is very low, and certainly I should say greatly below the standard of Christians in this country. . . . Falsehood is a very prominent part of their character [one is reminded here of Hume and Smith on national character]. . . . I think [their moral character] is a compound of servility, fraud, and duplicity. . . . That character may have originated in a considerable degree, in the despotism of the ancient government, which would naturally produce servility and deception, as the only guard against extortion; I do not think that their religion is calculated to correct it. Q: Are there any particular crimes that are directly inculcated by their religion?—A: Certainly: what would be called crimes in this country; for instance, such as the burning of widows on the funeral pile of their husbands. (XXV, 441)

Shore, unlike William Wilberforce as we shall see, was very cautious in his advocating evangelization; he urged a "judicious and prudent zeal" for the conversion of the natives (431). But as an evangelist he shared some basic presuppositions with his more zealous colleagues. First, as I remarked above, Indian society was still in the stranglehold of Oriental despotism. This despotism arrested the development of native society, and enslaved the minds and corrupted the morals of its populace. Neither Hinduism nor Islam could counter it. All of which had policy implications since despotism and native religion had rendered the people, in the words of the Marquis Wellesley, "submissive to all power, and incapable, in the present state of their manners, habits, and opinions, utterly incapable, of political freedom" (XXV, 715). Second, native religion, especially Hinduism, enjoins and sanctifies acts that would be criminal in Europe; for instance, sati, infanticide, suicide, self-torture; that sati tops the list indicates the close correlation in this discourse between the supposed status of women and level of civilization. This would become the dominant theme running throughout evangelical discourse on India and Hinduism over the course of the next 50 years. Lastly, confronted with an Indian "character" impossibly heterogenous (that is multiple, and composed of contradictory characteristics, themselves woven from complex and historically specific relations of power), evangelical discourse steadfastly proclaimed its unity, its homogeneity, its sameness.

This last point was probably the most difficult to maintain since throughout the course of the debates it came under repeated attack by many of the most prominent civil servants of the day. We have already seen Warren Hastings's critique of evangelical representations of Hindu society, but even a later generation of company servants shared many of Hastings's misgivings about facile generalizations of "native character." For instance, when

Lieutenant-Governor Sir John Malcolm was asked in the Commons to describe "what you consider to be the prevailing character of the Hindoos," he resolutely foregrounded the problem of heterogeneity:

> The character of the different classes of Hindoos, which compose a great proportion of the population of the subjects of the British government in India, varies in different parts of that empire, perhaps as much, if not more, than the nations of Europe do from each other. (XXV, 568)

Although he goes on to differentiate two "very distinct races" of Bengalis[60] (a southern one, "weak in body and timid in mind," and another northern race, "robust in frame of body" and with "fine qualities of mind"), the problem of heterogeneity and sameness in determining native character that Malcolm marks constantly haunts the debates around the charter. Charles Marsh, another "sentimentalist" in the House of Commons, attacked the "senseless cant" of the evangelicals in this way, "I have no scruple in saying, that this cant is founded on the falsest assumptions. I say nothing of the total want of philosophical precision in comprehending the mixed character of an immense population covering an immense territory with the terms of one general national description."[61] When asked of his opinion on the "civilization" of the Hindus, Colonel Thomas Munro responded cautiously, as if with perplexity:

> I do not exactly understand what is meant by the civilization of the Hindoos; in the higher branches of science, in the knowledge of the theory and practice of good government, and in an education, which, by banishing prejudice and superstition, opens the mind to receive instruction of every kind, from every quarter, they are much inferior to Europeans: but if a good system of agriculture, unrivaled manufacturing skill, a capacity to produce whatever can contribute to convenience or luxury; schools established in every village, for teaching reading, writing and arithmetic; the general practice of hospitality and charity amongst each other; and above all, a treatment of the female sex, full of confidence, respect and delicacy, are among the signs which denote a civilized people, then the Hindoos are not inferior to the nations of Europe; and if civilization is to become an article of trade between the two countries, I am convinced that this country will gain by the import cargo. (XXV, 786)

These famous words, spoken before the House of Commons on April 12, 1813, give a sense of the range of opinion on Indian character and civilization. As I noted above, the status of women became a common reference point for all sides in this debate, and Munro's position was definitely something of an anomaly. To have a sense of the specific valence of Munro's words we must keep in mind that by the second decade of the nineteenth century the idea that Hindu and Muslim women basically lived in a kind of elaborate prison was widely accepted. Missionary tracts were central in establishing the givenness of this idea; let us briefly consider some aspects of missionary discourse on native women.

As is well known, the specific nature of the subjection of women in India provided missionaries with probably their most effective scenes of horror and sympathy. Perhaps most tireless among these soldiers of Christ was Reverend Claudius Buchanan, former Bengal missionary of the Church Missionary Society and a disciple of the famous Cambridge divine, Charles Simeon. His *Christian Researches in Asia* (1812)[62] and *A Memoir of the Expediency of an Ecclesiastical Establishment for British India* (1806) were written in the fervid spirit of colonial evangelicalism, and in a context that was often openly hostile toward missionaries and missionizing. In his *Apology,* Buchanan sought to expose all those "circumstances of horror" that attended every form and practice of Hindu idolatry. In his preface he begins by citing two; I quote from the first:

> About the year 1796, the following most shocking and atrocious murder, under the name of suhumurunu, was perpetrated at Mujilupoor, about a day's journey south from Calcutta. Vaucha-ramu, a Brahman, of the above place, dying, his wife went to be burnt with the body; all the previous ceremonies were performed; she was fastened on the pile, and the fire was kindled. The funeral pile was by the side of some brushwood, and near a river. It was at a late hour when the pile was lighted, and was a very dark, rainy night. When the fire began to scorch this poor woman, she contrived to disentangle herself from the dead body, crept from under the pile, and hid herself among the brushwood. In a little time it was discovered that only one body was on the pile. The relations immediately took the alarm, and began to hunt for the poor wretch who had made her escape. After they had found her, the son dragged her forth, and insisted upon her throwing herself upon the pile again, or that she should drown or hang herself. She pleaded for her life, at the hands of her own son, and declared she could not embrace so horrid a death. But she pleaded in vain; the son urged that he should lose his caste, and that, therefore, he would die or she should. Unable to persuade her to hang or drown herself, the son and the others then tied her hands and her feet, and threw her on the funeral pile, where she quickly perished. (xiii-xiv)

A monstrous scene, as the missionary Alexander Duff would call it some 30 years later. Such scenes, truly the stock-in-trade of missionary discourse on India,[63] function as complex semantic units. They recall, in an inverted and distorted manner, the pathos that all Christians share in that primal theatre of horror, the crucifixion of Christ. A human injustice perpetrated through false religion—Hinduism substituted for Judaism. The pleasure of being "edified" through such pathos is never far from the pedagogical intent of such scenes. But the scenes are meant to do more than edify. They are meant to horrify—and there is nothing that horrifies more than the monstrous. That monster who cannot feel affection, who feels no ties of kinship, nor pangs of compassion—the creature without sympathy.

And this monstrosity was at its most monstrous in the treatment of women. In his *Lectures on India,* the missionary Caleb Wright declares that "Woman, by Heaven's appointment, is man's help-meet" (93), and goes on to argue that this holy union of man and woman is a relationship of benevolence, protection, and love. However, in such "unevangelized lands" as India women are "forced to perform the most perilous and menial services of the state and the family" (112). Under the false religions of the world, "The education of heathen females is entirely neglected"; women "are not at their own disposal in marriage" (96); and "Polygamy prevents the enjoyment of the husband's affection" (102). In lands "unaffected by the refining and elevating influences of Christianity," women are "trodden down as the mire of the streets by him whom Heaven created to be her protector and comforter." The itinerant preacher urges us to visualize those scenes where we can not but help pity the heathen woman: "We have seen unevangelized man everywhere, like the fabled generation of warriors springing from the serpent's teeth armed for the work of destruction, directing his chief malignities,—his most unfailing solace,—because her native timidity and weakness invite the violence and insult of a coward-arm! We have seen her lost to self-respect, dead to instinctive affection, ignorant of the rights with which her Maker has invested her, unacquainted with her relations to eternity, indulgent to the wildest passions of depraved nature, and plunged far down the abyss of unnatural crime. We have marked her wanderings, listened to her complaints, and seen her scalding tears. And have we no sympathy in her sufferings?—no arm that will extend to her relief?—no voice that will call her to Calvary?" (126–128).

What practices of gender emerge through such scenes of sympathy? It would seem that for such missionaries, to sympathize with the plight of the Hindu woman was to participate in the manly defense of the weaker sex. In this sense, sympathy for women seems to be a practice of masculinity in missionary discourse. Yet, as we had seen earlier, sympathy itself was linked to the affections and so was tied to a certain feminine agency. Moreover, if we take into account that during this time many women's organization in both England and the United States targeted the "deplorable condition of our Indian sisters" as an object of their philanthropic and evangelical crusade, the question of gender becomes rather more complicated. Could this be, I wonder, a possible explanation for the obsessive use of martial metaphors in missionary discourse?[64] The anxiety that perhaps God's work in India was not really manly work, or at least not as manly as military conquest? And so the "holy war" with the heathen to save the heathen had to be represented as a struggle against that implacable monster, Hinduism. No doubt, the drama of the righteous Christian, armed only with the Bible, struggling against all odds to win the heathen for Christ was a thoroughly apt subject of sympathy. In any case, what I am suggesting is that practices of sympathy and the genealogy of the affections complicated gender dichotomies such that any neat association with sex proves very difficult. Again we see how sympathy in various contexts could be a mobile and polymorphous technology of power.

Returning to the parliamentary debates, we can also see why it was that evangelical members like Charles Grant and Wilberforce targeted the seemingly relativistic benevolence of such romantic administrators as Munro and Hastings; the lingering anxiety of course was that the romantics were in some senses far more sympathetic to native culture and society than the evangelicals. Thus, in the ongoing reform of company practices and servant behavior, one of the central concerns was to combat the "Oriental infection" that had contaminated the civil service and compromised the British standards of morality. Embree suggests that the real opponents of the evangelicals "were the increasing number of people who, finding in Indian culture a deep and appealing wisdom, argued that the Indian people had a way of life that was valid for them, however different it might be from western civilization" (147–148). According to the evangelicals, one of the principal dangers threatening the British connection with India was that the civil servants, in the grip of a "deplorable infatuation," could undergo an "assimilation to Eastern opinions" and become "Indianized," instead of "retaining all the distinctions of our national principles, characters, and usages."[65]

And so the Evangelicals argued that real[66] sympathy meant something else altogether: To sympathize was both to identify and to improve, to know the other in all the recesses of her life and imagination (sexual and erotic imagery is not incidental to the discourse), to expose the other in all her horrific sufferings, and raise the other into the sphere of humanity. The problem for evangelical strategy in these debates was how to turn the sympathies of parliament away from a supposedly innocuous Hinduism, and channel those very sympathies for the active and radical conversion of South Asian society. They did this through a combination of massive public pressure, and through the discursive fabrication and deployment of the abstract human. And they took their cue, as we shall see, from the mobilization around the abolition of the slave trade.

What, exactly, did the evangelicals in parliament and in the country at large hope to accomplish through the Christianization of India? Of course there was the hope of saving "60 millions" souls from the degradations of their native religion and for a life in Christ. But as I have marked, evangelical thought on India had a decidedly practical element to it. And it mobilized huge numbers of British subjects. For instance, consider the unprecedented number of petitions (1,500 by one account)[67] that poured in from evangelical and missionary groups from all over Britain and Scotland. These petitions were themselves a sign of the growth of radical, woman-centered, and bourgeois male public spheres; that these petitions had as profound an impact as they did, despite the great opposition of the House of Commons and many of the most influential members of the Home Administration of the company, was an indication of parliament's grudgingly slow acknowledgment of the power and legitimacy of these publics. The class make-up of most of these petitioners was also crucial: The support for the mission campaign came from mostly Methodists, Baptists, Episcopalians, and the Evangelical clergy of the Church of England (men who were commonly thought to compose what was termed the "Low Church"). These were not insignificant populations. If we take the example of only one denomination, Wesleyan Methodists increased from 88,334 in 1800 to 319,770 in 1846; Primitive Methodism, which formed around 1810, had over 100,000 mostly working-class members by 1850.[68] But even in 1813, by the most conservative accounts, these petitions represented something of a mass movement. Often, these petitions had a common proemial:

> That your petitioners are deeply impressed with the moral degradation of the immense population of the British dominions in India, and lament that so little has hitherto been done to remove it. . . . Your petitioners . . . implore your lordships, that such provisions may be inserted in the new charter to be granted to the East India Company, as shall afford sufficient facilities to those benevolent persons, who shall be desirous of going to India for the purpose of communicating to its population the blessings of useful knowledge, and moral and religious improvement.[69]

We see clearly here what I have been calling the massification of colonial sympathy: The phrase the "moral degradation of immense population" became almost a fetish, an accepted and discreet object for the dutiful operation of benevolence; by invoking the degraded, and presumably helpless population these petitions both legitimated the project of evangelization and associated it with a strong, well-ordered empire.[70] The discourse, through such performative sleights of hand, created its own object while providing a pedagogy, or a subject-script for empire.

For the many petitioners as well as the parliamentary saints, useful knowledge and moral and religious improvement, as well as truth and divinity all had a common origin in Christianity. And for this reason Christianity provided a very practical argument for the longevity of empire. As the

"Protestant Dissenters' Petition for Promulgating the Christian Religion in India" put it, "That the petitioners firmly believing in the truth and divine authority of the Christian revelation, are also deeply impressed with a full conviction of its proportionate efficacy, to establish, on the most solid foundations, the fabric of social order, and all the highest and best interests of mankind . . . : and that . . . these petitioners are anxiously desirous that the light and blessings of Christianity should be gradually diffused over the immense empire of Great Britain in the East, which, instead of being . . . endangered, would . . . derive additional strength and stability from the spread of the Christian religion" (XXV, 765). "Idolatry and superstition," the accepted evangelical term for Hinduism, was not consistent with "the highest and best interests of mankind"; Christianity, by contrast, producing "moral virtue and human happiness," would strengthen and stabilize the immense Eastern empire. As I have suggested, there is a common protocol in these petitions. They narrate the desire that animates Christ's empire through a simple play and propriation of opposites. A distinct assertion of the identity between truth, morality, and Christianity; closely followed (or sometimes preceded) by a declaration of the degraded, and barbaric condition of the masses of Indian natives;[71] then an assertion of the duty of British sympathy and benevolence; a declaration of prudence and caution in missionizing ("to diffuse [Christianity] in a meek and peaceful manner" [XXV, 1091]); and a final assertion that evangelization is good imperial policy. Consider, finally, the following petition from the Missionary Society:

> That the inhabitants of the populous regions in India, which form an important portion of the British empire, being involved in the most deplorable state of moral darkness, and under the influence of the most abominable and degrading superstitions, have a pre-eminent claim on the compassionate feelings and benevolent services of British Christians; and that this sympathetic disposition has been powerfully felt throughout the kingdom, and plans have been formed . . . for the purpose of extending the knowledge of the Christian religion in India; . . . and that the Missionary Society, through the kindness of the executive government, . . . have for several years past had missionary stations in the colonies of the Cape of Good Hope, Demerara, Trinidad, Tobago, and also on the continent of India . . . ; and that the petitioners . . . are conscious that, in endeavouring to diffuse the principles of Christianity to the utmost extent of the British dominions and influence, they are acting on the purest principles of patriotism, and rendering the most important service to their country.[72]

I believe one can see clearly in this petition just how the "sympathetic disposition" could be a form of power through which colonial governmentality operated: The initial designation of a "massified" native population lost in moral darkness legitimates and activates the "compassionate feelings and benevolent services of British Christians." One might say that the sympathetic disposition is parasitic on this moral darkness; it needs something like Hinduism as a mass of "the most abominable and degrading superstitions" but cannot avow it, cannot affirm this necessary connection. Perhaps the anxiety of a connection disavowed gives rise to the patriotic hysteria toward the end of the quote? In any case, sympathy becomes a process of transforming and integrating the Indian native and his society: " . . . similarity of religious principle, while it removes many causes of jealousy and discord, leads to similarity of habits, and produces a new and powerful bond of affection."[73] This transformation partakes of the global struggle of European Christian light against the darkness that reigned throughout the colonized world—"the Cape of Good Hope, Demerara, Trinidad, Tobago, and also on the continent of India."

I close this chapter by considering the multiple contexts of a crucial exchange on the pious clauses (Resolution 13) between Stephen Lushington and William Wilberforce. As we shall see, what is at stake in these debates is the very nature of sympathy and colonial governance, and the fractures and torsions of the debate would provide crucial openings for Indian intellectuals resisting imperial domination later in the century. By contextualizing these two very different historical moments together, we begin to get a sense, it seems to me, of the overall terrain of struggle of sympathetic governmentality as well as the conditions of possibility for that very struggle. I turn first to the British contexts.

Wilberforce, on March 23, 1813, "animated" by an "unfeigned spirit of friendship for the natives of India," was the first to bring up the scandal of the resolution passed during the last charter debates (May 14, 1793), which enabled the Court of Directors of the company to neutralize the project for the "religious and moral instruction of India" (XXV, 255). This time the Saints would make no mistake. Wilberforce, as we have seen, was a crucial figure in the institutionalization of sympathy in England and the colonies; his labors of sympathy span the 50-year period from around 1780 until 1830. As the most forceful parliamentary supporter of evangelization, Wilberforce drew on his successes in the abolition of the slave trade, associating the evangelization of India with the "liberation" of Africa from slavery, and the "protection" of enslaved Africans in the West Indian colonies—all were acts that accorded with the most enlightened ideals of humanity. I think these exchanges before parliament are a crucial turning point in the history of imperial ideology and the emergence of sympathy as an institutionalized form of power in Britain and the colonies. In what follows I trace the structure, strategies, and play of anxieties that mark these exchanges. Wilberforce's speeches read today as a kind of planning agenda for most of the reforms that occupied British civil servants in India over the course of the next 50 years. But they are more than that. They are also the moment, prepared for many years by the exertions of Charles Grant and the other Clapham Saints, when a new kind of British subject finally became the dominant, or common sense model of the imperial ruler. At the very moment when the depraved Hindu assumed his final, abjected form, the purified, fully humanized Anglo-Indian assumed center stage in colonial history—all in the name of sympathy.

As Embree notes, perhaps the most significant result of the missionary clause and of the evangelical discourses that were deployed in the debates was that the nature of British power in India became a concern of a very large section of the British people in a way it had never been before. While Edmund Burke and his followers had denounced the behavior of company servants like Warren Hastings, William Wilberforce accused the whole British nation of abusing its trust in India. Next to the slave trade, as he said again and again, "the foulest blot on the moral character of the country was the willingness of the Parliament and the people to permit our fellow-subjects . . . in the East Indies to remain . . . under the grossest, the darkest and most degrading system of idolatrous superstition that almost ever existed upon earth."[74] Wilberforce was able to pursue this line of argumentation in his extended speeches on evangelization. Linking Christianity to the diffusion of Western science, he stressed that, according to the 13th Resolution, "We are to enlighten and inform the minds of the subjects of our East Indian empire":[75] "And after much reflection, I do not hesitate to declare that, from enlightening and informing them, in other words, from education and instruction, from the diffusion of knowledge, from the progress of science, more especially from all these combined with the circulation of the Holy Scriptures in the native languages, I ultimately expect even more than from the direct labours of missionaries" (832). This visionary expectation in fact became the foundation for the most ambitious evangelical project in India in the first half of the nineteenth century; over the next 50 years, missionaries and utilitarians (and, as in the era of Governor-General Lord Bentinck's "Age of Reform," roughly 1828–1840, Christian utilitarian administrators) would consider a comprehensive Christian education in English as the surest means of evangelizing and civilizing India. This newfound faith in education reflected the conjunctures and ruptures of a transforming class and social structure in England. With the steady rise in numbers and influence of men "engaged in trade and commerce," who demanded a different education for their sons from that obtainable in the old grammar schools; with the growth of dissenting (non-Anglican) academies, elaboration of the Bell and Lancaster systems of learning, and the founding of various educational societies—the evangelicals and Benthamites came together in a common cause.[76] Thus, when evangelicals began to consider the future of Britain's Indian education seemed to be the surest route to both stability and civilization. Which meant, necessarily, exposing the false religion of the Hindus: "The Hindoos err because they are ignorant; and their errors have never fairly been laid before them."[77]

But what errors? Why should we enlighten them? How are they enslaved? Throughout his speech, Wilberforce, at times silently, at times explicitly, draws on Charles Grant's influential 1792 tract *Observations on the State of Asia.* Grant had argued "we ought to study the happiness of the vast body of subjects which we have acquired" so that "we might continue to hold the advantage we first derived from them." For Grant, the company, "as part of the Christian community," was obligated to seek "the general welfare of the many millions under its government." By treating the natives as "exclusively and absolutely our subjects," the British, "with the affection of a wise and good superior . . . watch[ing] over their civil and social happiness," could remedy the disorders that prevailed in Indian society.[78] For Grant, as with all evangelicals, the cause of the disorders was plain: the character of the people and the prevailing system of religious values. "Abandoned selfishness was the distinguishing mark of Hindu character. . . . Discord, hatred, abuse, slanders, injuries, complaints, litigations, all the effects of selfishness unrestrained by principles, prevail to a surprising degree." Because of Hinduism, the "natural affection" of parents for children was lacking and conjugal love was unknown. Parents sold their children, not only in times of famine, but very often simply out of greed; women were doomed to a life of servitude and semi-imprisonment and a "violent and premature death."[79] In short, Grant was advocating that the company "take the initiative in instituting a programme of social change in India that aimed at the complete alteration of the basis on which the existing social structure rested."[80] As we shall see, Wilberforce repeats many of these arguments in his rather more eloquent and dramatic manner in parliament.[81]

Wilberforce spends the majority of this speech depicting in no uncertain terms the "true condition of the masses" of native society. (The reader would do well to recall Wilberforce's own words during the debates on abolishing the slave trade: "We must not forget what share we have had in converting them into an ignorant, low, peevish, and bloody, and thievish race. Our conduct to that unfortunate people has certainly had that tendency. Our cruelty also must have made them ferocious. It is very customary indeed to excuse cruelty, by saying it is necessary, and that its victims deserve it. We therefore wish to make these men every thing that is bad, in order to serve as an excuse for our own conduct.") "Immense regions, with a population amounting . . . to sixty millions of souls, have providentially come under our dominion. They are deeply sunk, and by their religious superstitions fast bound, in the lowest depths of moral and social wretchedness and degradation. Must we not then be prompted by every motive, and urged by every feeling that can influence the human heart, to endeavour to raise these wretched beings out of their present miserable condition, and above all to communicate to them those blessed truths which would not only improve their understandings and elevate their minds, but would, in ten thousand ways, promote their temporal well-being" (833–834). "Common humanity" called to the British to uplift these wretched beings; this was indeed true humanity: "[T]rue humanity consists, not in a squeamish ear, but in the feeling for the sufferings of others, and being forward and active in relieving them" (861). Wilberforce then quotes a mass of "authorities" on native India[82] to show that just as there is an intimate connection between virtue and humanity there is a near identity between depravity and cruelty. The list of Hinduism's crimes against humanity is long, but Wilberforce does not spare his audience the tedium: Sati, infanticide, bloody idolatrous rites (the Jagganath festival), and caste slavery top the list. There are two aspects of these crimes that need to be emphasized here. First, for Wilberforce, "the evils of Hindostan are family, fireside evils: they pervade the whole mass of the population, and embitter the domestic cup, in almost every family" (856). In other words, they enter into the very heart of native society, and infect the most intimate of relations, that between man and woman. Second, and this has to do with the rhetorical strategies that Wilberforce uses as well as the silences of the other evangelicals, the caste system is worse than slavery. It is worth quoting Wilberforce here:

> It is justly, Sir, the glory of this country, that no member of our free community is naturally precluded from rising into the highest classes in society. . . . Even where slavery has existed, it has commonly been possible (though in the West Indies, alas! artificial difficulties have been interposed), for individuals to burst their bonds, and assert the privileges of their nature. But the more cruel shackles of Caste are never to be shaken; as well might a dog, or any other of the brute creation . . . aspire to the dignity and rights of man. (856)

Linking the evangelization of India to the struggle to overthrow slavery, Wilberforce yoked two great evangelical imperial projects in the cause of benevolence. But Wilberforce was walking a fine line here: As Charles Grant had made amply clear in numerous company dispatches and parliamentary speeches, just because liberty and equality were British ideals of governance, that in no way applied to the colonial administration of India. For Grant, as for most British administrators at the time, Britain must rule India with a benevolent but firm despotism—(at times radically limited) "democracy" for Britain and despotism for India were the guiding principles of imperial policy. (What was the exact difference between British and Oriental despotisms of course would remain an open question.) But if Christianity will render the natives "partakers of the best blessings which we ourselves enjoy" (857) the very stability of the empire could be sacrificed.[83] For strategic reasons, Grant and the other evangelicals actually involved in colonial administration remained silent on these points so that Wilberforce could in fact establish both the contrasting identities of India and Britain, and the need for active sympathy.[84]

But did Wilberforce really have any sympathy for India or its natives? This was the question Lushington put to his adversary and to parliament. Lushington was himself a former Chairman of the East India Company, and knew British India "first-hand." Like Munro and Hastings, Lushington took exception to the mode ("fanatical") and substance ("contemptuous") of evangelical representations of India. And if the Clapham Saints were truly friendly to the Indian natives, Lushington declared, then they must rejoice in knowing that Hinduism was far from the degraded, animalistic orgy that it had been represented as. On June 28, 1813, Lushington spoke out against the evangelization of India. Declaring that his chief concern was the welfare and happiness of the natives of India, he lamented the ill-effects both on future civil servants of India and on the British public of the various evangelical publications.

> If the natives of India were represented as a race of beings devoid of all truth and honour—would not those, who, in the new order of things, visiting their shores, treat them with contempt and cruelty? The assertions, however, which had been made, from his own personal knowledge, he could distinctly contradict; and he should endeavour to remove the effects which seemed to have been created by them on the mind of one hon. member (Mr. Wilberforce), whose benevolence and kindness of heart, he was satisfied, would lead him to feel infinite delight at hearing calumnies of so foul and a so cruel a nature, clearly and positively refuted. The publications which were most conspicuously violent against the Hindoos, were those of Dr. Buchanan . . . ; they were deficient both in honour, honesty, gratitude, and charity. (XXVI, 944)

Many in the audience would be disgusted at these words; that any other religious system could promote honor, honesty, and charity seemed outrageous to a public that was beginning to identify evangelicalism with charity itself. Contrary to his opponents, Lushington goes on to argue that the literatures of India "were perhaps too much taken up with lessons of morality"; that the moral sentiments of Hindus toward women "were as good as ours, and their general practice, better"; and that Hinduism itself is "replete with devotion to God, and benevolence to man" (945–946). Instead of the mass of absurdities and degradations that the evangelicals saw, Lushington argued for a more expansive vision of Hinduism, one that would put the smooth functioning of the empire foremost in its consideration of the Orient. These themes, in their turn, would be picked up by other sentimental Orientalist in the Commons opposing the evangelical proposals. Taking his lead from Lushington's speech, Charles Marsh, for instance, pointed out the folly of evangelical representations of India, saying "if such is our opinion of our fellow subjects in India, we are unfit to govern them. It is a mischievous hypothesis, corrupting the very fountains of pure and beneficent administration. Hatred and contempt for those whom you govern, must, in the very nature of things, convert your government into a stern and savage oppression."[85]

What was at stake in this struggle was the very nature of sympathetic governance. And its implications did not escape the natives. For from another context, it would be precisely this struggle around the true nature of British sympathy that intellectuals of the Bengali renaissance would engage through their own sympathetic discourses on Hinduism, Christianity, colonialism, nationalism, and modernization. I suggest that the emergence of a certain nationalist reformism toward the end of the century must be contextualized not only within protest traditions within Hinduism and Islam but in fact through a genealogy of missionary sympathy, which immediately complicates any notion of colonial resistance without complicity. The role of the Brahmo Samaj was crucial in this form of a certain complicitous resistance in the later half of the nineteenth century. Formed by the famous reformer Rammohan Roy in 1828, the Brahmo Samaj drew on aspects of Unitarianism and a rationalistic Hinduism to articulate a form of elite centered reform Hinduism that sought to transform "native society" from the ground up. That Brahmoism in various forms led to a certain kind of nationalism, a compradour social reformism, and even in some ways to a more orthodox form of Hinduism signals its own double, mixed consciousness. And yet it enabled a specific kind of resistance to missionary colonialism. In their response to missionary endeavors to convert the "heathen" the Bengali Hindu elite launched projects of reconstruction, reformation, and reform that would have profound implications for the course of modernization and nationalism in India. The community of Brahmos played a crucial role in the genesis and development of nearly every major religious, social, and political movement in India from 1820 to 1930.[86] Part of the ideological impetus for the Brahmo Samaj was a universalistic, catholic theism, summed up in the phrase, "The fatherhood of God and the brotherhood of man." But all its major ideologues were Hindus of one sort or another, and various Hindu traditions mark every Brahmo institution throughout its history.[87] Much needs to be said about this movement and its specific relationship to Enlightenment sympathy; here I only note how one figure in the Brahmo movement used and adapted the sympathetic procedure to articulate a kind of critical if complicitous agency.

Crucial in the history of Brahmo reformism is the life and work of Keshub Chandra Sen. In his speeches delivered as the head of, first, the Brahmo Samaj of India (1866), and then the Nava Vidhan or New Dispensation (1879), Sen articulated a theory and practice of Hindu theism that attempted to syncretize Christianity, Buddhism, rationalism, positivism, and bhakti Vaishnavism (emotion or inspiration centered devotionalism). Sen's vision of reformed Hinduism changed and transformed throughout this period (roughly from 1866 until his death in 1884), but certain constant concerns mark his entire project of reform: Throughout his works, a complex negotiation is staged between what Sen considered the "divine Providence of British rule," Brahmo rationality, and racial and national difference.

Consider Sen's representation, then, of British Providence. In a speech delivered on May 5, 1866, "Jesus Christ: Europe and Asia,"[88] Sen tries to balance two civilizations through the figure of Christ, the savior. In this speech, Sen first claims a position of objectivity; such a position would be the hallmark of his Brahmoism, and its keywords would be brotherhood, science, history, fact, progress, and evolution; coinciding with Christian missionary discourses, Sen's Brahmoism would eschew all "vapory sentimentalism" (110), and would found a "science of inspiration" (192) that could teach the "stern realities of the spirit world" (397): "I will not soar into the ethereal regions of fairy dreams, nor spin out romantic fables and myths under the influence of morbid sentimentalism" (396–397). Instead, Sen stands "on the platform of brotherhood" to "disclaim the remotest intention of offending any particular class or sect" (18). From this platform of objective kinship, he attempts to "show how, under an overruling Providence, [the Church of Christ] has brought the Asiatic and the European races together, and made the East and West kiss each other in fraternal sympathy" (2). What has been the nature of this sympathetic kinship? First, through missionary endeavors, Western enlightenment has dawned over India; and hand in hand with this has come the blessing of an enlightened colonialism.

Fortunately for India, she was not forgotten by the Christian missionaries when they went about to preach the Gospel. [Cheers.] While, through missionary agency, our country has been thus connected with the enlightened nations of the West, politically, an All-wise and All-merciful Providence has entrusted its interests to the hands of a Christian sovereign. In this significant event worldly men can see nothing but an ordinary political phenomenon, but of you who can discern the finger of Providence in individual and national history will doubtless see here His wise and merciful interposition. [Hear, hear.] . . . It is to the British Government that we owe our deliverance from oppression and misrule, from darkness and distress, from ignorance and superstition. (20)

From out of the darkness of oriental despotism, India emerges into the day-light of British colonialism and Christianity. Sen goes on to extol those "en-lightened ideas," such as "freedom of thought and action," which having changed the "very life of the nation," have also wrought "such wondrous im-provement in Native society"—such are the "gifts of that Government" (20). All these considerations should lead to "our deepest gratitude and loyalty to the British nation and Her Most Gracious Majesty Queen Victoria . . . [Cheers.]"

One would imagine that such loyal sentiments would promote a state of "harmonious co-operation." "But does harmony actually prevail among us? . . . Does brotherly love subsist between the conquering and the con-quered races?" (21) Far from it. Indeed, the "flame of antipathy" between the races rages out of control, kindling the "bitterest rancour and hatred" to such an extent that "the worst passions of the heart are indulged with the ut-most recklessness" (21–22). (Let us not forget that the 1857 Indian "Mutiny" and the 1865 Morant Bay Rebellion were still fresh in the minds of his listeners.) In a word, racism rules the day.

> Among the European community in India there is a class who not only hate the Natives with their whole heart, but seem to take a pleasure in doing so. [Cheers.] . . . They regard the Natives as one of the vilest nations on earth, hopelessly immersed in all the vices which can degrade humanity, and bring it to the level of brutes. . . . Native ideas and tastes, Native customs and man-ners, seem to them odious and contemptible; while Native character is con-sidered to represent the lowest type of lying and wickedness. . . . I believe, and I must boldly and emphatically declare, that the heart of a Native is not nat-urally more depraved than that of a European or any other nation in the world. That fact is, human nature is the same everywhere—in all latitudes and climes; but circumstances modify it, and religion and usages mould it in dif-ferent forms. Educate the Native mind, and you will find it susceptible of as much improvement and elevation as that of a European. (23)

Under the banner of universalist humanism, whose progressivist agency is liberal education—both "gifts" of colonial rule—Sen opposes European racism. Yet, and not without contradiction, Sen also asserts the differentness of "Native ideas and tastes, Native customs and manners." Both a universal-ist progressivism and a difference-based nationalism marks Sen's reformist project. Note that Sen nowhere assimilates India to the British nation; all throughout his speeches, Sen is careful to mark, however subtly, this differ-ence between conqueror and conquered, between British and Indian. This difference enables him to contrast the "character" of each nation. As such, a tangential vector, or better, a side effect of this contrast would be the as-sumption of a certain Indian nationalism. Sen, thus, condemns European racism and at the same time asserts the need to educate the native mind; the defense of "Native character" is not a simple recourse to essence but also a plea for education (this was, in fact, one of Sen's major reformist projects, free compulsory education for the "masses").[89] The message, in short, is full of ambivalence. On the one hand, Sen gives an unequivocal pledge of loyalty to the British government. On the other hand, he qualifies this with an acknowledgment of a pervasive racism that disfigures British Providence. And finally, Sen pleads, in an almost defensive tone, for native education. Even though the plea is directed toward the British, there is a sense, and this would be a constant theme running throughout Brahmo reformism, that if we would be free, we must first free our minds and our souls—reform must start with ourselves.

Let us follow the track of this ambivalence in Sen's account of the two "national characters"—"Europeans and Indians." Declaring, "I rejoice, yea, I am proud, that I am an Asiatic" (33), Sen argues that the Indian "heart" is too "narrow and selfish." It wants sympathy.

> Its views and sympathies and aspirations are contracted. There is too much exclusiveness about a Native, which limits his thoughts and feelings within a small compass beyond which he can hardly extend them. His life is a round of selfish pursuits, and self-interest is generally the motive of his actions. . . . Selfishness . . . is a characteristic of our nation, and into this many of our national defects may resolve themselves. But this selfishness may be accounted for by the circumstances under which we live. . . . We are a subject race, and have been for centuries. We have too long been under foreign sway to feel anything like independence in our hearts. Socially and religiously we are little better than slaves. From infancy up we have been trained to believe that we are Hindoos only so far as we offer slavish obedience to the authority of the Shasters and the priests. (25–26)

Notice that what starts off as an anticolonial (and, always, even if in the background, anti-Mogul) argument slides seamlessly into a complaint against Hindu rigidity. A kind of pedagogy of universal sympathy shows how a subjugated Hinduism has contracted, narrowed our sympathies, and made our world too small; sympathy, in this context, functions as an ever-widening web of relations to the non-Hindu world. Hindus must free themselves from this slavish obedience if they would move toward "anything like independence." Again, reform must start with ourselves. Yet Sen does not spare his British listeners, either.

> The European . . . has a large and cosmopolitan heart. He can call the world his home, meet a distant call of charity, and offer his sympathy to all men, without any distinction of caste, creed, or colour. He enjoys and loves freedom,

which gives full scope to all the nobler instincts and sentiments of his heart, and leads him to follow, consistently and fearlessly certain high principles of action from which he thinks it unmanly and mean to swerve. [Hear, hear.] On reversing the picture, we find the Hindoo has certain excellences in which his European brother is rather deficient. The Hindoo is mild and meek. [Cheers.] . . . He is conciliating and forgiving, and would do all he can to enjoy the enviable felicity of having no enemy on earth. . . . But, however deplorable the abuse, I believe that if Native meekness be sustained and regulated by sound moral principles, it would prove an honourable virtue, and shed lustre on our national character. On the other hand, the European is full of energy and activity, and dislikes a quiet, smooth life. . . . In fact the European nature is rough, stern, impulsive, and fiery; it thinks meekness to be cowardice; it rejoices and glories in violence and vengeance. [Cheers.] How often do such qualities, overstepping all legitimate bounds, and defying all higher impulses, become frightful sources of mischief! And, alas! how sadly manifest is this in India? Many a European adventurer in this country seems to be believe that he has a right to trample upon every unfortunate nigger with whom he comes in contact. [Cheers.] This he believes to be heroism, and in this he seeks glory! But he forgets that to kick and trample upon one who is inferior in strength is not heroism, but base cowardice. [Deafening applause.] (29–30)

Deafening applause. A very odd characterization. Notice how the Native's narrow sympathies give way to something like their opposite, the elements of a future "honourable virtue"—forgiveness, mildness, and nonviolence (which in another part of his speech Sen links to the figure of woman, and the concept of femininity [28]). And, simultaneously, the widened sympathies of the European, when put in relationship to their racist actions sinks into "base cowardice."

What is to be done to end this state of racial antipathy? Sen argues for Christian sympathy, which at first seems to be another gift of a benevolent Europe.

If the European is at all anxious for the glory of his country and his God, he ought to seek it in a better and more generous treatment of the Natives. If he is conscious of his superiority, a Native should be all the more an object of his compassion and tender regards; and surely pity from a Christian heart he has every reason to expect. . . . It is the bounden duty of all Europeans in India so to prove their fidelity to [Christ] in all the avocations of their private and public life. . . . I regard every European settler in India as a missionary of Christ, and I have a right to demand that he should always remember and act up to his high responsibilities. [Applause.] (30–31)

In fact, European racism is a betrayal of Christ, and the mission of Christianity in India. If they would be true to Christ they must exercise compassion, pity, and tenderness toward their presumably inferior native brethren. Notice the language of the plea: "I have a right," declares Sen, "to demand" that Christ be the model subject for the colonizer. Again, a strange plea. Sympathy is urged but only by reinscribing the inequality between European and Indian within a rights-based discourse. Christian sympathy becomes Sen's own pedagogy to fashion a more humane colonialism governed by the rule of law.

But as it turns out, Christian sympathy, according to Sen, is not European at all, because, first, Christ was essentially oriental, and, second, because sympathy is in fact a fundamental principle of Vaishnavite Hinduism.[90]

> If . . . our Christian friends persist in traducing our nationality and national character, and in distrusting and hating Orientalism, let me assure them that I do not in the least feel dishonoured by such imputations. On the contrary, I rejoice, yea, I am proud that I am an Asiatic. And was not Jesus Christ an Asiatic? [Deafening applause.] Yes, and his disciples were Asiatics, and all the agencies primarily employed for the propagation of the Gospel were Asiatic. In fact, Christianity was founded and developed by Asiatics, and in Asia. When I reflect on this, my love for Jesus becomes a hundredfold intensified; I feel him nearer my heart, and deeper in my national sympathies. Shall I not rather say he is more congenial and akin to my Oriental nature, more agreeable to my Oriental habits of thought and feeling? (33)

Rather than turn the other cheek, Sen appropriates Christ to the Orient, to the Indian nation, and finally to Indian character. Notice, as with all appeals to "Oriental nature," history is eviscerated of all variation or heterogeneity, and movement or change, indeed of all difference in general. And against this homogenous background, the Orientalized Christ becomes an appropriate object for sympathetic identification. This Asiatic Christ, as Sen would put it years later,[91] "rivets our national sympathies":

> Recall to your minds, gentlemen, the true Asiatic Christ, divested of all Western appendages, carrying on the work of redemption among his own people. Behold, he cometh to us in his loose flowing garment, his dress and features altogether oriental, a perfect Asiatic in everything. Watch his movements, and you will find genuine orientalism in all His habits and manners. . . . Surely Jesus is *our Jesus*. (365)

A stunning passage fraught with desire, identification, and reversal. I would suggest that, subtly, Sen counters European racism by appropriating its chief symbol of moral progress to the orient. As such, his Christianity becomes something of an anti-Western, even protonationalist force in his spirituality.

But then what does Christ symbolize for Sen? Interestingly, Sen joins this figure of moral progress to the "ideal Hindu life." For Sen, Christ's central warning, as well as his central teaching, is that the "self is the greatest enemy of communion. . . . Never think of self, said he. Take no heed of what ye shall eat or what ye shall drink, or what ye shall put on, but seek ye first the kingdom of God and His righteousness. Surrender and resign yourselves completely to Him, and He will take care of you and feed you" (383–384). For Sen, Jesus was the prophet of self-denial; through his actions and his words, Christ "taught only one doctrine—divinity in humanity" (379). Divinity in humanity through the eradication of the self—such was the message of the Oriental Christ (and one wonders just how far Sen would take the identification of himself with Jesus). Sen argued that this message was necessarily also a message of love, and could be the "creed of salvation that is to save our nation."[92] We are very close to a national, even anticolonial gospel of sympathy here.

> Through love man is saved—thus saith the Lord. . . . What does love mean? A drawing together of hearts, they say. Men may be said to stand at some distance from each other in consequence of intervening barriers of selfishness. Love removes these barriers, brings different minds together, and binds them. . . . By love I mean that holy passion which removes all differences that estrange men, and reduced all differences that estrange men, and reduces a multiplicity of souls to unity. By it ten souls, yea, ten thousand souls, are so amalgamated as to form an indivisible unity. Love is nothing if it is not a thorough unification of hearts. . . . What I have said is true not only of the highest type of religious love, but also of the inferior passion which goes by the name of love in the world. There can be no love between man and woman unless they are identified, and made of one spirit. Husbands and wives surrender their hearts to each other. Their ideas tastes, inclinations, and hopes harmonize, and their sympathy with each other in joy and sorrow becomes so intense that they may be said to possess one heart. In true sympathy lies the secret of conjugal union and happiness. (211–212)

Notice how the national gospel of sympathy (or love) is always also a (heterosexual) family romance, the two are indeed indissociable. Love through sympathy would be the glue between individuals, tying husband to wife, and so the nation would be saved—through patriotism, the family and philanthropy: "The world calls him a patriot who loves not one of two of his countrymen only, but all his countrymen and countrywomen. His country as a totality, an aggregation of myriad souls, is interwoven, as it were, into his very being, and he may be said to live in them, the identification of interests is so complete" (213–214); philanthropic love "embraces countries and nations beyond number, yea all mankind. . . . The true philanthropist can and does embrace all mankind in his inmost heart. To him all men are as one, and with humanity he is identified" (214). As is true with every discourse of sympathy we have encountered in this study, difference must be eradicated, interests must be identified, multiplicity must be reduced to unity: "I have said salvation is to be worked out by love, such love as alone can effect a thorough spiritual unification, and convert multiplicity into unity" (214). In one of his last published speeches,[93] Sen would be much more explicit about what links together subjectivity, sympathy, and community. Sen argues that the two distinguishing characteristics of the New Dispensation is synthesis and subjectivity; it aims to synthesize all prior dispensations (Jewish, Christian, Buddhist, Muslim, Hindu) into a future-oriented unity, and it aims at transforming "subjectivity." The New Dispensation "endeavours to convert outward facts and characters into facts of consciousness" (470), the foremost fact being that "God is not only a Person, but also a character. As a Person we worship him; His Divine character we must assimilate to our own character" (471). But the New Dispensation has a powerful ally in the nature of human beings:

> Among the many theories of morals which the science of ethics deals with there is, as you are doubtless aware, one known as the Theory of Sympathy. Whatever its errors may be, and these are palpable, it has a substratum of truth. . . . It must be admitted that sympathy plays a most important part in the moral economy of the world. It is this noble sentiment which makes us go out of ourselves, and enter into the feelings and wants, into the difficulties and sufferings of others, with a view to afford the needed relief. Our selfishness keeps us in chains within ourselves. Sympathy breaks these iron chains, and drags us into the bosom of the sorrowing brother, so as to make us feel as he feels. We all know what this is. Whenever we see an object of pity, a man dying of starvation, a bleeding soldier, a poor disconsolate orphan, or a bedridden patient smarting under painful maladies, we unconsciously transfer ourselves in imagination to his position, and so closely identify ourselves with him as to feel at the time the very agony which he is suffering from. . . . Call it sympathy, or charity, or love, there is assuredly something in our nature which, though we ourselves may be happy and healthy, makes us feel and realize the wretchedness and disease and sorrow of our neighbours. It makes us one with others. It imperceptibly steals out of its own tenement, and gives it a temporary lodgment in the neighbour's breast that it may suffer and serve there. (474–476)

The last line is perhaps the most crucial one. Mark the similarity of language throughout this passage with that of Smith and Hume.[94] But for Sen, the mystic, the prophet, apostle, sympathy has no home, no final resting place other than with God, and God is with the world. It is essentially rootless, even diasporic.

> We are bound to love and serve all, however disagreeable and antagonistic
> they may be. We must love even our enemies. For though enemies, they are
> still our brothers and sisters . . . universal love means a going out of self and
> its absorption in humanity. Philanthropy makes the wide world its home, and
> dwells there . . . Deep sympathy makes us one with the world; its sorrows be-
> come our sorrows, and its joys our joys. True love is a pilgrim that has left
> home and gone away, never to return. Like a homeless traveler it wanders
> about it all parts of the world, and makes other people's homes its resting
> place. It is an eternal exile from home. (221)[95]

Sen is certainly in conversation with the eighteenth-century Western tradition of civic sympathy that I analyzed in chapter two. But there is also a profound shift in the project as a certain resistance nationalism and bhakti
spiritualism would seek to expand the parameters of Western civility toward
a new universalism. These strategies of deployment have everything to do
with the particular configuration of colonial power that the Brahmo Samaj
negotiated in its own rise to a certain dominance in the nineteenth century.
But what we have seen in these speeches is the profoundly protean nature of
sympathy: If in missionary discourses such as the one deployed by Wilberforce in the 1813 charter debates sympathy produces an abject figure of horror, in Sen's Brahmo reformism sympathy can, on one hand, serve to
legitimate a static and absolute difference between East and West, and on the
other, provide a trenchant critique of imperial racism. As the century progressed, Brahmoism and Indian reformism more generally would reduce
such national sympathy to various projects of social "betterment": female
education, workers rights, a more humane Hinduism. As such, elite social
sympathy was deployed as a tactic of a national regeneration.

I would suggest that these tactics of sympathy within Brahmo reformism
have a genealogy that must be traced to the charter debates of 1813. It was
then that the very idea of having sympathy for the heathen Hindu took hold
of the British imaginary in a completely unprecedented way. It was at that
moment that the parliamentary saints convinced not only parliament but the
nation at large that "Anglo-Indians" were somehow blinded when it came to
seeing the reality of native India. "There is a sort of inaptitude," declared
Wilberforce, "in what regards the subject of religion, which we discover in the
generality of Anglo Indians, which causes their judgement . . . to fail them
egregiously in this."[96] Arguing that "flatterers are not friends" (854), Wilberforce goes on to deny the charge that he hates India and Indians.

> I scarcely need to vindicate myself against such a charge, that it is not to exult
> over the melancholy degradation of these unhappy people, or to indulge in
> the proud triumph of our own superiority, that I have dwelt so long on this
> painful subject: but it is because I wish to impress you with a just sense of the

malignity of their disease, that you may concur with me in the application of
a remedy. . . . The most able of our opponents has told us, that some classes
of the natives are as much below others as the inferior animals are below the
human species. Yes, Sir, I well know it; and it is because I wish to do away
with this unjust inequality, to raise these poor brutes out of their present degraded state to the just level of their nature, that I am now bringing before
you their real character. (854)

What is crucial is that a posited inequality (civilizational, moral, intellectual,
social) is the occasion for Wilberforce's benevolence: He, through the agency
of evangelization, will do away with this "unjust inequality." There is to be
no exultation in civilizational superiority, rather difference, injustice, inequality is a disease to be remedied. But if we are thus to be their friends we
must acknowledge this difference and not give in to that false sympathy that
would blur it. And for this reason Wilberforce must also insist on the radical otherness of India to all that is truly British.

> Both their civil and religious systems are radically and essentially the opposites
> of our own. Our religion is sublime, pure and beneficent. Theirs is mean, li-
> centious, and cruel. Of our civil principles and condition, the common right
> of all ranks and classes to be governed, protected, and punished by equal laws,
> in the fundamental principle. Equality, in short, is the vital essence and the
> very glory of our English laws. Of theirs, the essential and universal pervad-
> ing character is inequality; despotism in the higher classes, degradation and
> oppression in the lower. (865)

If this was the radical difference, Christianity would be a radical, total "cure"—
its goal would be an absolute sameness. But then the process of evangelization
would eliminate its own raison d'être: unjust inequality. As I have been arguing, sympathy not only takes this difference as its object of transformation,
but, as an essential part of its procedure, produces it. It is this contradictory
play of identity and difference, of injustice and benevolence that structures the
discourse and practice of sympathy in evangelical reformism in India. Finally,
coming back to a theme that the Petitions had stressed again and again—the
basis of evangelization in good colonial policy—Wilberforce asserts that
Christianity is the best means of securing the natives's affections: " . . . would
we render ourselves secure against [France], let us endeavour to strike our roots
into the soil, by the gradual introduction and establishment of our own principles and opinions; above all, as the source of every other improvement, of
our religion, and consequently of our morals."[97] What we see in this exchange
is the tactical nature of sympathetic humanitarianism. We see also that precisely what was at stake at this historical moment was the nature of "real sympathy" and who or what would be its most proper agent. That in one context

such humanitarian evangelism could "make these men [into] every thing that is bad, in order to serve as an excuse for our own conduct," and excoriate precisely such strategies in other contexts shows further how sympathy could be adapted and transferred, delimited or extended: "Sentimental" abolitionists could take the form of real politicking imperialists in other contexts—and all in the name of sympathy. In these ways sympathy became unevenly integrated into various strategies of colonial governmentality.

No doubt, Lushington and his allies represented what was probably the last gasp of sympathetic Orientalism in the nineteenth century, as Charles Grant's monopolism was probably the last concerted defense of mercantilism—both were losing battles. By the provisions of the new charter, India was opened to all British merchants and all missionaries. As for the later, in addition to requiring the company to permit missionaries to go to India and creating an Indian Episcopal See, the charter provided that the governor-general could spend up to £10,000[98] a year on education from the public fund. In the event, the evangelicals won India for the missionaries, but Marsh would be proven right in the long run: The most profound and painful realization through the long nineteenth century was that Britain's rule of sympathy was in fact "a stern and savage oppression."

Conclusion

In the Name of Sympathy

This study has urged a rethinking of the history of sentiment through technologies of power and figurations of difference. I have lingered over those moments in sentimental fiction, parliamentary debates, moral philosophy, slave narratives and Hindu reformist discourses when sympathy seems to take the reader beyond the pale of humanity and civilization, and so (ex)poses the naturalness or givenness not only of the sympathetic relation but also of the proper boundary of the proper human itself: the contours of a certain matrix of power. Focusing on those aspects of sympathy where one can discern the limits of a certain logic of otherness and identification obliges us to consider the general textuality of the world and its histories of domination and resistance. For within this tradition, from inside a discourse that seems to abject relentlessly the racial other, we also come across those scenes where a (usually European) man or woman sympathizes with those who seem to be beyond the pale of humanity—savages and barbarians, or even Indians. And as if a tangent of sympathy were returning from some other space, or better from the space of the other, former slaves and colonial subjects also used this very sympathetic procedure in their own strategies of resistance. In this reading strategy can be discerned my own rearticulation of the legacy of sympathy: Sympathy can and must be practiced without turning the suffering other into an occasion to consolidate a subject in sovereignty. This other practice of sympathy, this non-propriative identification with others, can also be given another name: solidarity. In other words, what I have attempted is to write not simply another history of sympathy, but further to show that from this history, if listened to with another ear, other forms of sociality are audible. These social practices are certainly tied to the bourgeois European concept of sympathy—and so an interminable inventory of complicities is launched and relaunched with every movement—but through a persistent displacement of its eighteenth-century foundations in moral philosophy, literature, and political discourse another memory, and hence another future is possible.

For over two hundred years, sympathetic humanitarianism has been the dominant modality of social intervention in the West. Today, we must pose our own relationship to the pedagogy of sympathy staged with such force through strategies of horror and sentiment in eighteenth- and nineteenth-century discourses and institutions. Here I will briefly return to questions I have posed throughout this study: Do we read with sympathy? And if so, what kind of sympathy is it? Can we fracture the imbrications between sympathy and the police? What political positions are possible in the name of sympathy? Today, do scenes of sympathy thrill us with horror, move us with pity, and so humanize us? If "enlightened" Europeans could sympathize with enslaved Africans, what blocked the extension and transference of this sympathy to exploited workers, or colonized Indians? Who or what is excluded . . . in the name of sympathy? I will address these questions through a consideration of the specific arguments made throughout this study: How the sympathetic procedure relates to questions of gender, of difference, of humanity, and of justice.

The Gender of Sympathy

I have argued that the question of gender was central to the elaboration of sympathy as a mode of power. First, by elaborating and extending certain aspects of Foucault's theory of governmentality, I have shown how the heterosexual family was *both* target (as modality) and instrument (as model) of a technology of power linked to sentiment and morality. In other words, as a *model of governing* the patriarchal family was not eliminated from the history of governmentality—the articulation of paternalistic and evangelical sensibilities with new mechanisms of governmentality is what gave the family-as-model a "new career in domination." Moreover, as I noted in chapter three, meditations on the delicacy of the body and its susceptibility to pain also enabled the construction of essential differences between both the sexes and civilizations: at the very moment when "sex as we know it was invented," sympathy, sensibility, and benevolence would come to characterize woman's natural role (Pamela) and England's civilizational status (above, say, Hindoos). The feminine and feminized body bore the burden of the sympathetic gaze. In short, a whole matrix of power converged around the sentimental figuration of women's bodies. This notion of women's natural susceptibility to pain and suffering became an index of civilization, giving new meaning to both human misery and human history.

And yet, as a pedagogy of femininity, sympathy also provided the emerging middle-class British woman with a new arena of agency: social causes that were aimed at "uplifting" the downtrodden, enslaved, and abjected and consolidating a new feminine subject as good "domestic policy." This originally feminine agency became a model of bourgeois social intervention toward the end of the eighteenth century. This marked the dawn of a new era that to our present day would tie discipline to sympathy. If before the constitution of "man," then, sympathy was a feminine pedagogy, I have also shown that as this gender genealogy was both repressed and incorporated (for instance in parliamentary debates around abolition and evangelization) sympathy was more and more assimilated to the twin projects of civilization and nation-building (legible in the martial rhetoric of missionary sympathy). What this study shows, it seems to me, is that there was a certain disciplining of sympathy itself such that its feminized, nonrational, even occult excesses were normalized through a pedagogy of the abstract human. As such, sympathy was articulated with older forms of gender and civilizational discourses that assimilated the figure of the active agent of sympathy to a masculinized (but never only male) colonial and civilizing project. This suggests, finally, that the gender of sympathy was itself polymorphous and adaptive.

Difference in Sympathy

One of the central arguments throughout *Rule of Sympathy* is that as a form of power sympathy was adapted in overall technologies of normalization and propriation. As a discursive practice, sympathy was a pedagogy of identification: Sympathy was predicated on procedures, rules, and fantasies of identification (for instance, in slavery or evangelization). At the same time, it was a paradoxical mode of power. The cultural or gender differences that divided the object and agent of sympathy was precisely that which must be bridged, effaced even, through a certain process of identification. Yet without such differences, which were inequalities of power, sympathy could not function; sympathy produced the very inequality it sought to bridge. I have argued that the necessary distance in sympathy (the production and elaboration of a certain difference), and the imaginative bridging of it through a kind of identification—the double movement of the gaze of sympathetic power— would be the effective paradox of the sympathetic relation in both abolitionism and missionary discourse. Indeed, as I argued in chapter four, in the new genre of the Gothic sympathy provided a representational matrix to figure the savagery of slavery. The pained body, the distanced, sympathizing observer, the archaism of the detached scene of horror, the moral uplift of sublime terror, the ambivalent, anxious demarcation of savagery and civilization, and finally, the relentless haunting of those millions of Africans murdered in the slave trade and in the slave colonies—these Gothic practices as we have seen found their way into both evangelical abolitionism and missionary representations of Africa and India. Such scenes also helped to suture the discourse of sympathy to a movement that could be named propriation.

As we saw in our consideration of moral philosophy, the movement of sympathy both appropriates and makes proper all forms of otherness: the other's body is embodied in pity; the savagery of the racialized other is both renarrativized and normalized in the story of the "social affections"; the effeminacy of sentiment is made proper to the civilized, re-masculinized, universal human. In other words, sympathy founds the being (proper) of the (social) subject—through sympathy the subject comes to know the mode of sociality proper to the moral order; sympathy renders the other an object of identification, and so the other seems to be knowable, accessible, and so appropriable. Moreover, through this economy the other of sympathy is rendered an attribute of the sovereign self.

At the same time, there is another movement that haunts sympathy's propriative drive. Recall reasonable Jane's murderous struggle against the black spectre of superstition, even as she acknowledges that sympathies "baffle mortal comprehension." I showed that while sympathy animates Jane's various projects of propriation, it also names a fundamental mystery that cannot be integrated into the realist, rationalist logic of the text. It was this opening that obliged me to return repeatedly to a seemingly insignificant parentheses in the history of the word sympathy: an "affinity between certain things, by virtue of which they are similarly or correspondingly affected by the same influence, affect or influence one another (esp. in some occult way), or attract or tend towards each other." In my analyses of various discourses this parenthetical becomes crucial. I asked, what if through sympathy a kind of premodern (real or supposed) occultism, even mysticism, came to be adapted by modern modes of power? What if, in sympathy, a principle, at once nonrational, and nonsecular is operative, at least in terms of a certain haunting, and yet without being irrational or Christian? These questions lead us to another memory, another genealogy of sympathy, one that cannot be contained within a narrow European Christian tradition, one that finally opens on to another possibility.

The Sympathetic Human

This study locates the emergence of sympathy and liberal humanist sentiment within that broader shift in modes of domination that Michel Foucault called governmentality. What we have seen is that discipline was enabled by, and security legitimized through sympathy for the other—the poor, the heathen, criminals, delinquents, deviants, prostitutes, slaves, colonial subjects, and the insane were to be sympathized with, and their condition ameliorated. In other words, sympathy was central in making the other proper to the self, and so a way of habituating the self to propriety. We have seen how the practice of sympathy aimed to create a specific kind of subject in and through sentimental and gothic fiction. These genres were closely tied to new ideologies of the "feminine," and, in different ways, associated to the new practices of middle-class politeness. Sympathy was yoked to the work of constructing a viable bourgeois civil society through the production of a particular kind of gendered, national, and racial subject.

This humanized subject, whose experience of pain elicits a certain response in the observer, was also moored to specific religious traditions of Puritan, latitudinarian, and—later in the century—evangelical benevolence and charity. I argued in my analysis of *Pamela,* for instance, that the narrative of sympathy inaugurates B's progress toward the sympathetic human. This human it turns out is also thoroughly market savvy: the "temporality" of sympathy, I argued, operates as a kind of market discipline through the production of a future-oriented, utility calculating sensibility. Sympathy is a pedagogy of bourgeois humanism in so far as it constructs and sutures (through identification) a subject who looks at the suffering of another and learns to benefit by it, and so perfects him- or herself through that suffering. In moral philosophy, the principle of sociality that was to found a new, bourgeois civil society was sympathy; in *Pamela,* the sympathetic subject can also function as an agent of the "police." Moreover, we have seen how, using sentimentalist and Gothic idioms, tropes, figurations, and imaginings, antislavery and missionary discourses articulated practices of governing racialized populations and producing sympathetic selves. The practices associated with evangelical humanity became the index for the proper treatment of enslaved (and, at around the same time, colonized) populations. This human was the ideal object of sympathy; conversely, to sympathize with such humanity was also a means to normalize difference: racial, cultural, civilizational difference would come to be the horrific signs of a static savagery or barbarism. Thus, just as Pamela is a force of civility, health, and economy, abolitionist sympathy draws once benighted Africans into the circuits of civilization and commerce: Recall that even Cugoano's proposals for the emancipation of enslaved Africans is not only a period of mourning for those murdered by the trade but also Christian missionary "instruction" that will produce tractable, obedient, useful, dutiful, and good colonial subjects. In my analysis of the subject of moral philosophy, I marked what I think are the contradictions and openings in this structure of the sympathetic human: Representation (culture) inaugurates the naturally sympathetic subject; the sovereignty of the agent of sympathy is predicated on the suffering other;

such a subjectivity must both bridge and reproduce endlessly a certain difference, and so on. Finally, this open structure is precisely what allowed me to pose questions that would take the sympathetic human to the limits of its own discourse, and beyond—into histories of domination and resistance that give the lie to the aura of benevolence that has swathed this strange figure to this day.

Another Sympathy, Another Justice

The history of sympathy is not closed. Its history did not end with modernity, nor will it dissolve in the triumphalism of the postmodern. As the most recent "War on Terror" shows, sympathy certainly has not lost its political usefulness: As smart bombs and lunch boxes seem to be the weapons of choice in the West's new-found crusade against Islamic "evil," humanitarian aid has once again been harnessed to the project of legitimating military intervention. And yet, what I have tried to show throughout this study is that there is another sociality heralded in this history—the right of "humanitarian intervention" that the West has arrogated to itself in the name of a universal sympathy, through a mission to police the world and protect its own interests, is both a problem and a possibility. And this for specific reasons: From its inception, the modern practice of sympathy has always also been tied to the interminable movement of a justice that is both complicit with, and irreducible to the police. With the rise of European humanitarianism, we saw that sympathy enables the struggle against injustice; it inaugurates a relational identity that legitimates social intervention.[1] But this movement and this subjectivity have always been circumscribed by a propriative drive and a disciplining pedagogy. So, on the one hand, almost every project of reform in modern England was in some ways tied to an emergent sensibility that reticulated sympathy with a fundamentally new vision of a better policed citizen. As such sympathy became a modality of elite intervention against perceived "injustice": the injustice of immorality, of slavery, of heathenism, of wage slavery, and so on. On the other hand, questions of colonial and domestic "policy" always also delimited the justice of sympathy. And so we saw how arguments around "uplifting" the enslaved African reached their limit when sympathetic humanitarianism had to deal with wage slaves breaking the chains of property at home. If, by linking civilization to humanity and benevolence, evangelical abolitionists were able to identify the cause of civilization with good government, that is better policy, and thus with justice and humanity, it was precisely this linkage that would allow these same evangelicals to call sympathetically for the Christian colonization of the world. Again, the propriative drive of sympathetic humanitarianism moors justice to the proper human. Thus, I have emphasized the tactical nature of sympathetic humanitarianism. For Wilberforce and the Saints, what was at stake was the nature of "real sympathy" and who or what would be its most proper agent; "sentimental" abolitionists could take the form of real politicking imperialists in other contexts—all in the name of sympathy. In these ways, sympathy became unevenly integrated into various strategies of colonial governmentality.

But another question can orient us toward another future: If justice and humanity are tied to the practice of sympathy, who is to say where sympathy should stop? There are moments where sympathy seems to spill beyond good policy, embodying an entirely different strategy. Harley speaks out against colonialism sympathizing with barbarians, Ezra produces an inexplicable response from Blake; Cugoano fashions his sympathetic abolitionism into a call for a radical justice; Jane seems to travel hundreds of miles through a sympathetic reverberation; and Sen demands racial justice in the name of a universal sympathy. These moments point to another structure, a different movement that has always haunted the history of sympathetic humanism. They open on to a strategy of sympathy that questions and in some ways undermines the movement of propriation and all calculations of profit, the gift, sovereignty, and the rational subject: Linking slave revolt to anticolonialism to early proletarianism demands a vision of justice that would see the overlapping structures, the mutually ramifying discourses of what was then a new global mode of political domination and economic appropriation. I have tried to give this movement, this difference, other names, but it will have been in the name of sympathy that such a difference activates another memory, another history, and the need for imagining another future.

Notes

Preface

1. "Humanitarian Intervention: A Forum," in *The Nation,* May 8, 2000, 21–26.
2. David Owen, *English Philanthropy, 1660–1960* (Cambridge, MA: Belknap, 1965), 14; qtd. in Ellis 15.
3. Running a word search of "solidarity" on the Internet (MSN search engine) yielded the following results: 1) www.igc.org/solidarity ("This socialist, feminist, labor rights party has literature explaining its principles and information on issues where it is active."); 2) www.labornet.org/solidarity/contMain.html ("American socialist, feminist, activist org. Includes description of philosophy, principles and aims, links, features, magazine, and articles."); 3) www.igc.org/cubasoli ("InfoMed USA is an organization working to provide computer network technology to Cuba's medical community. This site contains updated health news from Cuba, background information on the U.S. blockade of Cuba and links to related sites."); 4) www.socepp.de ("Solidarity Committee for Ethiopian Political Prisoners presents its objectives, an archive of press releases and news articles, a list of disappearances, and its contact details."); 5) http://www.solidarity.com/ (A celebration of Labor in America.). This last had had twelve thousand hits. A similar search for "sympathy" yielded first a Malayali-German diasporic home page inexplicably entitled sympathy.org (still under construction, with five hundred hits); and, second, a review article, "Sympathy for the devil."
4. Friedrich Nietzsche, *The Will To Power,* Walter Kaufmann and R. J. Hollingdale, trans., Walter Kaufmann, ed. (New York: Vintage, 1968), 49.
5. In certain postcolonial critiques of authoritarian masculinity, by contrast, sympathy can function as a kind of counter-pedagogy. Thus, in an article that challenges Western feminist's rejection of motherhood in analyzing women's resistance, Rohini Hensman asks, "Why do so many men allow themselves to be drawn into actions which go against all norms of humanity? I believe the answer lies in the ideology and practice of masculinity, which on the one hand allows men to feel no shame or guilt about the most brutal exercise of power over other human beings, and on the other hand

fails to train boys in the skills of caring and nurturing. Like all processes of learning, this involves internalizing appropriate responses to specific stimuli to a point where they become second nature. . . . If your normal response to the sight of a baby is a feeling of tenderness, you won't find it easy to throw it in a fire or dash its head against a wall. If your normal response to the sight of a person in pain is an answering pang of sympathy, your muscles will resist the motions of inflicting torture" ("Women's resistance to authoritarianism," in *Women and Politics in the Third World,* Haleh Afshar, ed. [New York: Routledge, 1996], 69). Of course, that sympathy has been a norm of Western humanity for two centuries is precisely what obscures an interrogation of sympathy as a mode of power.

6. *Times of India,* November 4, 1999, 1.

7. Friedrich Nietzsche, *On the Genealogy of Morals,* W. Kaufmann and R. J. Hollingdale, trans. (New York: Vintage, 1989), 6; *The Will to Power,* W. Kaufmann and R. J. Hollingdale, trans., W. Kaufmann, ed. (New York: Vintage, 1968), 149 (see also 58, 158). In terms of the gendering of Nietzsche's own discourse, consider this passage from the *Will to Power:* "Two type of morality must not be confused: the morality with which the healthy defends itself against incipient decadence—and another morality with which this very decadence defines and justifies itself. . . . The former is usually stoical, *hard,* tyrannical . . . ; the latter is enthusiastic, sentimental, full of *secrets;* it has the *women* and 'beautiful feelings' on its side . . ." (153; emphasis mine). That woman should be tied to the secret of sentimentality presents us with a key lever for the critique that follows.

8. "Nietzsche, Genealogy, History," *The Foucault Reader,* Paul Rabinow, ed. (New York: Pantheon, 1984), 80.

9. It was the insightful scholarship of Paul Gilroy that in part inspired me to take up this project. In the *Black Atlantic,* he wrote in opposition to the "nationalist or ethnically absolute approaches" that continue to dominate transnational/postcolonial/cultural studies today. Instead, Gilroy wanted "to develop the suggestion that cultural historians could take the Atlantic as one single, complex unit of analyses in their discussions of the modern world and use it to produce an explicitly transnational and intercultural perspective" (Gilroy, 15). This stunning suggestion functioned as a much needed wake-up call to contemporary cultural critics. But then I must ask, Why frame this history by the Atlantic? And why situate "one" race at its center (although let us not forget the difference that constitutes the "African" both today and historically)? Ironically, the danger here is a kind of geographical, if not biological, absolutism. Of course, I am quite sympathetic to the argument that one must begin and end somewhere. But the problem is sympathy never did.

10. Michel Foucault, "What is Critique?" Lysa Hochroth, trans., *The Politics of Truth* (New York: Semiotexte, 1997), 60.

11. Jacques Derrida once remarked on the strategy of inversion in an interview in *Points* thus: " . . . this inversion or reversal . . . is also unavoidable in the strategy of political struggles: for example, against capitalist, colonialist, sex-

ist violence. We must not consider this to be a moment or just a phase; if from the beginning another logic or another space is not clearly heralded, then the reversal reproduces and confirms through inversion what it has struggled against (84). See also his brilliant and not unrelated exposition on "epistemological liberation" in *Of Grammatology,* 83; and the two strategies of deconstruction in "The Ends of Man," *Margins of Philosophy,* Alan Bass, trans. (Chicago: University of Chicago Press, 1982), 133–136.

12. Gayatri Chakravarty Spivak, "Deconstructing Historiography," *Selected Subaltern Studies* (New York: Oxford University Press, 1988), 8–9.

13. Jacques Donzelot, *The Policing of Families,* Robert Hurley, trans. (New York: Pantheon, 1979), xxv.

14. Michel de Certeau, *The Writing of History,* Tom Conley, trans. (New York: Columbia University Press, 1988), 30.

15. I think it was with such dangers in mind that Jacques Derrida once argued for a "pluri-dimensional" history, in which meaning is not subjected to successivity, or to the order of logical time, the order, also, of phallogocentrism. "This pluri-dimensionality does not paralyze history within simultaneity, it corresponds to another level of historical experience, and one may just as well consider, conversely, linear thought as a reduction of history. It is true that another word ought perhaps to be used; the word history has no doubt always been associated with a linear scheme of the unfolding of presence, where the line relates the final presence to the originary presence according to the straight line or the circle" (Derrida, *Of Grammatology,* 85).

16. I use the terms discourse and practice as a way to get at these discontinuities. In "Nietzsche, Genealogy, History," Foucault defines genealogy as a new, "effective" form of "historical" inquiry. First, "discourses" and "practices" are central to such an analysis. He defines discourse "as the group of statements that belong to a single system of formation"; we can, says Foucault, for instance, speak of "clinical discourse, economic discourse, the discourse of natural history, psychiatric discourse" (Foucault, in *The Archaeology of Knowledge* [1968], 107–108). For Foucault, "Discursive practices are characterized by the delimitation of a field of objects, the definition of a legitimate perspective for the agent of knowledge, and the fixing of norms for the elaboration of concepts and theories. Thus, each discursive practice implies a play of prescriptions that designate its exclusions and choices. . . . Discursive practices are not purely and simply ways of producing discourse. They are embodied in technical processes, in institutions, in patterns for general behavior, in forms for transmission and diffusion, and in pedagogical forms which, at once, impose and maintain them. . . . These principles of exclusion and choice, whose presence is manifold, whose effectiveness is embodied in practices, and whose transformations are relatively autonomous, are not based on an agent of knowledge (historical or transcendental) who successively invents them or places them on an original footing; rather, they designate a will to knowledge that is anonymous, polymorphous, susceptible to regular transformations, and determined by the play of identifiable dependencies." (Foucault, "History of Systems of

Thought," in *Language, Counter-memory, Practice,* Donald Bouchard, trans. [Ithaca, NY: Cornell University Press, 1977], 199–202).

17. See Michel de Certeau, *The Practice of Everyday Life,* Steven Rendall, trans. (Berkeley: University of California Press, 1984), 45.

18. Foucault, "Nietzsche, Genealogy, History," *The Foucault Reader.* Paul Rabinow, ed. (New York: Pantheon, 1984), 76. Foucault's genealogical method, in its concern for effectivity, bears some relationship to Deleuze and Guattari's concept of the "rhizomatic," recently redeployed by Patricia Clough: "A certain way of reading and writing is required, something more like what Deleuze and Guattari refer to as rhizomatic, that brings conceptualizations from various writings together, assembling them on the same plane so that these concepts can be made to provoke a problematization. In *What is Philosophy?*, Deleuze and Guattari argue that a concept is better understood as the construction of a question that urges a new perspective. The concept in this sense has a 'becoming' that refers to its relationship with other concepts on the same plane: 'here concepts link up with each other, support one another, coordinate their contours, articulate their respective problems'" (Clough, *Auto-Affection* [Minneapolis: University of Minnesota Press, 2000], 6–7).

19. De Certeau, 35–36.

20. Michel de Certeau, *The Practice of Everyday Life,* Steven Rendall, trans. (Berkeley: University of California Press, 1984), 43. For an insightful experiment in this non-dialectic historiography, see Gayan Prakash, *Another Reason,* 201–226.

21. My "final intention" (to quote Derrida) is parasitic on Marx's analysis. "The discovery of gold and silver in America, the extirpation, enslavement and entombment in mines of the indigenous population of that continent, the beginnings of the conquest and plunder of India, and the conversion of Africa into a preserve for the commercial hunting of blackskins, are all things which characterize the dawn of the era of capitalist production. These idyllic proceedings are the chief moments of primitive accumulation. Hard on their heels follows the commercial war of the European nations, which has the globe as its battlefield. It begins with the revolt of the Netherlands from Spain, assumes gigantic dimensions in England's Anti-Jacobin War, and is still going on in the shape of the Opium Wars against China, etc." (Marx, *Capital,* 915). We have yet to attain to a historiographical practice that is in keeping with this insight.

22. De Certeau, 49.

23. De Certeau writes on the "unevenness of terrain" when a critical discourse "has to advance over an area where there are no longer any discourses" (61). "An individual science can avoid this direct confrontation. It grants itself a priori the conditions that allow it to encounter things only in its own limited field where it can 'verbalize' them. It lies in wait for them in the gridwork of models and hypotheses where it can 'make them talk.' . . . Theoretical questioning, on the contrary, does not forget, cannot forget that

in addition to the relationship of these scientific discourses to one another, there is also their common relation with what they have taken care to exclude from their field in order to constitute it." I believe we must not forget that these exclusions continue to affect, to structure, even speak our own discourses, and that to write the history of a practice that is both discursive and material, archival and bodily, we must give in to this haunting, perhaps even commune with it.

24. See Derrida's analysis of the keepers of the archive in *Archive Fever,* Eric Prenowitz, trans. (Chicago: University of Chicago Press, 1995), 2–4.

25. Prakash, *Another Reason* (Princeton, NJ: Princeton University Press, 1999), 237.

Chapter One

1. David Brion Davis, "Quaker Ethic and Antislavery International," in *The Antislavery Debate,* Thomas Bender, ed. (Berkeley: University of California Press, 1992), 61.

2. Michel Foucault, "Governmentality," Colin Gordon, trans., in Graham Burchell, Colin Gordon, Peter Miller, eds., *The Foucault Effect* (Chicago: University of Chicago Press, 1991), 103.

3. Colin Gordon, "Governmental Rationality. An Introduction," in Graham Burchell, Colin Gordon, Peter Miller, eds., *The Foucault Effect* (Chicago: University of Chicago Press, 1991), 10. The English word "policy," as we shall see, became a kind of irradiating center in all discourses of Evangelical humanitarianism.

4. Foucault, "Governmentality," 93.

5. What is a strategy of power? By tactics and strategies of power I do not mean practices resulting from the masterful manipulations of a governing "caste." As David Brion Davis pointed out in the case of abolitionism, few "historians would maintain today that abolitionists were hypocrites who consciously exploited humanitarian sentiments for ulterior aims" ("Reflections on Abolitionism and Ideological Hegemony" in *The Antislavery Debate,* Thomas Bender, ed. [Berkeley: University of California Press, 1992], 176). Indeed, in analyses of power, notions of simple hypocrisy or sinister conspiracies have been radically questioned by Foucault's elaboration of "force relations." In his famous chapter on "Method" in the *History of Sexuality, Vol. 1,* Foucault remarks that the exercise of power as a grid of intelligibility of the social order must be sought in the "moving substrate of force relations, which, by virtue of their inequality, constantly engender states of power, but the latter are always local and unstable" (*"c'est le socle mouvant des rapports de force qui induisent sans cesse, par leur inégalité, des états de pouvoir, mais toujours locaux et instables"*). Power is produced from one moment to the next, in every relation it inhabits; it is permanent, repetitious, inert, and self-reproducing; it names, finally, a "complex strategical situation in a particular society." For precisely this reason, relations of power, for Foucault, are both intentional

and nonsubjective: First, because power is always exercised with a series of aims and objectives. But, although "the rationality of power is characterized by tactics that are often quite explicit at the restricted level where they are inscribed," and thus the logic may be quite clear, the aims decipherable, it is often the case, argues Foucault, that "no one is there to have invented them, and few who can be said to have formulated them" (*History of Sexuality: An Introduction,* Robert Hurley, trans. [New York: Vintage, 1990], 93–95; *Histoire de la Sexualité* [Paris: Gallimard, 1976], 122–125). It is this sense of an intentional but nonsubjective tactic, which, by attracting and propagating other tactics, become connected to form "comprehensive systems" (*dispositifs d'ensemble*). For instance, tactics of "bio-power": "Tactics, the art of constructing, with located bodies, coded activities and trained aptitudes, mechanisms in which the product of the various forces is increased by their calculated combination are no doubt the highest forms of disciplinary practice" (*Discipline and Punish,* 167). This is also, I should say, my vision of the workings of hegemony.

6. Foucault's argument here echoes a certain Marx. If the epoch of capitalism coincides with the control of capital over the production process, under mercantilism, which is a specific mechanism of control over the exchange of products for money, the *form* of capital existed without the essential social relations upon which capitalism is based. Marx in *Capital III* argued that merchant capital is "incapable by itself of promoting and explaining the transition from one mode of production to another," and that "this system presents everywhere an obstacle to the real capitalist mode of production" (quoted in "Merchant Capital" in *A Dictionary of Marxist Thought,* Tom Bottomore, ed. [Cambridge, MA: Basil Blackwell, 1983], 332–333). Interestingly, this argument is also central to the debates around the relationship between capitalism, imperialism, and underdevelopment in the Marxist tradition.

7. To be clear, this strategic exclusion certainly does not mean that Foucault forgot about the family. As scholars such as Ann Stoler have consistently pointed out, Foucault's later researches in the history of sexuality, race, and bio-politics were precisely about the transformations in the structure and discourse of the family—as a target of discipline. What I am suggesting, however, is that as a *model of governing* the patriarchal family was not eliminated either—the articulation of paternalistic and evangelical sensibilities with new mechanisms of governmentality is what gave the family-as-model a new career in domination. This argument extends a certain line within Foucauldian discourse—see for instance, Donzelot's careful analysis of the paternalism of the state in juvenile courts in "The Tutelary Complex," *The Policing of Families,* 96–168.

8. Michel Foucault, "Society Must be Defended," Robert Hurley, trans., in *Ethics,* Paul Rabinow, ed. (New York: The New Press, 1997), 57.

9. I have been guided here by Gayan Prakash's work on science and governmentality in colonial India. In *Another Reason,* Prakash argues that Foucault's "concept of governmentality illuminates the processes at work in the formu-

lation of disciplines directed at preserving life and governing bodily conduct" (124). But consistent with his rigorous critique of the myth of Western self-fashioning, Prakash insists that "Colonial governmentality . . . could not be the tropicalization of its Western form, but rather was its fundamental dislocation" (125). What I attempt to show, with the help of Prakash's own history, is that in fact the "Western form" of governmentality, *as Foucault articulates it,* was already haunted by the exclusion of the other(s): religion and the family.

10. See Prakash, *Another Reason,* 17.
11. Michel Foucault, "What is Critique?" Lysa Hochroth, trans. in *The Politics of Truth* (New York: Semiotexte, 1997), 23–82.
12. See, for instance, Foucault, "The History of Sexuality," in *Power/Knowledge,* Colin Gordon, ed. (New York: Pantheon, 1980), 183–193, and *History of Sexuality: An Introduction,* Robert Hurley, trans. (New York: Vintage, 1990); Roy Porter and Lesley Hall, *The Facts of Life: The Creation of Sexual Knowledge in Britain* (New Haven, CT: Yale University Press, 1995) 1–121; Michael Mason, *The Making of Victorian Sexuality,* 2 vols. (New York: Oxford University Press, 1994); Thomas Laqueur, *Making Sex: Body and Gender from the Greeks to Freud* (Cambridge, MA: Harvard University Press, 1990); for the articulation of concerns around domesticity and working class sanitation, see Mary Poovey, *Making a Social Body : British Cultural Formation, 1830–1864* (Chicago: University of Chicago Press, 1995), 115–131; Jacques Donzelot, *The Policing of Families,* Robert Hurley, trans. (Baltimore: Johns Hopkins University Press, 1997); Phillipe Aries, *Centuries of Childhood: A Social History of Family Life,* Robert Baldick, trans. (New York: Vintage Books, 1962). I would like to thank David Staples for this suggestion. See also Ann Stoler's consistent work that has long argued for a Foucauldian critique of a politics of sentiment, as well as her researches in to the specificities of the "alienation of affections" and "disaffections" that form the anxieties of colonial governance and shape its interventions in the home—"A Sentimental Education: European Children and Native Servants," in *Fantasizing the Feminine: Sex and Death in Indonesia,* Laurie Sears, ed. (Durham, NC: Duke University Press, 1995), "Sexual Affronts and Racial Frontiers," in *Comparative Studies in Society and History,* 34:2 (July 1992): 514–51; *Race and the Education of Desire: Foucault's History of Sexuality and the Colonial Order of Things* (Durham: Duke University Press, 1995) and (edited with Frederick Cooper) *Tensions of Empire: Colonial Cultures in a Bourgeois World* (Berkeley: University of California Press, 1997). See also Julia Adams, "The Familial State: Elite Family Practices and State-making in the Early Modern Netherlands," *Theory and Society,* 23 (Summer 1994), 505–539; Lynn Hunt, *The Family Romance of the French Revolution* (Berkeley : University of California Press, 1992); and Françoise Vergès, *Monsters and Revolutionaries : Colonial Family Romance and Métissage* (Durham: Duke University Press, 1999). While both Hunt and Vergès draw on Freud's theory of the psychosexual family "drama" and, for better or worse, extend it to the psychosocial,

I find that their historical elaborations of the relationship between the discourse of the family—qua discourse—and forms of rule support my overall argument that the family as model for social relations was much more widely deployed than Foucault considered.

13. Jacques Donzelot, *The Policing of Families,* Robert Hurley, trans. (New York: Pantheon, 1979), xx.

14. Donzelot, xxi.

15. Although Foucault himself is arguing against the unicity of the state, his relegation of the family to "residual themes" opens his analysis to a critique of his own metaphysics. It would be the analysis, I think, of a certain trace-structure that would thoroughly problematize the periodicity, the linearity of some of his analysis. It would place difference at the moment of rupture, that is, at the origin of governmentality. Which would mean there is no absolute origin. I attempt such a situating in my argument. I am drawing here on the work of Jacques Derrida (not to mention Foucault himself in such texts as "Nietzsche, Genealogy, History"): "The trace is not only the disappearance of origin . . . it means that the origin did not even disappear, that it was never constituted except reciprocally by a nonorigin, the trace, which thus becomes the origin or the origin. From then on, to wrench the concept of the trace from the classical scheme, which would derive it from a presence or from an originary nontrace and which would make of it an empirical mark, one must indeed speak of an originary trace or arche-trace. Yet we know that that concept destroys its name and that, if all begins with the trace, there is above all no originary trace. . . . *The (pure) trace is difference.* It does not depend on any sensible plenitude, audible or visible, phonic or graphic. It is on the contrary, the condition of such a plenitude" (*Of Grammatology,* Gayatri Chakravorty Spivak, trans. [Baltimore, MD: Johns Hopkins University Press, 1976], 61–62).

16. Hunt writes, "I am interested . . . in the ways that people collectively imagine—that is, think unconsciously about—the operation of power, and the ways in which this imagination shapes and is in turn shaped by political and social processes. Central to this collective imagination are the relations between parents and children and between men and women" (*The Family Romance of the French Revolution* [Berkeley: University of California Press, 1992], 8). Hunt goes on to mark the transformations in the deployment of the term "fraternity" in revolutionary discourses.

17. Stoler, *Race and the Education of Desire,* vii.

18. McClintock, Anne, "Gender, Race, and Nationalism," in *Dangerous Liaisons,* McClintock et al., eds. (Minneapolis: University of Minnesota Press, 1997), 91.

19. Prakash, *Another Reason,* 218.

20. John Stuart Mill, *The Subjection of Women,* Wendell Robert Carr, ed. (Cambridge, MA: MIT Press, 1970), 34–36.

21. Elizabeth Barnes, *States of Sympathy: Seduction and Democracy in the American Novel* (New York: Columbia University Press, 1997), ix–x.

22. Barnes, 2; emphasis mine. She links this familial model of sympathy to the erasure of two specific kinds of difference. First, as a pedagogy of reading, American democratic sympathy employs a "method of affective representation that dissolves the boundaries between 'self' and 'other'"; as such, Barnes sees sympathy as a practice that "reinforces homogeneity" (4). Second, as a rhetorical strategy tied to an aesthetic of verisimilitude, sympathy, in order to be effective, is "dependent upon the author's ability to contract the distance, or, rather, to *obscure the difference,* between reality and representation, reader and character" (4). Although I am not able to pursue this connection further here, one could interrogate this specifically "American" sympathy, in its naturalization of family as state, as an oblique trace of a racial unconscious. Could the centrality of familial sympathy in America be a distorted image of how the system of slavery was founded on the relentless destruction of African and later African American community and kinship bonds? Such a line of questioning would also immediately transnationalize anything like an "American" identity. Keep in mind that British antislavery discourse, as it gathered pace in the late 1780s in anticipation of the parliamentary debates surrounding slave-trade abolition, sought to render spectacularly visible how slavery, in Hannah More's words, broke apart "the fond links of feeling Nature. . . . / The fibres twisting round a parent's heart, / Torn from their grasp, and bleeding as they part" (More, "Slavery, a Poem," qtd. in Ferguson, 151).

23. Henry Abelove notes that from 1681 to 1831 the population in England increased from 4.93 million to 13.28 million; by 1831, 8 percent of all births were illegitimate (about half of all first births were either illegitimate or prenuptial). He links this enormous increase in population and rise in sexual activity to new capitalist technologies and discourses of "production." He argues further that in the earlier part of the eighteenth century, "before the big rise in production and in the incidence of sexual intercourse so-called, was an era of relatively late marriage, low illegitimacy and prenuptial pregnancy rates, and relatively high rate of nonmarrying for women." Which does not mean that these men and women were not sexually active. "They practiced mutual masturbation, oral sex, anal sex, display and watching . . . , and much else besides, on a cross sex basis and in some now uncertain measure on a same-sex basis as well." See Henry Abelove, "Some Speculations on the History of 'Sexual Intercourse' During the 'Long Eighteenth century' in England," in *Nationalisms and Sexualities,* Andrew Parker, Mary Russo, Doris Sommer, and Patricia Yaeger, eds. (New York: Routledge, 1992), 336, 339–40.

Chapter Two

1. In *The Order of Things,* Foucault situates sympathy as a kind of integrative or assimilative epistemological technology, a dominant rhetorical device in the "Prose of the World." Sympathy plays freely through the universe, says Foucault; it exerts a power over things such that from a distance they are

drawn together. But that is not all. Sympathy displaces qualities of one thing onto or into another; it causes individuality to disappear, rendering foreign what was the same. "Sympathy transforms"—but always in the direction of identity. Put in a Lacanian register (which I think Foucault silently assimilates here) sympathy condenses and displaces difference. But always toward a homogeneous mass, "to the featureless form of the Same." Indeed, this power is so strong according to Foucault's account of premodern epistemology, that a countervailing force of antipathy is essential; antipathy preserves the "ferocious appetites [of beings] in opposition to all sympathy." These counterbalancing "twins" assure that things can both resemble other things and yet maintain their singularity. "The identity of things . . ." (23–25) "[a]nd yet the system is not closed." So Foucault starts his next section of *The Order of Things* ("Signatures," 25–30). This is a fascinating account of the rhetorical mode of sympathy in the premodern age. One danger, as Foucault senses I think in the negation, is precisely that it is closed. Another problem, it seems to me, is that for Foucault sympathy in its condensing and displacing function works unidirectionally, always toward identity, homogeneity, the Same. Hence his positing its structuralist twin antipathy. He doesn't pose the prior question: was sympathy ever that? When we come to consider the role of sympathy later in the eighteenth century, as it became a principle of bourgeois socialization, as it became the organizing principle of institutions of humanitarianism, as it became, that is, a discursive practice— it must be understood as a rhetorical mode (articulating both an integrative and repulsive force) and as a paradoxical mode of power (which both bridges inequalities and reinscribes them).

2. I find this parenthetical crucial in some ways. What if through sympathy a kind of premodern occultism, even mysticism, came to be adapted by modern modes of power? What if, in sympathy, a principle, at once nonrational, and nonsecular is operative, at least in terms of a certain haunting, and yet without being irrational or Christian? Toward the end of this chapter, I gesture toward a practice and history that offers other possibilities to these questions.

3. Consider the definition from Microsoft's *Bookshelf Dictionary:* sym-pa-thy, noun plural sym-pa-thies 1.a. A relationship or an affinity between people or things in which whatever affects one correspondingly affects the other. b. Mutual understanding or affection arising from this relationship or affinity. 2.a. The act or power of sharing the feelings of another. b. Often sympathies. A feeling or an expression of pity or sorrow for the distress of another; compassion or commiseration. See synonyms at pity. 3. Harmonious agreement; accord: He is in sympathy with their beliefs. 4. A feeling of loyalty; allegiance. Often used in the plural: His sympathies lie with his family. 5. Physiology. A relation between parts or organs by which a disease or disorder in one induces an effect in the other.

4. Aristotle, *Rhetoric,* W. Rhys Roberts, trans. (Chicago: Encyclopedia Britannica, 1978), 54 vols., Vol. 9, Book II, Chapter 8, 632.

5. Thomas McCarthy, *Relationships of Sympathy: The Writer and the Reader in British Romanticism* (Aldershot, UK: Scholar Press, 1997), 1.

6. Terry Eagleton, *The Ideology of the Aesthetic* (Cambridge, MA: Basil Blackwell, 1990), 31.

7. Eagleton, 32.

8. McCarthy, 2.

9. Keep in mind here that Roget's Thesaurus lists the following connotational chains for "artlessness": 1. artlessness, simplicity, simple-mindedness; 2. naïveté, ingenuousness, guilelessness, innocence; 3. inexperience, unworldliness; unaffectedness, unsophistication, naturalness, freedom from artifice, plainness; 4. sincerity, candor, frankness; 5. bluntness, matter-of-factness, outspokenness, veracity; 6. truth, honesty, probity; 7. uncivilized state, primitiveness, savagery; 8. darkness, barbarism, no science, no art, ignorance. This associational chain would be exploited strategically, and at times brilliantly, by writers taking up the "noble savage" mystique in critiques of European civilization—Montaigne's "Of Cannibals" is exemplary here.

10. Markman Ellis, *The Politics of Sensibility* (New York: Cambridge University Press, 1996), 7.

11. Ellis, 8.

12. As Eagleton reminds us, capitalist agriculture, at least in so far as wage labor and commodity production is concerned, was already operative in England as early as the sixteenth century—see *The Ideology of the Aesthetic* (Cambridge, MA: Basil Blackwell, 1990), 31.

13. Paul Langford, *A Polite and Commercial People: England 1727–1783* (New York: Oxford University Press, 1989), 461–518; qtd. in Ellis, 17.

14. McCarthy is drawing on the work of J. Engell here, see *The Creative Imagination: Enlightenment to Romanticism* (Cambridge, MA: Harvard University Press, 1981), 143–149.

15. Alexander Gerard, *Essay on Genius* (1774); qtd. in McCarthy, 2.

16. This was suggested to me by McCarthy's argument that sympathy can be understood as a "simultaneous exercising of the intellect and the emotions, an event most often depicted as the physical metaphor of reaching, rising or lifting oneself out of oneself and into the other's body and being" (3).

17. The passage reads: 31:13. If I have rejected the cause of my manservant or of my maidservant, when they brought a complain against me; 14. what then shall I do when God rises University Press? and when he makes inquiry, what shall I answer him? 15. Did not he that made me in the womb make him? and did not one fashion us in the womb? The verses continue thus: 16. If I have withheld anything that the poor desired, or have caused the eyes of the widow to fail, 17. or have eaten my morsel alone, and the fatherless has not eaten of it 18. (for from his youth I reared him as a father, and from his mother's womb I guided him); 19. if I have seen any one perish for lack of clothing, or a poor man without covering; 20. if his loins have not blessed me, and if he was not warmed with the fleece of my sheep; 21. if I have raised my hand against the fatherless, because I saw help in the gate; 22. then

let my shoulder blade fall from my shoulder, and let my arm be broken from its socket.

18. Rev. Samuel Stanhope Smith, *The Lectures, Corrected and Improved which have been delivered for a series of years, in the College of New Jersey; on the subject of Moral and Political Philosophy* (Trenton, NJ: 1812), 2 vols. vol. 1, 251–252.

19. McCarthy, 10.

20. Talal Asad, *Genealogies of Religion* (Baltimore, MD: Johns Hopkins University Press, 1994), 76–77.

21. Terry Eagleton, *The Ideology of the Aesthetic* (Cambridge, MA: Basil Blackwell, 1990), 13. For an important analysis on the relationship between sentimentalism and the body in early republican America see Bruce Burgett, *Sentimental Bodies: Sex, Gender, and Citizenship in the Early Republic* (Princeton, NJ: Princeton University Press, 1998), 1–23.

22. Eagleton, 13.

23. John Locke, *An Essay Concerning Human Understanding;* qtd. in Steven Bruhm, *Gothic Bodies: The Politics of Pain in Romantic Fiction* (Philadelphia: University of Pennsylvania Press, 1994), 2.

24. Bruhm, 3.

25. Bruhm, 5.

26. Burgett, 15.

27. For the crucial German contexts of the rise of aesthetics, see Eagleton, *The Ideology of the Aesthetic* (Cambridge, MA: Basil Blackwell, 1990), chapters 3–6.

28. Terry Castle, Explanatory Notes, in Ann Radcliffe, *The Mysteries of Udolpho,* Bonamy Dobrée, ed. (New York: Oxford University Press, 1998), 675.

29. Bruhm, xx; 1.

30. Bruhm, 11.

31. Albrecht von Haller, *An Essay on the Vital and other Involuntary Motions of Animals* (Edinburgh, 1758), 318–319; qtd. in Susan Bourgeois, *Nervous Juyces and the Feeling Heart: The Growth of Sensibility in the Novels of Tobias Smollett* (New York: Peter Lang, 1986), 2. Bourgeois's argument builds on the fact that Smollett was himself trained in the medical profession and published works on midwifery and the "external use of water" (14–15); see also Laqueur, 112.

32. We should note that for moral philosophers of the Scottish Enlightenment, such as David Hume, the physiological and the moral were by no means discrete realms of inquiry. In an abstract to *A Treatise of Human Nature* (1739), subtitled, "An attempt to introduce the experimental Method of Reasoning into Moral Subjects," Hume declared that he intended his theory of human nature "for a system of the sciences." See Bourgeois, 8.

33. See Michel Foucault, *Discipline and Punish,* Alan Sheridan, trans. (New York: Pantheon, 1979); Bruhm, 6.

34. Colin Jones and Roy Porter, Introduction, in *Reassessing Foucault* (New York: Routledge, 1994), 11; see also Foucault, *The Birth of the Clinic,* A. M. Sheri-

dan Smith, trans. (New York: Pantheon Books, 1973), *Madness and Civilization,* Richard Howard, trans. [1965] (New York: Vintage, 1988), and *History of Sexuality: An Introduction,* Robert Hurley, trans. (New York: Vintage, 1990); Catherine Gallagher and Thomas Laqueur, eds., *The Making of the Modern Body* (Berkeley: University of California Press, 1987) and Jennifer Terry and Jaqueline Urla, eds., *Deviant Bodies* (Bloomington: University of Indiana Press, 1995).

35. Extending this line of argumentation, Donzelot remarks that childhood underwent an educative reorganization during this period which was "centered on the spread of household medicine, that is, a set of knowledges and techniques designed to enable the bourgeois classes to rescue their children from the negative influence of servants and to place them under the parents' observation" (*The Policing of Families,* 16). He also notes that the other pole of this reorganization "aimed at the consolidation, under the label of 'social economy,' of all the forms of direction of the life of the poor, so as to diminish the social cost of their reproduction and obtain an optimum number of workers at minimum public expense: in short, what is customarily termed philanthropy." Indeed, medicine and the family enjoyed a very intimate relationship as a new dispensation around the body sought to close up the bourgeois family against negative influences (domestic servants, social promiscuities, etc.), while privileging medicine's alliance with the mother, "favoring the advancement of women by virtue of this recognition of their educative usefulness" (18). We will have occasion to return to this "educative usefulness" in the context of *Pamela* and *Jane Eyre.*

36. Christopher Lawrence, "The Nervous System and Society in the Scottish Enlightenment," in *Natural Order: Historical Studies of Scientific Culture,* B. Barnes and S. Shapin, eds. (London: Sage, 1979), 27; qtd. in Ellis, 19.

37. Bruhm, 11.

38. Robert Whytt, emphasis mine; qtd. in Bruhm, 11, 14.

39. Bruhm, 12. See John Mullan, *Sentiment and Sociability: The Language of Feeling in the Eighteenth Century* (Oxford: Clarendon Press, 1988); and Dorinda Outram, *The Body and the French Revolution: Sex, Class and Political Culture* (New Haven, CT: Yale University Press, 1989).

40. Bruhm, 14–15.

41. Thomas Laqueur, *Making Sex: Body and Gender from the Greeks to Freud* (Cambridge, MA: Harvard University Press, 1990), 149.

42. Mary Sheriff, "Fragonard's Erotic Mothers and the Politics of Reproduction," in *Eroticism and the Body Politic,* Lynn Hunt, ed. (Baltimore, MD: Johns Hopkins University Press, 1991), 22.

43. Donzelot, *The Policing of Families,* 20–21.

44. Randolph Trumbach, "Erotic Fantasy and Male Libertinism in Enlightenment England," in Lynn Hunt, ed., *The Invention of Pornography: Obscenity and the Origins of Modernity* (Cambridge, MA: MIT Press, 1993), 255–256.

45. Burgett, 16–17. See also Robyn Wiegman, *American Anatomies: Theorizing Race and Gender* (Durham, NC: Duke University Press, 1995); Londa

Schiebinger, *The Mind has no Sex?* (Cambridge, MA: Harvard University Press, 1989).

46. Laqueur, 196–197.
47. Laqueur, 196.
48. Laqueur, 200–201.
49. Qtd. in McCarthy, 3.
50. For an analysis of the twin economies of repression and incorporation, see J. Derrida, *The Gift of Death,* David Wills, trans. (Chicago: University of Chicago Press, 1995), 21.
51. Edmund Burke, *A Philosophic Enquiry into the Origin of Our Ideas of the Sublime and Beautiful,* James T. Boulton, ed. (Notre Dame, IN: University of Notre Dame Press, 1986), 113. My emphasis.
52. Such a suggestion requires that we move away from assigning aesthetics a merely supplementary role in the creation of material reality. Ian Hunter argues that the limits that have been established for aesthetics

> are those of a knowledge or practice of cultivation segregated from the driving forces of human development—labor and politics—and retarding further development by diverting culture into the ideal realm of ethics and taste. Given this specification, the way to transcend these limits is clear. The narrowly ethical practice of culture associated with aesthetics must be subsumed within culture as the whole way of life. Then it will be possible to actualize the promise of self-realization by harnessing aesthetics to the processes of economic and political development. ("Aesthetics and Cultural Studies," *Cultural Studies,* Lawrence Grossberg, Cary Nelson, and Paula Treichler, eds. [New York: Routledge, 1992], 348)

Thus, aesthetics has often been incorporated into a utopian-metaphysical narrative of ontological and epistemological self-completion, where the economic, the political, and the social spheres would operate by representing society as a domain in which humanity is alienated from its true being, or declared incomplete, through "objective analogues" of the aesthetic divisions: analogues such as the divisions between law and inclination, labor and self-actualization, dominating and dominated classes, utility and desire. One way to conceptualize aesthetics beyond this reduction, I think, is to consider critically Foucault's genealogy of ethical subjects. In these genealogies, Foucault sought to show how, through various "modes of subjection," "people are invited or incited to recognize their moral obligations" (Michel Foucault, "On the Genealogy of Ethics: An Overview of Work in Progress," *Michel Foucault: Beyond Structuralism and Hermeneutics,* Paul Rabinow and Hubert L. Dreyfus, eds. [Chicago: University of Chicago Press, 1983], 239).

53. Burke, 42–43.
54. Burke, 44–46. Burke also emphasizes the theatrical qualities of sympathy—the mise-en-scène of suffering or pleasure is indispensable to its functioning (he notes, for instance, the important role of sympathy in tragedy).

55. Burke, 45.
56. Bruhm, 33.
57. Bruhm, 34.
58. James T. Boulton, introduction to Edmund Burke, *A Philosophic Enquiry into the Origin of Our Ideas of the Sublime and Beautiful* (Notre Dame, IN: University of Notre Dame Press, 1986), xlvii.
59. Burke, 32.
60. Burke, 39–40.
61. Burke, 134.
62. Burke, 135–136.
63. Suleri, *The Rhetoric of English India* (Chicago: University of Chicago Press, 1992).
64. See Brantlinger, *Rule of Darkness.*
65. Sara Suleri, *The Rhetoric of English India* (Chicago: University of Chicago Press, 1992), 36.
66. Suleri, 37.
67. Suleri, 112.
68. Burke, 144. We would do well to recall Frantz Fanon here. Fanon's famous passage of a white girl fixing him with her horrified gaze is cited in Homi Bhabha's argument concerning stereotypes: "On one occasion a white girl fixes Fanon in look and word as she turns to identify with her mother. It is a scene which echoes endlessly through his essay, 'The Fact of Blackness': 'Look, a negro . . . Mamma, *see* the Negro! I'm frightened. Frightened.' 'What else could it be for me,' Fanon concludes, 'but an amputation, an excision, a hemorrhage that splattered my whole body with black blood'" (Bhabha, "The Other Question," 80).
69. As Young writes, aesthetics and race were increasingly to be intertwined throughout the nineteenth century: " . . . the cultural and class fix of the formulations of racial difference are particularly obvious in the aesthetic dimension that is so often emphasized in the distinctions between the races. It is telling that the physician Franz Joseph Gall, who invented the apparently irrefutable scientific tests of craniometry, nevertheless simply classified the races according to criteria of 'beauty' or 'ugliness.' Aesthetic characteristics are generally most evident in depictions of physical differences, in which African faces, contrived to resemble apes as much as possible, are contrasted to European faces (or types) that are illustrated by Greek sculpture, such as Apollo Belvedere" (Young, *Colonial Desire,* 96).
70. Qtd. in Bruhm, 37. See also Terry Castle's Explanatory Note to *The Mysteries of Udolpho,* 687.
71. Michel Foucault, *Discipline and Punish,* 136.
72. See Smith, quoted above; Foucault, *Discipline and Punish,* 137.
73. See Jeffrey Minson, *Genealogies of Morals* (New York: St. Martin's Press, 1985), 3–5.
74. Ellis, *The Politics of Sensibility,* 12.
75. Ellis, 15.

76. Mary Poovey, *A History of the Modern Fact: Problems of Knowledge in the Sciences of Wealth and Society* (Chicago: University of Chicago Press, 1998), 147. See also Ellis, 12.
77. On "tactics," see chapter one, note 5.
78. David Hume, *Inquiry Concerning The Principles of Morals,* Charles W. Hendel, ed. (New York: Liberal Arts Press, 1957).
79. Emmanuel Levinas writes, "We respond: in our relation with the other is it a matter of *letting be?* Is not the independence of the other accomplished in the role of being summoned? Is the one to whom one speaks understood from the first in his being? Not at all. The other is not an object of comprehension first and an interlocutor second. The two relations are intertwined. In other words the comprehension of the other is inseparable from his invocation" ("Is Ontology fundamental?" *Basic Philosophic Writings,* A. Peperzak, S. Critchley, R. Bernasconi, eds. [Bloomington: Indiana University Press, 1996], 6). This invocation of the other will be crucial for my reading of the work of sympathy, and I will return to Levinas in my conclusion.
80. *An Inquiry Into The Original Of Our Ideas Of Beauty And Virtue, In Two Treatises* [1738], *An Essay on the Nature and Conduct of the Passions and Affections* [1742], *A system of moral philosophy* [1755], *Thoughts on laughter ; and, Observations on The fable of the bees : in six letters* [1758]. As Bourgeois notes, Hutcheson's empiricism was a shift away from precursors such as the earl of Shaftesbury (4–6). Writing in *A system of moral philosophy,* he contended that a true system of morals "could not be the produce of genius and invention, or of the greatest precision of thought in metaphysical reasonings, but must be drawn from proper observations upon the several powers and principles which we are conscious of in our own bosoms, and which must be acknowledged to operate in some degree in the whole human species" (xiv; qtd. in Bourgeois, 6).
81. Francis Hutcheson, *Inquiry concerning Moral Good and Evil,* III.viii, qtd. in D. D. Raphael and A. L. Macfie, Introduction, in Adam Smith, *Theory of Moral Sentiment* (Indianapolis: Liberty Fund, 1984), 12.
82. Ellis, 13.
83. Hume *A Treatise of Human Nature,* L. A. Shelby-Rigge, ed. (Oxford: Clarendon Press, 1888), II: 386; qtd. in Bourgeois, 8.
84. Founding happiness and social order on "natural" sympathy would be one of the central projects of moral philosophic thought in the eighteenth century. Kames argues that " . . . for besides that [sympathy] is the great cement of human society, we ought to consider, that, as no state is exempt from misfortunes, mutual sympathy must greatly promote the security and happiness of mankind. And 'tis a much more comfortable situation, that the prosperity and preservation of each individual should be the care of the whole species . . ." (Henry Home Kames, *Essays on the Principles of Morality and Natural Religion* [1751] [New York: Garland, 1976], 16–17).
85. A certain logic of proximity is followed here. That sympathy diminishes as the distance from the self increases was in fact common to moral philoso-

phy. Kames, Ferguson, and Smith all deploy it at some point in their thought on the moral. And yet it is precisely in this space of distance that sympathetic representation would take hold. Kames, for instance, writes "The principal objects of man's love are his friends and relations. He has to spare for his neighbours. His affection lessens gradually in proportion to the distance of the object, 'till if vanish altogether. But were this the whole of human nature, with regard to benevolence, man would be but an abject creature. By a very happy contrivance, objects which, because of their distance, have little or no influence, are made by accumulation, and by being gathered together, in one general view, to have the very strongest effect; exceeding in many instances the most lively affection that is bestowed upon particular objects" (Henry Home Kames, *Essays on the Principles of Morality and Natural Religion* [1751] [New York: Garland, 1976], 84–85). The absolute other cannot be an (natural) object of sympathy, but simultaneously sympathy gathers the other together in this gap of difference, and so refashions the absolute other into a candidate for the benevolent relation. Another name for this gathering and refashioning would be propriation, and it is linked to specific modalities of power. This logic and this movement, I we shall see, will haunt abolitionist discourse.

86. Kames argues that sympathy, self-approbation and justice work naturally together. "Sympathy with our fellow-creatures is a principle implanted in the breast of every man: we cannot hurt another without suffering for it, which is an additional punishment. And we are still further punished for our injustice, or ingratitude, by incurring thereby the aversion and hatred of mankind" (68). We will return to this question of approbation below in our consideration of Adam Smith.

87. Propriation names that associational chain which links proper, propriety, property, and appropriation to the ethic of cleanliness. Spivak glosses Derrida's critique of the proper in this way: "The investigation and critique of the 'proper' has been a very large part of Derrida's work. His speculations have circled about the implications of the *proprius* and *propre*. Property as distinguishing predication and as self-possession; the proper as that which is so self-proximate that it is self-adequate or self-identical; the proper name, a genealogical mark, as the most intimate legal sign of this adequate predication, this self-proximity of self-possession. Why can we not do without these conceptual practices, these hierarchical judgements? What do they conceal, reveal, make (im)possible? . . . In French the *propre* is not merely proper but also clean. Derrida has written on the strange kinship between *propriété* (property, propriety) and *propreté* (cleanliness). . . . How do cleanliness and the sign 'connect'? . . . The language of philosophy professes to be 'clean'. It is also the shortest distance between truth and sign. No metaphoric detours to truth are allowed there. All adventitious material (empirical or exceptional, depending on the kind of philosophy you choose) must be excluded in order to build its route. This cleanliness is not only next to, but on the way to, the godliness of truth, a truth that is vouched for in the name of the

god that is its own cleanliness. . . . It is this obsessive 'cleanliness' or rigour that Derrida questions, and points here and there at how all projects of philosophical cleanliness must conceal their own befoulment, and, more important (though this point is far less often grasped), that cleanliness is constituted by varieties of befoulment which, being implicit in all originary concepts of cleanliness, are methodologically irreducible" (Spivak, "Speculations on reading Marx: after reading Derrida" in *Poststructuralism and the Question of History*, 46–47). Also see Jacques Derrida, *Given Time*, Peggy Kamuf, trans. (Chicago: University of Chicago Press, 1992), 22.

88. Amy Louise Erickson, *Women and Property in Early Modern England* (New York: Routledge, 1993), 4.

89. I am drawing on Jacques Derrida's notion and application of "textuality." In the Afterword to *Limited Inc*, Derrida writes, "One of the definitions of what is called deconstruction would be the effort to take this limitless context, and thus to an incessant movement of recontextualization. The phrase which for some has become a sort of slogan, in general so badly understood, of deconstruction ('there is nothing outside the text' [*il n'y a pas de hors-texte*]), means nothing else: there is nothing outside context" (136). And: "I wanted to recall that the concept of text . . . is limited neither to the graphic, nor to the book, nor even to discourse, and even less to the semantic, representational, symbolic, ideal, or ideological sphere. What I call 'text' implies all the structures called 'real', 'economic', 'historical', socio-institutional, in short: all possible referents. Another way of recalling once again that 'there is nothing outside the text'" (Afterword, *Limited Inc*, Samuel Weber, trans. [Evanston: Northwestern University Press, 1988], 148). The strategic exclusion of these referents, in philosophic discourses that dissimulate their own impurity and so their own violence, haunt the text (narrowly construed). By opening the ear to this more general textuality I hope to open myself to this haunting.

90. Quoted Ellis, 53; also qtd. in Carretta, Explanatory Notes, in Cugoano, *Thoughts and Sentiments on the Evil of Slavery*, Vincent Carretta, ed. (New York: Penguin, 1999), 178–179. Carretta reminds us that Hume was also critical of slavery at least in "ancient times"—see Hume's "Of Populousness of Ancient Nations," in *Political Discourses*. As Ellis notes, "Of National Characters" is a "significant representation of Hume's position on the relation between humanity, the environment and differing characters of nations"; the footnote was apparently added in response to Montesquieu's *Esprit des Lois* (1748), 52.

91. "One law, and one manner shall be for you, and for the stranger that sojourneth with you; and therefore, all things whatsoever ye would that men should do to you, do ye even so to them."

92. Cugoano, *Thoughts and Sentiments on the Evil of Slavery*, Vincent Carretta, ed. (New York: Penguin, 1999), 88–89.

93. Smith and Hume were close friends. From 1752 to 1776, there are 40 letters extant from Hume to Smith; and from 1763 to 1766, 15 letters from Smith to Hume (see Bourgeois, 10).

94. Bourgeois, 11.
95. Markman Ellis, *The Politics of Sensibility: Race, Gender and Commerce in the Sentimental Novel* (New York: Cambridge University Press, 1996), 107.
96. Randolph Trumbach, "Erotic Fantasy and Male Libertinism in Enlightenment England," 255–256.
97. And if the familial bond is a result of "natural habituation," its absence is monstrous: "A parent without parental tenderness, a child devoid of all filial reverence, appear monsters, the objects, not of hatred only, but of terror" (220). Of course, this is no sublime terror, but that which is intolerable, that which cannot withstand reason and investigation (Radcliffe would term it horror). We will return to this figure of the terrifying monstrosity of the affection-less parent when we turn to missionary discourses on Hinduism.
98. Smith explicitly draws on Kames's moral theory here (he refers to him as "an author of very great and original genius"; Kames had also been largely responsible for Smith's Glasgow appointment to the Chair of Moral Philosophy in 1752). Kames had argued that humans have a "strong Attachment" to "Objects of Distress" (1).
99. But we should remember that the word identification nowhere occurs either in Hume or Smith in relation to sympathy; the connection would be a nineteenth-century achievement whose conditions of possibility I suggest are to be found in the political and discursive imbrications of eighteenth-century moral philosophy.
100. By "ethical implications," I am stressing the relationship between representation and ethics. As soon as something can hide behind the onto-theological enigma of "nature" the responsibility of situating that something seems to disappear. Of course, Smith's distinction between natural and secondary representations was central to eighteenth-century moral philosophy. And the distinction would always turn on the body. Consider this passage from Adam Ferguson's *Institutes of Moral Philosophy* (1773) (New York: Garland Publishing, 1978): "Language, in the most general sense, comprehends all the external signs of thought, sentiment, or will. Signs are, either original, or conventional. Original signs are such as men are led by instinct to employ, and to interpret. Such are, tones of the voice, change of features, and gestures. Conventional signs are such as men have agreed upon, or rendered customary" (43–44). As we shall see, Smith's text leaves open the fissure between origin and convention, which could be the starting point for another reading of this tradition.
101. And again: "He . . . appears to deserve reward, who to some person or persons, is the natural object of a gratitude which every human heart is disposed to beat time to, and thereby applaud" (69).
102. Emmanuel Levinas, "Transcendence and Height," in *Basic Philosophic Writings,* A. Peperzak, S. Critchley, R. Bernasconi, eds. (Bloomington: Indiana University Press, 1996), 12. Glossing Levinas's complex relation to violence, otherness, and the "spiritual life," Hent de Vries has recently argued that whenever the self and the other are related to each other, "not as totally other

(as they should be), but as alter egos, as each other's mirror images, each other's negations or, what amounts to the same thing, each other's (rational or irrational, diffuse or anonymous and neutral) totality. Wherever the self relates the other to the sameness of its own horizon, the other's singularity will be effaced. But conversely, wherever the self is overtaken or absorbed by the other . . . violence has taken place" ("Violence and Testimony: On Sacrificing Sacrifice," in *Violence, Identity, and Self-Determination,* Hent de Vries and S. Weber, eds. [Palo Alto: Stanford University Press, 1997], 15). It is the structure of this complex violence that I am charting here.

103. This is a connection that is central to Kames also: For him, there is no moral action that is not beautiful, pleasurable, and useful. See Kames, *Essays on the Principles of Morality and Natural Religion* (New York: Garland, 1976), 44, 50, 88.

104. This figure would reappear in Immanuel Kant's *Reflections on Anthropology* (1799) as *der Unpartheyische Zuschauer*—see Rafael and Macfie, 31.

105. Motives are fourfold for Smith. As Bourgeois notes, Smith "divides proper motive into four classes of sentiments. We can give our approval to sentiment through sympathy with the motives of the agent of an action; through entering into the gratitude of those who receive the benefit of an action; through observing conduct which has been agreeable to the general rules by which the first two sentiments, sympathy with motive and gratitude, generally act; or through considering an action as part of a system of behavior which promotes the happiness of either the individual or of society" (11).

106. Much could be said about this mirror relation that Smith posits as the condition for subject formation. Of course, the proleptic identification with the mirror-other (which implies an irreducible spacing and lag) has been most rigorously elaborated in the field of Lacanian psychoanalysis. See Jacques Lacan, *The Four Fundamental Concepts of Psycho-Analysis,* Alan Sheridan, trans. (New York: Norton, 1981); Samuel Weber, *Return to Freud,* Michael Levine, trans. (New York: Cambridge University Press, 1991); Homi Bhabha, "Of Mimicry and Man: The Ambivalence of Colonial Discourse," *The Location of Culture* (New York: Routledge, 1994), 85–92; *Reading Seminar XI,* Richard Feldstein, Bruce Fink, and Maire Jaanus, eds. (New York: SUNY Press, 1995); Henrietta Moore, "Gendered Persons: Dialogues between Anthropology and Psychoanalysis," *Anthropology and Psychoanalysis: An Encounter through Culture,* Suzette Heald and Ariane Deluz, eds. (New York: Routledge, 1994), 131–152. My reading is parasitic on this complex literature.

107. Derrida, and perhaps we can hear Levinas through him, reminds us that to locate duty within the semantic horizon of propriation, of the calculable, of the knowable, is already to reduce the absolute uniqueness of the other as other, to master the risk that duty entails: "Duty or responsibility binds me to the other, to the other as other, and ties me in my absolute singularity to the other as other. God is the name of the absolute other as other and as unique. . . . As soon as I enter into a relation with the absolute other, my ab-

solute singularity enters in relation with his on the level of obligation and duty. I am responsible to the other as other, I answer to him and I answer for what I do before him. But of course, what binds me thus in my singularity to the absolute singularity of the other, immediately propels me into the space or risk of absolute sacrifice" (*The Gift of Death,* David Willis, trans. [Chicago: University of Chicago Press, 1995], 68; see also Afterword, *Limited Inc,* 116, 122, 148).

108. Michel Foucault, "On the Genealogy of Ethics: An Overview of Work in Progress," in *Michel Foucault: Beyond Structuralism and Hermeneutics,* Paul Rabinow and Hubert L. Dreyfus, eds. (Chicago: University of Chicago Press, 1983), 239. This is much more explicitly articulated in Kames's text: " . . . by [our moral sense] we perceive some actions under the modification of being *fit, right,* and *meet* to be done, and others under the modification of being unfit, unmeet, and wrong. When this observation is applied to particulars, it is an evident fact, that we have a sense of *fitness* in kindly and beneficent actions. We approve of ourselves and others for performing actions of this kind . . . What is here asserted, is a matter of fact, which can admit of no other proof than an appeal to every man's own feelings" (59). Note that this "fitness" of sympathetic actions is another form of what I have been marking as a logic of propriation in moral philosophy. Later in the text, Kames attributes this sense of dis/approbation to something he calls our "conscience"—Smith takes this much further.

109. Foucault, *Discipline and Punish,* 160.

110. Haskell, "Capitalism and Humanitarian Sensibility, 1," in *The Antislavery Debate,* Thomas Bender, ed. (Berkeley: University of California Press, 1992), 111.

111. I am adapting Haskell's formulation here—see Haskell, 129. This argument should not be taken to mean that Smith in any simple way articulated his theory of sympathy as a kind of ideological prelude to his free-trade economic theory in *Wealth of Nations.* Indeed, in that later text, he argues that humanitarianism has nothing to do with market relations: "It is not from the benevolence of the butcher, the brewer, or the baker that we expect our dinner, but from their regard to their own interest. We address ourselves, not to their humanity but to their self-love, and never talk to them of our own necessities but of their advantages" (13). What I am arguing is that sympathy, in its temporality and in its relationship to virtue, interest, and difference was quite in keeping with a consideration of "self-interest." As we shall see in subsequent chapters, humanitarian struggles were fought precisely on this double terrain: justice and policy.

112. Poovey also marks this genealogical link—see *A History of the Modern Fact,* 147–148.

113. Derrida, *Given Time,* 23.

114. All throughout his *Essays on the Principles of Morality and Natural Religion,* Kames insistently differentiates social passions and civilization from solitary passions and savagery. Throughout history, and around the globe. "The

laws, which govern sociable creatures, differ widely from those which govern
the savage and solitary. Nothing more natural nor more orderly among solitary creatures, who have no mutual connection, than to make food one of
another" (39); "Remove those principles of action which operate by reflection, and whose objects are complex and general ideas, and the necessary
consequences will be, to double the force of the appetites and passions,
pointing at particular objects; which is always the case with those who act by
sense, and not by reflection. They are tyrannised by passion and appetite,
and have no consistent rule of conduct. No wonder, that the moral sense is
of no sufficient authority to command obedience in such a case. This is the
character of savages. . . . Even the greatest savages [are not] destitute of the
moral sense. Their defect rather lies in the weakness of their general principles of action, which terminate in objects too complex for savages readily to
comprehend. This defect is remedied by education and reflection; and then
it is, that the moral sense, in concert with these general principles, acquires
its full authority, which is openly recognised, and chearfully submitted to"
(142); "And when we run over the history of man, it will be found to hold
true in fact, that savages, who are most possest with the opinion of evil spirits, have, of all people, the least idea of a Deity; and, that as all civilized nations, without exception, entertain the firm belief of a Deity, so the dread of
evil spirits wears out in every nation, in proportion to their gradual advances
in social intercourse" (347). The historical refinements in the nature of man
(mark the paradox) by "culture and education" (143) eventually produce the
most delicate feelings even in savages (a word whose function would be filled
later in the text by "infants and rusticks" [280]). Let us simply note that an
entire program of discipline for a certain European bourgeois subjectivity is
legible in this problematic.

115. I am aware that the twentieth-century connotations of race do not strictly
apply to Smith's thought; the word, in fact appears no where in his text. In
her *History of the Modern Fact,* Poovey goes to some length to repudiate this
kind of historical blurring (22–23). I believe, on the contrary, the risks are
too great not at least to attempt to make these connections. I will insist on
this odd word, "race," understanding it as a discourse that would comprehend but never totalize the complex history of "family," "culture," "nation,"
"civilization," and "character." See Robert Young, *Colonial Desire* (New York:
Routledge, 1995); George Stocking, *Victorian Anthropology* (New York: Free
Press, 1987); Raymond Williams, *Marxism and Literature* (New York: Oxford University Press, 1985); Anne McClintock, *Imperial Leather* (New
York: Routledge, 1995); Paul Gilroy, *The Black Atlantic.* I will return to this
argument in subsequent chapters.

116. Equiano, *The Interesting Narrative of the Life of Olaudah Equiano, or Gustavus Vassa, the African, Written by Himself,* Vincent Carretta, ed. (New York:
Penguin, 1995), 45. Equiano is quoting from Acts 27:26.

117. Of course, as I pointed out above, reason was itself a problem for moral philosophy. Both Hume and Smith, for instance, argue that reason is not equal

to the task of founding a moral ontology, other sensibilities—a naturally sympathetic one, for instance—would be necessary. This problematization of reason is itself part of the rationality I am mapping here.

118. Why is the limited agency of the object of sympathy not a concern for eighteenth-century moral philosophy? My sense is that the other of sympathy (the object in this case) is not a concern for these thinkers because one of the chief imperatives of moral philosophy at this time was to render the other (and otherness more generally) an attribute of the self through that economy of propriation I analyzed above.

119. Again, to return to a point I made earlier, it is clear that these aporias did not function as self-conscious problems in the discourse of moral philosophy. In this I agree with Poovey. But to demarcate the conditions of (im)possibility of this discourse and its various practices is to open my analysis of sympathy to another history. It is this opening of the other in the history of sympathy that calls me to think at the limits of the episteme. Thought may fail us, but let us not fail (again) to hear the call.

120. Which does not mean that this representation of sympathy is an "epistemological unit." This is Mary Poovey's term. See her *A History of the Modern Fact* (Chicago: University of Chicago Press, 1998), xiii, 9. As she explains about "facts": "In the seventeenth and early eighteenth centuries, natural philosophy was only one in an ensemble of knowledge-producing practices, and what I am calling the modern fact was only one of the available epistemological units called 'a fact.' . . . To designate the epistemological unit whose history I am discussing 'the modern fact' is not to deny the historical existence of this natural historical variant of the fact or its importance in the seventeenth and early eighteenth centuries" (9). It seems to me that the sympathetic representation functions as not only one among other "epistemological units," but rather problematizes epistemology itself. Which is why its history and procedure is marked by crucial aporias.

121. Of course, slave narratives and the broader discourse of abolition was thoroughly enmeshed in the system of relations that sympathy superintends. In other words, the complicity between, say, Equiano's demand for justice and sympathy and the project of European civilizing is irreducible if also fraught. This complicity is legible in all counter-strategies of sympathy. What I am suggesting, however, is that to break this circuit the absolute alterity of the suffering object must be the starting point for another practice of sociality beyond propriation. It is this practice of sociality that I would want to name solidarity.

122. Which does not mean, of course, that Levinas is not aware of this history—in one sense, it names his entire philosophical enterprise. See Hent de Vries, "Violence and Testimony: On Sacrificing Sacrifice," in *Violence, Identity, and Self-Determination,* Hent de Vries and S. Weber, eds. (Palo Alto: Stanford University Press, 1997), 16–17.

123. Solidarity [ad. Fr. *solidarité,* f. solidaire, solid: see solidary a.]: 1. a. The fact or quality, on the part of communities, etc., *of being perfectly united or at one in*

some respect, esp. in interests, sympathies, or aspirations; spec. with reference to the aspirations or actions of trade-union members. b. Const. of (mankind, a race, etc.). c. Const. between or with (others). 2. Community or perfect coincidence of (or between) interests. 3. Civil Law. *A form of obligation involving joint and several responsibilities or rights* (*Oxford English Dictionary;* emphasis mine). According to the *Oxford English Dictionary,* the term solidarity entered the English language around 1841, most probably through the developing discourse of trade union organizing and Chartist agitation. The French adjective *solidaire* usually means "binding on several; jointly and separately liable; interdependent, bound up with" (*Cassell's French Dictionary*). Lynn Hunt notes how the linkage between solidarity, fraternity, and equality changed throughout the course of the French Revolution; she remarks that fraternity "was an idea associated with political solidarities and the drawing of political and social boundaries within the community." From early associations of the term fraternity could mean solidarity with almost anyone who would participate in the community. After the radical years of 1792–1794, "fraternity was used more often in a narrow and fearful sense; fraternity defined a kind of 'us' and them of revolutionary politics" (*The Family Romance of the French Revolution,* 12–13). Also writing from the French context (but with implication far beyond France), Jacques Donzelot notes that it was after the civil war of 1848 that the republic develops a discourse of solidarity to legitimate social legislation and economic intervention. Solidarity, in other words, was a modality for the rational mobilization of society: Solidarity enabled the organization of sociality through the criterion of similarities of social and professional conditions (e.g., trade unionism); by privileging the principle of the interdependence of individuals, social solidarity also is that principle which enables the state to intervene more forcefully, more dynamically into the sphere of "natural associations" (i.e., the family). "It is in the name of social solidarity that the republican state develops its social legislation and, subsequently, its economic intervention. The concept of solidarity makes it possible to arrive at a situation where the state itself is no longer at stake in social relations, but stands outside them and becomes their guarantor of progress" (Jacques Donzelot, "The Mobilization of Society," in *The Foucault Effect,* Graham Burchell, Colin Gordon, and Peter Miller, eds., [Chicago: University of Chicago Press, 1991], 173). Affirming the contradictions, divergent lines of force and resistance in this history, it seems to me, is absolutely indispensable if we are to think anew the complicities and ruptures in forms of sociality that are both tied to propriation and to justice. This will be the basis for my next set of researches into modern forms of sociality—a history of solidarity as at once a strategy of cohesion, a form of resistance, and the practice of a non-propriative relationship to a struggling, living other.

Chapter Three

1. Michel Foucault, "Governmentality," Colin Gordon, trans., in *The Foucault Effect,* Graham Burchell, Colin Gordon, and Peter Miller, eds. (Chicago: Uni-

versity of Chicago Press, 1991), 87–104. I have been guided here by Gayan Prakash's suggestive work on science and governmentality in colonial India. In *Another Reason,* Prakash argues that Foucault's "concept of governmentality illuminates the processes at work in the formulation of disciplines directed at preserving life and governing bodily conduct" (124). But consistent with his rigorous critique of the myth of Western self-fashioning, Prakash insists that "Colonial governmentality . . . could not be the tropicalization of its Western form, but rather was its fundamental dislocation" (125).

2. For "contrapuntal" reading strategies, see Edward Said's *Culture and Imperialism* and Jean and John Comaroff's *Of Revelation and Revolution.*

3. Roland Barthes, *S/Z,* Richard Howard, trans. (New York: Hill and Wang, 1974), 12.

4. Markman Ellis, *The Politics of Sensibility* (New York: Cambridge University Press, 1996), 2. Ellis goes on to argue that the sentimental novel was widely recognized as an "innovative, even radical, event in literary history." Although the new audiences of the sentimental novel thought of novel reading as a pursuit of leisure that did not require "extensive intellection or education," this same audience, disenfranchised and lacking power in political life, created a new political role for literature (3).

5. Mary Poovey, *A History of the Modern Fact: Problems of Knowledge in the Sciences of Wealth and Society* (Chicago: University of Chicago Press, 1998), 152.

6. See Samuel Richardson, *Pamela,* 2 vols. (New York: Dutton, 1962), II: 136, 255, 461.

7. Ferguson, *Subject to Others,* 92.

8. Watt, *The Rise of the Novel* (Berkeley: University of California Press, 1957), 19–21.

9. Firdous Azim, *The Colonial Rise of the Novel* (New York: Routledge, 1993), 15–33.

10. In the French context, Lynn Hunt argues that the novel was the most influential source for new attitudes about both fathers and children. Linking these shifts to changing ideas of the family, she argues, "The rise of the novel and the emergence of interest in children and a more affective family went hand in hand. It is in fact impossible to tell which—the novel of the child-centered family—was cause and which effect. As sensibility and individual subjectivity, even for children, came to be more and more emphasized, the role of the father was bound to change. A stern, repressive father was incompatible with the new model of the family as emotional center for the nurturing of children and the new model of the individual as an autonomous self" (*The Family Romance of the French Revolution,* 21).

11. Catherine Gallagher, *Nobody's Story: The Vanishing Acts of Women in the Marketplace, 1670–1820* (Berkeley: University of California Press, 1994), 166. See also John Mullen, *Sentiment and Sociability: The Language of Feeling in the Eighteenth Century* (New York: Oxford University Press, 1988); Janet Todd, *Sensibility: An Introduction* (New York: Methuen, 1986); Fred Kaplan, *Sacred Tears: Sentimentality in Victorian Literature* (Princeton, NJ: Princeton

University Press, 1987); David Marshall, *The Surprising Effects of Sympathy: Marivaux, Diderot, Rousseau, and Mary Shelley* (Chicago: University of Chicago Press, 1987).

12. McCarthy, 24.
13. Bruhm, 3.
14. Ellis, 16.
15. G. A. Starr, "Sentimental Novels of the Later Eighteenth Century," in *The Columbia History of the British Novel,* J. Richetti, J. Bender, D. David, and M. Seidel, eds. (New York: Columbia University Press, 1994), 181.
16. Starr, 183–184; I pursue the Christian contexts of sympathy below.
17. As Ellis notes, the "Latitudinarians maintained that the foundation of morals was in revelation rather than reason. Dwelling on the moral constitution of men, they stressed the necessity and blessedness of being righteous, and promoted the religious value of human works that increased justice, love and mercy" (14).
18. Starr, 187.
19. Starr, 189–190.
20. Hayden White, "The Value of Narrativity in the Representation of Reality," in *On Narrative,* W. J. T. Mitchell, ed. (Chicago: University of Chicago Press, 1980), 1. White also notes that the etymological root of narrative is the Sanskrit word *gna,* to know.
21. Chatman, "What Novels Can do that Films Can't," in *On Narrative,* W. J. T. Mitchell, ed. (Chicago: University of Chicago Press, 1980), 118.
22. Ellis, 72.
23. Barnes, 8; see also David Brion Davis, "Reflections on Abolitionism and Ideological Hegemony," in *The Antislavery Debate,* Thomas Bender, ed. (Berkeley: University of California Press, 1992), 178–179.
24. See Ferguson, 147.
25. Ellis, 24.
26. Anonymous reviewer in *Critical Reviewer* [February 1789], 237; qtd. in Ferguson, 163.
27. Nancy Armstrong, *Desire and Domestic Fiction: A Political History of the Novel* (New York: Oxford University Press, 1987), 3.
28. See Armstrong, 21. I am aware that I may be overstating Armstrong's position in order to make this point. But I think my argument is indicative of a certain theoretical ambivalence in Armstrong's own text. To be absolutely clear, in arguing that gender not sex is central to the constitution of the modern subject I am suggesting that a complex and mobile gender subordination is central to the project of modernity itself.
29. See Barnes, 13.
30. Ellis, 86.
31. See Ferguson, 242–245. As Karen Sanchez-Eppler notes for the American context, "In feminist writings the metaphoric linking of women and slaves proves ubiquitous: marriage and property laws, the conventional adoption of husband's name, or even the length of fashionable skirts are explained and de-

cried by reference to women's 'slavery.' This strategy emphasizes the restrictions of women's sphere, and despite luxuries and social civilities, classes the bourgeois woman among the oppressed" (*Touching Liberty: Abolition, Feminism and the Politics of the Body* [Berkeley: University of California Press, 1993], 3).

32. I am aware that the repetition of such "terrible spectacles" in my own work, "[r]ather than inciting indignation" could "inure us to pain by virtue of their familiarity" (for a crucial intervention in this dehumanizing circuit of specularity see Saidiya V. Hartman, *Scenes of Subjection: Terror, Slavery, and Self-Making* [New York: Oxford University Press, 1997], 3). My sense of the ethical stakes in the analyses of such scenes is twofold. First, one must acknowledge a certain irreducible complicity in the spectacle. The examples of tortured bodies that recur throughout *Rule of Sympathy* are enabled by discourses that are invested in certain contexts of domination and injustice. I cannot disavow in any simple way my own specific participation in these contexts even as I wish to transform them. Second, it brings to mind (again) the necessity for a persistent critique, a kind of inventory of infinite traces, in the ethical relations of one's own discourse, one's own desire. This is something that I negotiate throughout this study in a series of parasitic, supplementary footnotes. But finally if the affirmation of complicity and the inventory of infinity have any effectivity at all it will be indexed in the openings and possibilities left to the other, to the other reader.

33. Frederick Douglass, *Narrative of the Life of Frederick Douglass, an American Slave*, Houston A. Baker, Jr., ed. (New York: Penguin, 1986), 50–51.

34. Hartman, 3. See also Jenny Sharpe's brilliant "'Something Akin to Freedom': The Case of Mary Prince," in *differences*, 1996 (8:1), 31–55.

35. What came first, abolitionism or Gothic? If we go by timelines, the answer is clear (the Gothic), but in fact if we consider the movement of memory, commodities, history, language, and, of course, bodies for (unpaid) labor, the tales of usurpation and tyranny that obsessed England from around 1760 to 1820, a period of intense abolitionist agitation not to mention four revolutions (French, American, Haitian, and the "revolution" in British Bengal), the problem becomes rather more complex. To me it seems impossible today to try to understand the political and cultural contexts of the gothic movement without reference to the European enslavement, rape, and brutalization of millions of African men and women and the struggles to end slavery, and without understanding the displacement of this horrific history in missionary-colonial discourses.

36. Bruhm, 3.

37. Bruhm, 3–4.

38. Walpole to William Cole, 9 March, 1765; qtd. in E. J. Clery, Introduction, in Horace Walpole, *The Castle of Otranto, A Gothic Story*, W. S. Lewis, ed. (New York: Oxford University Press, 1996), vii.

39. Clery, xii. As Clery notes, when Walpole declared in his second Preface to *Otranto* that the "great resources of fancy have been dammed up, by a strict adherence to common life," he seems to have had the run of the mill sentimental

novel in mind (specifically Richardson's *Pamela* and *Clarissa*). And so "a god, at least a ghost, was absolutely necessary to frighten us out of too much senses" (letter to Hertford, March 18, 1765; qtd. in Clery, xiii).

40. Clery, ix.

41. Matthew C. Brennan, *The Gothic Psyche* (Columbia, SC: Camden House, 1997), 1.

42. Thus, when Clery remarks that the "frequent use of southern European settings in gothic fiction is generally attributed to a mixture of Protestant prejudice and a stereotyped notion of strong Mediterranean passions" (*Castle of Otranto,* note for pg. 5, 116), perhaps what is being forgotten is that the "southern passions" of the Gothic is also tied to the history of Muslim stereotypes. How can we make sense of Theodore's forced sojourn in Algiers in *Otranto* (84) without a sense of this genealogy?

43. It is no accident, therefore, that Freud's "The Uncanny" is the psychoanalytic text of choice for Gothic critics. That it has also exerted such a profound impact on colonial discourse analysis should cause us to pause over the possible connections between Gothicism and colonialism. See "'The 'Uncanny,'" in *Collected Papers,* Joan Riviere, ed. and trans. (New York: Basic Books, 1959), 5 vols., 4:368–407.

44. Brennan, 1–2.

45. Norman Bryson, *Tradition and Desire from David to Delacroix* (New York: Cambridge University Press, 1987), 205; qtd. in Steven Bruhm, *Gothic Bodies: The Politics of Pain in Romantic Fiction* (Philadelphia: University of Pennsylvania Press, 1994), xiv.

46. Clery writes, "The concept of romance as social allegory made the literature of the past at once comprehensible and palatable for the enlightened reader. It followed that eighteenth-century society must have its own characteristic style of literary production and, given that this society is peaceful, commercial, civilized, well ordered, it ought to produce nothing but 'polite' literature. From this historicist perspective, Walpole's airy proposal to combine ancient and modern romance is not only monstrous, but transgressive. . . . *Otranto* and other pioneering gothic romances tended to generate anxiety and provoke denunciation from the critics because they implied that there must be something awry in the contemporary social order itself. A gothic revival in literature disturbed the comfortable vision of historical progress" (xxv).

47. Edward Young, *Conjectures on Original Composition;* qtd. in Brennan, 2.

48. Terry Castle, Explanatory Notes, in Ann Radcliffe, *The Mysteries of Udolpho,* Bonamy Dobrée, ed. (New York: Oxford University Press, 1998), 675.

49. Bruhm xx; 1.

50. E. J. Clery, Introduction, in Horace Walpole, *The Castle of Otranto, A Gothic Story,* W. S. Lewis, ed. (New York: Oxford University Press, 1996), ix.

51. George Haggerty, "The Gothic Novel, 1764–1824," *The Columbia History of the British Novel,* John Richetti, ed. (New York: Columbia University Press, 1994), 221.

52. Clery, xxxi–xxxii.

53. Haggerty 223, 231. Haggerty quotes part of this famous passage from *Otranto* (New York: Oxford University Press, 1998): "The lower part of the castle was hollowed into several intricate cloisters; and it was not easy for one under so much anxiety to find the door that opened into the cavern. An awful silence reigned throughout those subterraneous regions, except now and then some blasts of wind that shook the doors she had passed, and which grating on the rusty hinges were re-echoed through that long labyrinth of darkness. Every murmur struck her with new terror;—yet more she dreaded to hear the wrathful voice of Manfred urging his domestics to pursue her" (27). Such typical Gothic passages give force to the interpretation that what is at stake in the Gothic is "the spectral presence of a dead-undead mother, archaic and all-encompassing, a ghost signifying the problematics of femininity which the heroine must confront" (Claire Kahane, "The Gothic Mirror," in *The (M)other Tongue: Essays in Feminist Psychoanalytic Interpretation;* qtd. in Haggerty, 226). See also Clery, xv.
54. Clery, xvii–xviii.
55. See the groundbreaking essays collected in *The Female Gothic,* Juliann E. Fleenor, ed. (Montreal: Eden Press, 1983).
56. Peter Sabor, ed., *Horace Walpole: The Critical Heritage,* 81–82; qtd. in Clery, xxiv. This last point should remind us that the Gothic novel shared many of the anxieties and a large part of the discursive terrain with the novel of sensibility. Thus, although Walpole abhors Richardson's novels, his own is replete with figures of pathos and scenes that excite pity. See, for instance, Walpole, *Castle of Otranto,* 10, 15.
57. One of the most influential figures in the early abolitionist movement, Anthony Benezet was born at St. Quintin, in France, in 1713. His family fled religious persecution following the revocation of the edict of Nantes, spending some years in London (1715–1731), and finally settling in Philadelphia. An evangelical Quaker and fervid pacifist, Benezet spent most of his life teaching children of both European and African descent. See Anon, "Memoirs of Anthony Benezet," in *Park's Travels in Africa* (London, 1816), 29–33.
58. Jean Camaroff and John Camaroff, *Of Revelation and Revolution: Christianity, Colonialism and Consciousness in South Africa,* 2 vols. (Chicago: University of Chicago Press, 1991), 1, 93.
59. Alexander Duff, "Explanatory Statement Addressed to the friends of the India Mission of the Church of Scotland, as it Existed Previous to the Disruption in May 1843" (Edinburgh: John Johnstone, 1844), 5. This statement was written at a moment when the Church of Scotland was fracturing over doctrinal and practical issues. For Duff, sympathy for the benighted other harbors the hope of fusing antipathetic elements within the Church of Scotland; sympathy for the missionary endeavor, in other words, could bind together what would otherwise be implacable enemies in a common humanity, a common imperial citizenship.

60. Samuel Richardson, *Pamela*, 2 vols. (New York: Dutton, 1962). The language of barbarism in consistently linked to aristocratic men like B; see, for instance, II: 180, 458.

61. Foucault, "The Politics of Health in the Eighteenth Century," in *Power/Knowledge,* 170.

62. Donzelot, *The Policing of Families,* 6.

63. Ainslie Thomas Embree, *Charles Grant and British Rule in India* (New York: Columbia University Press, 1962), 247.

64. This was a hugely influential tract, which after the 1813 charter debates, gained even greater prominence because of the fact that Wilberforce quoted it in his speech on the evangelization of India, and urged others to read it.

65. Embree, 247.

66. Charles Grant to Lord William Bentinck, April 17, 1807; qtd. in Embree, 247.

67. Equiano, *The Interesting Narrative of the Life of Olaudah Equiano, or Gustavus Vassa, the African, Written by Himself* (Halifax, 1814).

68. James Walvin, *Black Ivory* (Washington, DC: Howard University Press, 1992), 27; the region was tropical rain country, and criss-crossed by trade routes, one of them leading south by foot, and then, by the River Ase, on to the major slave-trading region of the coast. The economy was agricultural, using both male and female labor.

69. Equiano, *Interesting Narrative,* 234.

70. Ellis, 55.

71. Charlotte Brontë, *Jane Eyre* (New York: Norton, 1987), 369.

72. Interestingly, it seems Brontë here puts the reader in the position of Smith's impartial spectator. Recall that in the last chapter, I had noted that "when we make a decision to act, it is always in reference to this spectator, even if the reference is occult, hidden from view, or even secret. 'Whatever judgement we can form concerning [our own sentiments and motives] must always bear some secret reference, either to what are, or to what, upon a certain condition would be, or to what, we imagine, ought to be the judgement of others. We endeavour to examine our own conduct as we imagine any other fair and impartial spectator would examine it.'" Even in secret the impartial spectator judges our past actions, and watches over our future behavior.

73. Gilbert and Gubar, Jenny Sharp, Gayatri Spivak, Terry Eagleton, Elsie Michie, and Jean and John Camaroff, among others, have written incisively about this complex text.

74. Afterwards, when all have left Jane to her punishment (to "stand half an hour longer on that stool"), and even when Helen comes to comfort her, she "remained silent as an Indian" (59).

75. See also Stuart Piggin, *Making Evangelical Missionaries, 1789–1858: The Social Background, Motives, and Training of British Protestant Missionaries to India* (Sydney: Sutton Courtenay, 1984).

76. Jean and John Camaroff, *Of Revelation and Revolution: Christianity, Colonialism and Consciousness in South Africa,* 2 vols. (Chicago: University of Chicago Press, 1991), Vol. 1: 50.

77. Quoted in Piggin, *Making Evangelical Missionaries, 1789–1858: The Social Background, Motives, and Training of British Protestant Missionaries to India* (Sydney: Sutton Courtenay, 1984).

78. Although the space does not permit us to pursue this opening, it would be important to analyze the moment and contexts of Wesley's "conversion" (May 24, 1738), coming as it did just months after his failed two-year mission to the Native American "heathens" in Georgia; consider this despairing plea from his *Journal:* "I went to America to convert the Indians; but O! who will convert me!" (January 24, 1738). Such startling and self-probing reversals would also become central to John Wesley's evangelicalism.

79. Camaroffs, 59.

80. See Piggin, 115.

81. "Memorial, addressed by the Baptist Missionaries to the Right Honourable Gilbert Lord Minto" (dated Mission-House, Serampore, 30th September 1807; signed W. Carey, Jo. Marshman, Wm. Ward, Wm. Moore, Josh. Rowe, Felix Carey), rpt. in Buchanan, 172–186.

82. John Bentley, *Essays relative to the Habits, Character, and Moral Improvement of the Hindoos* (London, 1823), 65; original emphasis.

83. But maybe memory is what Jane gives to Helen? Perhaps the return Jane makes on Helen's sympathy is her very narration.

84. This did not go unnoticed by contemporary reviewers, some indeed were inclined to wax hysterical because of it. Elizabeth Rigby, writing in the *Quarterly Review* (December 1848), opined: "It is true Jane does right, and exerts a great moral strength, but it is the strength of a mere heathen mind which is a law unto itself. No Christian grace is perceptible upon her. . . . Jane Eyre is proud, and therefore she is ungrateful too. It pleased God to make her an orphan, friendless, and penniless, yet she thanks nobody, and least of all Him. . . . Altogether the autobiography of Jane Eyre is pre-eminently an anti-Christian composition. There is throughout it a murmuring against the comforts of the rich and against the privations of the poor, which, as far as each individual is concerned, is a murmuring against God's appointment . . . there is a pervading tone of ungodly discontent which is at once the most prominent and the most subtle evil which the law and the pulpit, which all civilized society in fact has at the present day to contend with. We do not hesitate to say that the tone of mind and thought which had overthrown authority and violated every code human and divine abroad, and fostered Chartism and rebellion at home, is the same which has also written *Jane Eyre*" (qtd. in Norton Edition, 442).

85. This is the OED definition of "brownie": [dark elves of the Edda. A 'wee brown man' often appears in Scottish ballads and fairy tales.] 1. A benevolent spirit or goblin, of shaggy appearance, supposed to haunt old houses, esp. farmhouses, in Scotland, and sometimes to perform useful household work while the family were asleep.

86. As the Comaroffs argue, Charles Dickens, and in a somewhat more ambivalent way, Charlotte Brontë, "was convinced that the work to be done at

home as far more urgent and important; to him, the call for missionization overseas, or for grand colonial schemes, simply distracted attention from the dire social and political problems that beset England" (51).

87. As Ferguson tells us, "Bermuda, at the time Mary Prince was born, was a self-governing British colony lying about 600 miles from the coast of Virginia in the western North Atlantic ocean. Now one island but an archipelago of seven major and over 150 smaller islands and rocks that encompass about twenty square miles, 'just under the size of Manhatten,' Bermuda was proclaimed a Crown colony in 1684" (Introduction, 2).

88. Mary Prince, *The History of Mary Prince, A West Indian Slave, Related by Herself,* Moira Ferguson, ed. (Ann Arbor: University of Michigan Press, 1997).

89. For Ferguson it was Mary Prince's sovereign will, intentional and present to itself, that transformed her into "the first black British spokeswoman for general emancipation. . . . Her collective spirit is manifest to the end" (23). What is the image of the black slave-woman that emerges from Ferguson's analysis? First, for Ferguson, Mary Prince is a sovereign subject who resists through multiple, conscious strategies—mistress of them all. Second, Mary Prince is a subject who speaks an authentic truth. Ferguson insists that there is not "much to quibble about regarding the authenticity of the narrative, despite its being so transparently pressed into the service of antislavery propaganda and censored by evangelical dictates. . . . New information about her father and her owners incontrovertibly establishes the veracity of her narrative" (25). For Ferguson, then, Mary Prince is a sovereign agent whose resistant and authentic truth reverses the relations of power that define slavery. Under Ferguson's gaze, Mary Prince becomes the humanized heroine of late twentieth-century feminist criticism. Oddly, what is lost in all this is, precisely, Mary Prince—not to mention a critique of what exactly constitutes the "human."

90. Which would not mean that such a reading would be antifeminist. Far from it. I think indeed as Jenny Sharp's careful analysis suggests the impulse of justice within feminism receives its most rigorous critique but also its most hopeful vision through a vigilant attending to the silences that give voice to power.

91. Sharpe, "Something Akin to Freedom," in *differences,* 8.1 (1996), 31–55.

92. The Moravian Church was the American branch of the Renewed Church of the Unity of the Brethren, an evangelical Protestant denomination organized in Germany in 1727. The Moravian Church is governed by the conferential system; its ministry includes bishops, elders, and deacons. The church is divided into northern and southern administrative provinces, which have headquarters at Bethlehem, Pennsylvania, and Winston-Salem, North Carolina. Provincial synods exercise legislative authority. The American, German, and British branches of the church are under the overall jurisdiction of a general synod, which meets every ten years. The Moravians have no specific creed, but their tenets basically agree with the Apostles' Creed and the Augsburg Confession; the Bible is the only guide to faith and conduct. In-

fant baptism is practiced, and full church membership requires only a voluntary profession of faith. A liturgical form of worship is practiced, and the Moravian Church places special stress on fellowship and missionary work. In the early 1990s the Moravian Church in America reported about 52,200 members.

93. Emmanuel Levinas, "Truth of Disclosure and Truth of Testimony," in *Basic Philosophical Writings*, A. Peperzak, S. Critchley, and R. Bernasconi, eds. (Bloomington: Indiana University Press, 1996), 100.

94. Henry Mackenzie, *The Man of Feeling* [1771] (New York: Garland, 1974).

95. Quoted in Ellis, 16.

96. Kenneth Slagle, Introduction, in Henry Mackenzie, *Man of Feeling* (New York: Norton, 1958), x.

97. The word comes from the Middle English Bedlem, which was in fact the name of the Hospital of Saint Mary of Bethlehem, an institution in London for the mentally ill.

98. This sympathy with the colonial other can also be seen in John Shebbeare's *Lydia; or, Filial Piety* ([London, 1755] 2 vols.), where, even as the Noble savage serves as a foil for Europe, the native American subject can also detest the Europeans "for broken Faith, and fraudulent Treaties, for the Persuasions of his Countrymen to arm and engage in their Defence, and then shamefully deserting them at the Moment of their Necessities; their Wives and Children borne off to Slavery, or murdered by the Hands of the Enemies, were the Consequences which he conceived to have followed from the faithless Behaviour of the English" (I: 7–8).

99. See Eric Stokes, *The English Utilitarians and India* (New York: Oxford University Press, 1959), 20–21.

100. See Stokes, 332; Ellis, 124–125.

101. And yet, should we be surprised to hear echoes of Harley in the words of elite Hindu reformers almost a century later? In the next chapter, I will consider the work of Keshub Chandra Sen, who as the head of, first, the Brahmo Samaj of India and later the New Dispensation, began his long struggle to reconcile a Vaishnavite bhaktism with a firm commitment to natural revelation and rational faith—arguing for the necessary commingling of "East and West."

102. Cugoano also, we should keep in mind, draws explicitly on Wesley's abolitionist writings, which would again complicate the too neat separation between European/elite versus Ex-slave/subaltern discourses.

103. Cugoano, *Thoughts and Sentiments on the Evil of Slavery*, Vincent Carretta, ed. (New York: Penguin, 1999), 27.

104. Revelation 13:10: If any one is to be taken captive, to captivity he goes; if any one slays with the sword, with the sword must he be slain. Here is a call for the endurance and faith of the saints. 18:1–3: After this I saw another angel coming down from heaven, having great authority; and the earth was made bright with his splendor. And he called out with a mighty voice, "Fallen, fallen is Babylon the great! It has become a dwelling place of demons, a haunt of every foul spirit, a haunt of every foul and hateful bird;

for all nations have drunk the wine of her impure passion, and the kings of the earth have committed fornication with her, and the merchants of the earth have grown rich with the wealth of her wontonness."

105. We should never forget that part of Cugoano's proposals for the emancipation of enslaved Africans is not only a period of mourning for those murdered by the trade but also Christian missionary "instruction" that will produce tractable, obedient, useful, dutiful and good colonial subjects—see 104–107.

106. Levinas, "Truth of Disclosure and Truth of Testimony," 102.

Chapter Four

1. See C. A. Bayly, *Imperial Meridian* (New York: Longman, 1989), 136–138.

2. James Walvin, *Black Ivory* (Washington, DC: Howard University Press, 1992), 36–37.

3. Qtd. in Bready, 331.

4. Speech of General Isaac Gascoyne, February 28, 1805; III, 641. For the link between abolition and sentimentalism see speech of Lord Sheffield, May 16, 1806; VII, 235; for "philosophy" see the speech of Robert Peele, May 1, 1806; VI, 1022.

5. Speech of Sir William Young, February 28, 1805; III, 652.

6. Although generally a throwaway suggestion by some proplanter members, the idea of sending "East India Sepoys" to, first, police and, then, to replace the enslaved Africans needs to be noted. See *Parliamentary Debates,* III, 654, 666. By 1840, more and more people were taking this suggestion seriously, as "coolies" were substituted for "sepoys."

7. James Walvin, *Black Ivory: A History of British Slavery* (Washington, DC: Howard University Press, 1994), 32, 302. As he remarks on the rise and fall of this company, "The British Royal African Company had been hugely successful. It had built forts, dispatched 500 ships and transported 100,000 Africans, exported £1.5 million worth of goods and imported 30,000 tons of sugar. But by the 1720s its time had passed. It no longer made a profit and had created a demand it could no longer supply. Henceforth, the markets of the Americas were satisfied by individual traders and companies, largely unfettered by any trace of restrictive economic philosophy and seeking only to ferry as many live Africans as they could" (34).

8. Walvin, 301–302.

9. Walvin, 301.

10. Walvin, 314.

11. Briefly, then: The *Zong,* a slave ship owned by a large Liverpool slaving company, sailed from West Africa with a cargo of 470 slaves bound for Jamaica in 1781. Twelve weeks later, more than 60 Africans and 7 of the 17-man crew were dead of disease. As there seemed to be no end in sight to slave deaths, Captain Luke Collingwood suggested to his officers that sick slaves should be thrown overboard to secure the rapidly dwindling supplies of

water and to allow the shipping company to claim their loss as insurance. Two weeks after the news of the mass murder reached London, Olaudah Equiano, the former slave who had emerged as the most prominent spokesperson for the black community living in London, called on Granville Sharp, the famous abolitionist, to discuss the implications of the case and what could be done; they resolved to pursue criminal proceedings against the *Zong* crew. In the event, although Lord Justice Mansfield ordered a new trial, the case went no further: There was no trial, and for all intents and purposes the planter-slaver interests suppressed the case. See F. O. Shyllon, *Black Slaves in Britain* (New York: Oxford University Press, 1974), 189–190; Walvin, 19.

12. By "Saints," I am referring to all those members of parliament who were part of or allied with the Clapham sect of Evangelicals, who pushed for, and obtained, missionary rights for India in 1813, pushed through legislation abolishing the slave trade, and passing prison and other social reforms (people such as Hannah Moore, the Thorntons, Thomas Babington, Zachary Macaulay, Charles Grant, John Shore, etc.).

13. Leonard Cowie, *William Wilberforce, 1759–1833. A Bibliography* (New York: Greenwood Press, 1992), 5.

14. Or, as Sir William Young put it, "It was an easy matter for an English country gent. sitting by his fire side, to amuse himself with declaiming against the imaginary cruelty of the gentlemen of the West India islands to their slaves, upon false and exaggerated accounts; but the West-India gentleman did not advert to the many severities and oppressions imposed upon the labouring poor throughout England, by the arbitrary hand of the country justices and the different parish officers, of which so many severe cases came before the Court of King's Bench, on appeals respecting the poor-laws" (June 12, 1804; II, 660).

15. In the early nineteenth century, the term "white slaves" (found often in William Cobbett's writings, as well as in such minor works as James M. Rymer's *The White Slave. A Romance for the Nineteenth Century* [1844] and G. W. M. Reynolds's *The Seamstress; or the White Slave of England* [1853]) was fraught with political antagonisms. At one and the same time it articulated a critique of capitalist social relations, as well as an ambivalent, oblique even, racial identity. Ambivalent because the term "white" could be read in at least two ways: (1) that a certain form of (industrial) slavery could ensnare white men and women in the nineteenth century is a crime against both British Liberty and God's order, since only blacks, given their natural inferiority, can be slaves, and since no slavery can exist on British soil; or, and sometimes simultaneously, (2) like our black brothers and sisters, for whom Jesus died so that they may be free, like these who are chained, brutalized, and oppressed by the tyrannical slave captain and the West Indian planter, we white Christians are also slaves—of the despotic British manufacturer and our unsympathetic, aristocratic representatives in parliament. As such, "white slavery" could be deployed in a declaration of solidarity between exploited laborers across race, as well as in a reinscription of racist ideology that

argued for the emancipation of labor in terms that both naturalized racial domination and championed the British nation. The discursive field of this articulation was fashioned through religious, most often evangelical idioms of sympathy, love, humanization, salvation, and piety.

16. C. Brooke, February 28, 1805; III, 645.

17. Speech on February 28, 1805; III, 642–643.

18. Speech of General Tarleton, February 28, 1805; III, 656.

19. Speech of George Rose, June 27, 1804; II, 868.

20. Surprisingly, Wilberforce here is departing from arguments made by Wesley and Anthony Benezet around the piety of African peoples. Wesley in his *Considerations* argues that "All the Mahometan negroes constantly go to public prayers three times a day: there being a priest in every village, who regularly calls them together . . ." (10); and "The accounts we have of the natives of the kingdom of Benin is, that they are a reasonable and good-natured people, sincere and inoffensive, and do no injustice either to one another or to strangers.—They are civil and courteous" (13). This kind of non-propriative narrative suggests that another memory, even another possibility of sympathy is part of abolitionist history.

21. See G. Stocking, *Victorian Anthropology* (New York: Free Press, 1987); Robert J. C. Young, *Colonial Desire* (New York: Routledge, 1995); Jean and John Camoroff, *Of Revelation and Revolution,* vol. 1 (Chicago: University of Chicago Press, 1991).

22. Speech of Earl of Rosslyn, February 5, 1807; VIII, 669. Consider the words of Lord Glenville in the House of Lords on the suffering of the enslaved peoples. "His lordship then glanced at the consideration of the middle passage, the miseries and horrors of which were acknowledged by all, save those whose hearts were steeled against every emotion of humanity. . . . No circumstance . . . on the face of the habitable globe, could exhibit so great a portion of human misery, condensed into such a narrow compass, as did this middle passage. . . . [T]he object of this middle passage . . . was to tie and shackle the unhappy wretches who survived it, to hopeless bondage and never ending labour, in the burning climate of the West Indies! rising up and laying down, day after day, under the lash of an imperious and unfeeling task master! to those 'Hope never comes which comes to all!'" (June 24, 1806; VII, 304).

23. We should mark the language of "good policy" that was used during the debate on stopping the importation of enslaved Africans to the newly occupied French colonies; the speaker is the Earl of Moira: "If . . . slaves were to be considered as merchandize, they must be considered as the raw material. It had always been considered as highly impolitic to export to foreign states any raw material from this country, which was afterwards to be worked up into manufactured articles. Upon this principle, therefore, it was surely extremely to allow slaves, which were the raw material with respect to the produce of our colonies, to be exported by British subjects to the colonies of the enemy" (May 7, 1806; VII, 34). Walvin simplifies the euphemism "working up": He called it breaking the slaves in—see *Black Ivory,* 69–103.

24. See II, 454–455.
25. Of course, it was something of an open secret that emancipation was Wilberforce's ultimate object, as he had made clear in personal correspondence, and speeches in and out of parliament. But in terms of the discourses in parliament, such vacillations and concessions that I have marked are themselves managed by other kinds of closures.
26. Speech on June 27, 1804; II, 870.
27. Speech on May 16, 1806; VII, 233.
28. Praise for Wilberforce poured in from all corners of England. In it, he seems to emerge as the quintessential man of sympathetic humanitarianism. The *Times of London* reported the following words of the *Edinburgh Review* on September 12, 1807: "Most of all, let our gratitude be testified to that man who has begun and led this glorious struggle—who has devoted to its success all his days and all his talents—who has retired from all recompense for his labours, save the satisfaction of doing good to his fellow-creature—who giving up to mankind what others have sacrificed to party, has preferred the glory of living in the recollection of a grateful world to the shining rewards of a limited ambition. Had he failed, as entirely he is now likely to succeed, in the great object of his exertions, his name would have equally merited a place among the benefactors of our species. But men will always judge by the event; and we now rejoice to contemplate this distinguished person standing, as it were, on the brink of his final triumph, in the greatest battle ever fought by human beings, and an object, we really think, of just envy to the most ambitious of mortals."
29. February 28, 1805; III, 673.
30. See also John and Jean Comaroff, *Of Revolution and Revelation, Vol. 1* (Chicago: University of Chicago Press, 1991), Chapter 6.
31. See Holt, *The Problem of Freedom: Race, Labor, and Politics in Jamaica and Britain, 1832–1938.*
32. See Saidiya V. Hartman, *Scenes of Subjection: Terror, Slavery, and Self-Making in Nineteenth-century America* (New York: Oxford University Press, 1997), 52–53.
33. See Hobsbawm and Rude, *Captain Swing* (New York: Norton, 1975 [1968]); Raymond Williams, *The Country and the City* (New York: Oxford University Press, 1983).
34. Ainslie Thomas Embree, *Charles Grant and British Rule in India* (New York: Columbia University Press, 1962), 262.
35. Speech of Charles Grant, May 31, 1813, *Parliamentary Debates,* XXV, 464. See also Embree, 163.
36. Embree, 164.
37. As Adam Smith declared: "The discovery of a passage to the East Indies . . . opened perhaps a still more extensive range to foreign commerce than even that of America. . . . [T]he empires of China, Indostan, Japan, without having richer mines of gold or silver, were in every other respect much richer, better cultivated, and more advanced in all arts and manufactures than either

Mexico or Peru . . . But rich and civilised nations can always exchange to a much greater value with one another than with savages and barbarians. Europe, however, has hitherto derived much less advantage from its commerce with the East Indies than from with America. . . . No great nation in Europe has ever yet had the benefit of a free commerce to the East Indies. . . . The trade to the East Indies, by opening a market to the commodities of Europe, or . . . to the gold and silver which is purchased with those commodities, must necessarily tend to increase the annual production of European commodities, and consequently the real wealth and revenue of Europe" (*The Wealth of Nations* (New York: Everyman's Library, 1991), Bk. IV, Ch. 1, 394–395).

38. Adam Smith, qtd. in Embree, 165.
39. Embree, 172.
40. Embree, 129.
41. Embree, 264. Some sense of the governance structure of the East India Company during this period would be useful to the general reader. After the scandalous investigation of company servants in the early 1780s, Pitt's India Act (1784) created a government appointed Board of Control that gave the British government an effective voice in the company's administration. The company, for its part, governed its affairs through what Embree has termed a "kind of bicameral legislature": the General Court (or Court of Proprietors) and the Court of Directors. The General Court was made up of all the company shareholders, and met four times a year. During these meetings the 24 members of the Court of Directors were elected and all matters of concern for the company were debated; the General Court could also pass bylaws that were binding on the company, and also controlled all grants exceeding £600. The Court of Directors was the executive of the General Court, and it had virtually complete control of the company's administration. As Embree points out: "Since the Company not only managed a great commercial enterprise but still administered the political and military affairs of India under the Board of Control, the Court of Directors performed all the normal duties of a government secretariat in addition to the functions of a trading corporation" (125). The company had about 4,500 British employees at the beginning of the nineteenth century, of whom close to 3,500 were officers in the military service; their combined salaries were about £3,400,000 (around $429,000,000 in today's US currency).
42. On questions of free trade, see Embree, 262–264; see also the crucial wording of the hundreds of petitions on free trade and the renewal of the charter in *Hansard's Parliamentary Debates* (London, 1813), Vol. XXII, 231, cxxxi, clix; Vol. XXIV, 356–358, 675. As the "Petition from Paisley, Swansea and Birmingham" put it, by ending the company monopoly "new and extensive markets will be opened for reception of British manufactures, which will render this country more independent of all commercial relations with the continent of Europe, and contribute to the financial resources of the empire" (XXII, 236; presented to Commons on April 8, 1812). This idea that one

way both to extend Empire and to combat Napoleon was to open fully Eastern commerce became perhaps the most contentious issue in the subsequent
debates, the "Company Members" (MPs friendly to the company) arguing
that this would lead to colonization (and hence the eventual loss of the "our
Eastern possessions"—America was still very much on the minds of the
British) and that Indian natives could neither afford European products nor
had any taste for them. Thus, the role of Christianity in creating a properly
receptive, enlightened, and, most important, docile colonized population
seemed not only morally right but politically sound.

43. The strategic exclusion of Islam from the consideration of what "native" culture is can be accounted for it seems to me by the necessity to homogenize
Indian culture, as well as the assumption on the part of most British states-
men and historians that Islam and Muslims were basically foreigners in
South Asia.

44. Later, out of what seems to me to be sheer exhaustion, the House appointed
a Select Committee to continue examining witnesses.

45. Developed in the wake of the Enlightenment (and later codified in the Utilitarian) critique of the *ancien régime,* the divine right of kings, and aristocratic privilege, the discourse of oriental despotism posited an essentially
Western Order as a civilizational corrective to Eastern irrationality. In the
field of Indology, Ronald Inden argues incisively that the central principles
of that Order were "mutual exclusion, unity, centeredness, determinacy, and
uniformity. The transcendental knower of Indological discourse proceeds by
discovering mutually exclusive categories, as in a taxonomy, and reducing
them to a single order. The universe that is so constituted is centered . . . and
it is stable and uniform (and therefore predictable) in its movements. It is a
determinate world, where there is a place for everything and where single
events can be explained by single causes. It is also a moderate and reasonable
world" (88). The representatives of this moderate and reasonable world
would confront (and eventually dominate) their supposed opposites in the
colonial mirror of nineteenth-century discourse. This confrontation between
Order and its Other would be predicated not only on the isolation of a discreet and clearly identifiable figure, that of the Oriental despot, but also on
a certain geographical determinism. Inden depicts this famous confrontation
in this way: "Characterized by a salubrious mixture of topographic zones and
a temperate climate, Western Europe is inhabited by temperate peoples of
wide-ranging skills and organized into nations of a moderate to small size.
Asia, with vast river valleys juxtaposed to its uplands and a climate either hot
or cold, is inhabited by peoples of extreme temperament and organized into
large empires" (52). These inherent differences logically and naturally gave
rise to two radically different traditions of political and economic organization. For Europe, a constitutional monarchy or republic would be the characteristic form of polity, while the capitalist mode of production its
characteristic economic institution (Ronald Inden, *Imagining India* [Cam-
bridge, MA: Blackwell, 1990], 53). For the East, despotism, the arbitrary or

capricious rule by fear of an all-powerful autocrat over docile and servile masses, would be the normal and distinctive form of government; these peasant masses, distributed over innumerable, self-sufficient villages, engaging in a mixture of low-grade agriculture and handicrafts, make over to the despot the surplus of what it produces in the form of a tax, and subsist on the remainder—a mode of production that Marx termed "Asiatic." For an interesting reappraisal of Marx's thesis, see Irfan Habib, "Processes of Accumulation in Pre-colonial and Colonial India," *Indian Historical Review,* vol. xvi, nos. 1–2 (July, 1989–January, 1990), 137–148; and G. Spivak, *A Critique of Postcolonial Reason* (Cambridge: Harvard University Press, 1999).

46. *Hansard's,* Vol. XXV, 845; see also *Hansard's,* Vol. XXV, 863–864, 881, 906, 973.

47. For instance, Munro one of the conservative romantic administrators, answered the question of consumption through a simple calculus of demand, supply, use and wealth, and the distant hope of commerce: "It has been . . . said, that the natives have a prejudice against the manufactures of Europe; the Hindoos have no prejudice against the use of any thing that they can convert to an useful purpose, whether European or native manufacture . . . ; but they have one prejudice which I believe also is very common in this country, against the paying a higher price for a worse commodity, and until we can undersell them . . . we have no hope of extending the use of our own manufactures in India." (XXV, 785); "If the manners and customs of the Indians are to be changed, I think it likely that they will be changed by commerce; but commerce doesn't seem to have produced much effect upon them" (XXV, 809–810).

48. XXV, 553–554.

49. This ongoing diatribe against "adventurers" is an indication of the class valences of the monopolist position. Warning against the insolent behavior of soldiers, seamen, and "common" merchants, the monopolists wanted to protect the ignorant masses of India from the ignorant masses of England. As Hastings put it before the House of Lords: "'Since we became masters of the country;' 'our native subjects,' and other phrases of a similar import constantly occur in our books, in our writings, as well as in the language of familiar conversation. These ideas in the lower orders of British subjects rise to the height of despotism" (XXV, 555). Note the curious and complex play of a kind of benevolent, even self-critical imperialism and class domination. Or consider how Charles Grant tried to reconcile his defense of monopoly with his advocacy of missions: "Free trade would . . . prevent the working out of the kind of moral and spiritual improvement that he advocated, for the 'low and licentious' Englishmen who would flock to India would 'vex, harass and perplex the weak natives,' who driven desperate by mistreatment, would revolt and drive the British out" (Embree, 169). The figure of the low and licentious Englishman recurs throughout these debates, marking the contours of a class discourse imbricated within an imperial imaginary.

50. XXV, 415–416.

51. Ainslie Thomas Embree, *Charles Grant and British Rule in India* (New York: Columbia University Press, 1962), 237.

52. As another former employee put it, the natives are of "very quick sensibility; peculiarly susceptible of affront with respect to their religious prejudices; impatient of opposition with regard to their religious superstitions; quick and jealous of affront with respect to their women. I think a promiscuous intercourse of Europeans with the natives of India might lead to the most mischievous consequences" (XXV, 493); and another respondent put it in even more stark terms: "It would neither be consistent with the security of the British empire in India, to treat the religions established in the countries of their dominion with contempt and opprobrium; for with common humanity. If such a declaration of war was made between the religions of the country, between the professors of ours and those of the established religions, I know not what would be the consequences. There have been among the Mahometans, bigots more ferocious than any that have shed the blood of their brethren in Europe. If a fanatic should arise amongst them, and preach the doctrine inculcated in their Koran, I do not think it impossible that he might excite the zeal of thousands of abetters, and a religious war be the consequence of the first provocation" (XXV, 428).

53. Embree, 239.

54. Embree, 271. How do we account for this shift? I would suggest that by 1813, one effect of evangelical (mis)representations of a degraded and uncivilized India was to place Indians beyond the pale of those who could be animated by a "spirit of English liberty" (see my analysis of K. C. Sen's use of an anti-racist sympathy below).

55. Embree, 239.

56. Embree, 247.

57. This was a hugely influential tract, which, after the 1813 charter debates, gained even greater prominence, because Wilberforce quoted it in his speech on the evangelization of India, and urged others to read it.

58. Embree, 247.

59. Charles Grant to Lord William Bentinck, April 17, 1807; qtd. in Embree, 247.

60. We should keep in mind that in the early nineteenth century, "Bengal" extended many hundred of miles further north and south that it does today, including present-day Bihar and most of Orissa.

61. *The Parliamentary Debates from the Year 1803 to the Present Time,* published under the superintendence of T. C. Hansard (London, 1813), Vol. XXVI, 1037.

62. This would be a particularly influential text in the coming years, even though India figures in the *Researches* for only a third of the text. These sections, sensational and graphic, would be reprinted in 1858, in a version (edited by the former "missionary chaplain" of Gwalior) aimed at bolstering and promoting a wavering missionary spirit in England—see *Christian Researches in India; With the Rise, Suspension, and Probable Future of England's Rule as a Christian Power in India,* William Henry Foy, ed. (London, 1858).

Citing Buchanan's argument on the moral and religious influence of British rule, Foy defends the excessive reprisals during the Mutiny as just retribution in "this our holy war" (104).

63. Staughton for instance writes that after an ill person begins to wane, he or she is carried to the Ganges and "there instead of receiving from his friends any of the tender consolations of sympathy, to alleviate the pain of his departing moments, his mouth, nose and ears, are stuffed with clay, or wet sand, while the by-standers crowd close around him, and incessantly pour torrents of water upon his head and body" (131).

64. To cite only one magnificent passage from Duff: "These men,—call them missionaries, or preachers, or apostles, or by any other name more grateful to fastidious ears, as the name cannot alter the nature of the recorded fact,— these men came with no ensign but that of the cross,—no ammunition but the Bible—the sword of the Spirit,—no commissariat but the Gospel graced shining in their walk and conversation. The came, they saw, they conquered. Through the blessing of God on their bloodless warfare, the savage islanders were subdued under the power of Christian truth. Their idols were destroyed; their sacred groves cut down or deserted; their sanguinary sacrifices abolished. By becoming Christians, they became civilized;—and thus were laid the foundations of that noble fabric, civil and religious, under whose shadow we have gradually risen to the rank of the greatest, the wisest, and the happiest of nations" (408). Of course, with self-conscious irony, Duff is speaking here of the evangelizing of England itself.

65. Charles Grant, Dispatch of 1798 to Wellesley; qtd. in Embree, 190. Such writers as Q. Craford (*Sketches Chiefly Relating to the Historical Learning and Manners of the Hindoos,* 1790), William Hodges (*Travels in India during the Years 1780–83,* 1793), William Robertson (*An Historical Disquisition concerning the Knowledge the Ancients had of India,* 1791), and the famous orientalist Sir William Jones widely disseminated their "infectious enthusiasm for Indian studies," some even claiming that India, not Egypt or Greece, was the original home of the arts and sciences—see Embree, 148–149.

66. That neither the sentimentalists (such as Munro and Lushington) nor the evangelicals (such as Wilberforce or Grant) were interested in the actual conditions of the peoples of India is evident by the offhand dismissal of charges of oppression in the countryside in Bengal (by Wilberforce) and the stunning silence of both members on the testimony of witnesses denying that weavers in Bengal were beaten and extorted out of their earnings.

67. Embree quotes one "enthusiastic account" claiming that nearly 1,500 different groups sent in petitions (272). For a discussion of these petitions, see Embree, 271–272.

68. John Wolffe, *God and Greater Britain: Religion and National Life in Britain and Ireland, 1843–1945* (New York: Routledge, 1994), 25.

69. XXV, 457.

70. As two of the petitions phrased it: "The imperious duty to do every thing in their power to promote the best interests of so great a multitude of their fel-

low subjects, by procuring for them . . . the invaluable blessing of the knowledge of the gospel"; "and that such permission [to send out missionaries] . . . the petitioners humbly conclude to be not only consistent with the safety and peace of the empire, but of the greatest importance to its interests" (XXV, 1084–1085; 1091).

71. Fellow "subjects" "now sitting in darkness, practicing horrid cruelties under the name of religious rites, and addicted to the most detestable usages" was how the petition from the synod of Fife put it (XXV, 1084).

72. XXV, 817–818.

73. XXV, 1091.

74. Wilberforce to J. Butterworth, February 15, 1812; qtd. in Embree, 273.

75. XXVI, 832.

76. See Embree, 198.

77. Charles Grant, *Observations on the State of Asia;* qtd. in Embree, 150.

78. Qtd. in Embree 143–145.

79. Qtd. in Embree, 145.

80. Embree, 152.

81. In the England of 1793, still reeling from the American debacle and in the midst of an anti-Jacobin reaction, the main fear of his opponents was not, as it would be 20 years later, that the preaching of missionaries would offend the religious feelings of the people, but rather of the political effect education and the Christian religion might have on a subject population. Grant responded to these objections by arguing that it had been the lack of education and religion that had left the French masses a prey to "Jacobinical impostures and delusions, by which they were hurled into the atrocities of anarchy and atheism." As for a feeling of independence being inculcated by Christianity, the "spirit of English liberty is not to be caught from a written description of it, by distant and feeble Asiatics" (qtd. in Embree, 154).

82. He quotes from Nathaniel Brassey Halhed, Edward Gibbon, Charles Grant, Francois Bernier, Luke Scrafton, Orme, J. Z. Holwell, Robert Clive, Verelst, John Shore, John Macpherson, Lord Cornwallis, James Mackintosh, Lord Wellesley, and Claudius Buchanan.

83. This is precisely what another opponent fixed on in his critique of the evangelical position. Charles Marsh argued that interfering with native religion would "shake our empire . . . to its very centre" (XXVI, 1019). He derided the "diseased degree of enthusiasm" that had wound up parliament to the highest pitch of fanaticism and folly (1023). But if evangelization succeeded, Marsh countered, what then? "You will have destroyed that peculiarity of national character, that singular contexture of moral properties, which has given you an immense territory, and immense revenue, and 60 millions of subjects" (1029).

84. But the silence of the other evangelicals on the Thirteenth Resolution had a further significance to it as well. As we have seen, all throughout the debates the defenders of the monopoly—which included both Grant and Thornton (the two other prominent evangelicals in the Commons)—had been arguing

that free trade in India would be useless because the natives were fixed in their habits, customs, and practices. But if this were so, then evangelization was doomed to failure, and, as Wilberforce put his opponents's position, religious "conversion is utterly impracticable" (834). But Wilberforce absolutely denies the validity of this position, citing the "successes" of the permanent settlement, and reforms in the judicial system and military as examples of changes in the civil institutions of India, which not only did not cause a general insurrection but were supposedly welcomed as beneficial. He then uses the multiplicity of religious traditions within the subcontinent (Islam, Sikhism, Buddhism, Syrian Christianity) as proof that religious tolerance is part of native culture—which finally shows that "there is nothing in the nature or principles of a Hindoo which renders it impossible for him to become a Christian" (XXVI, 836). Wilberforce goes on to denounce his opponents, who, like the "French sceptical philosophers" of the last century, try to "discredit Christianity" by arguing that "the Hindoos are so good, their morals are so pure"—these people are infected with Jacobin and revolutionary ideologies. A telling reversal since at the time of the French Revolution, Wilberforce and his allies had been accused of the very same crimes. But this position was not consistent with the monopolist argument, and the odd silence of the other evangelicals is a reminder of this contradiction. For a discussion of these contradictions by one of their opponents see Charles Marsh's speech, XXVI, 1036.

85. XXVI, 1037–1038.
86. David Kopf, *The Brahmo Samaj and the Shaping of the Modern Indian Mind* (Princeton, NJ: Princeton University Press, 1979), xiii.
87. For instance, from 1843 (the year Debendranath Tagore institutionalized Rammohun Roy's ideology of Hindu reform by founding a more institutionalized form of the Brahmo Samaj) until about 1851, Brahmos based their reformation on the Vedas, proclaiming these texts the authentic scriptural source of Hinduism. After 1851, when the "idolatry of the scriptures" was rejected, new forces vied for dominance in the theology and spirituality of the Samaj; Vaishnava theists, led by Bijoy Krishna Goswami, struggled with rationalist Vedantists, led by Sitanath Tattvabhusan, for control of the movement.
88. In Keshub Chunder Sen, *Lectures in India* (New York: Cassell, 1901), 1–47.
89. Sen considered an "unsectarian, liberal, sound and useful education" the best missionary force in India (Sen, *Keshub Chunder Sen in England,* Prem Sunder Basu, ed. [Calcutta: Writers Workshop, 1980], 344). It also could have the most beneficial effects on the status of Indian women. "An education that will not patronize any particular Church, that will not be subservient or subordinated to the views of any particular religious community, and education free and liberal, and comprehensive in its character, an education calculated to make Indian women good wives, mothers, sisters and daughters" (*Keshub Chunder Sen in England,* 365).
90. This assimilation of Christ to Asia was a long standing strategy in Brahmo discourse. Consider these words written by Rammohun Roy in 1823: "Al-

most all the ancient prophets and patriarch venerated by Christians, nay even Jesus Christ himself, a Divine incarnation and the *founder* of the Christian faith, were ASIATICS, so that if a Christian thinks it degrading to be born or to reside in *Asia,* he directly reflects upon them" (qtd. in Killingley, 118). However, this kind of orientalism is also discernible within Unitarian and nonconformist Christianity as in the acknowledgment that "Our Bible is Eastern"—see W. J. Fox, "A Discourse on the Occasion of the Death of Rajah Rammohun Roy" (1833).

91. In a speech delivered April 9, 1879, "India Asks: Who is Christ?" in Keshub Chunder Sen, *Lectures in India* (New York: Cassell, 1901), 359–393.

92. "Behold the Light of Heaven in India," January 23, 1875, in Keshub Chunder Sen, *Lectures in India* (New York: Cassell, 1901), 194–241.

93. "We Apostles of the New Dispensation," January 22, 1881, in Keshub Chunder Sen, *Lectures in India* (New York: Cassell, 1901), 443–492.

94. In "Regenerating Faith" (January 24, 1868, in Sen, *Lectures in India,* 95–127), Sen elaborates a theory of ethics and sin in language that is haunted by Smith's elaboration of "conscience": "Whereas the prayer of heaven's creed is—That God's will may be done on earth as it is in heaven. In the one, religion is subordinated to man's judgement and wishes, and from the decrees of Providence there is always an appeal to human prudence for final decision. In the other, God's will is absolute and immutable law, and His judgement final and irreversible. In the one we see a stereotyped code of moral duties to be performed on the authority, and under the government, of conscience, the vicegerent of God in the human mind; but in every case it is the interpretation arbitrarily put upon the code by prudence and expediency which actually rules the heart" (98); in *Viveka o Vairagya* (*Conscience and Renunciation,* J. K. Koar, trans. [Calcutta: Navavidhan Publications]), Sen put it thus: "If you wish to attain the Holy Spirit take refuge in conscience and purify the mind and heart. Inherent in human nature as the vicegerent of the Spirit of Truth conscience protects man from sin and evil setting him on the path of purity" (6).

95. "Behold the Light of Heaven in India," January 23, 1875, in Keshub Chunder Sen, *Lectures in India* (New York: Cassell, 1901), 194–241.

96. XXVI, 851.

97. XXVI, 1069.

98. Around $1,260,000 in today's currency.

Conclusion

1. See Michael Hardt and Antonio Negri's very popular reading of this mobilization of universal values in the present moment of a United Nations-led *Empire.* They write, "No longer, as under the old international ordering, do individual sovereign states or the supranational (UN) power to intervene only to ensure or impose the application of voluntarily engaged international accords. Now supranational subjects that are legitimated not by right

but by consensus intervene in the name of any type of emergency and superior ethical principles. What stands behind this intervention is not just a permanent state of emergency and exception, but a permanent state of emergency and exception justified by the appeal to essential values of justice. In other words, the right of the police is legitimated by universal values" (*Empire,* 18). We might also add that what stands behind this universalism is the changing pattern of American hegemony, backed by Europe. In other words, universal values have also always been screen-metaphors for specific political and economic interests. Nowhere is this more spectacularly confirmed than in the self-serving conversion of George W. Bush to a kind of global feminism in the recent "crusade" against Islam.

Bibliography

Abelove, Henry. "Some Speculations on the History of 'Sexual Intercourse' During the 'Long Eighteenth Century' in England." *Nationalisms and Sexualities.* Ed. Andrew Parker, Mary Russo, Doris Sommer, and Patricia Yaeger. New York: Routledge, 1992. 335–340.

Adams, Julia. "The Familial State: Elite Family Practices and State-making in the Early Modern Netherlands." *Theory and Society.* 23 (Summer 1994), 505–539.

Anon. "Memoirs of Anthony Benezet." *Park's Travels in Africa.* London, 1816. 29–33.

Aries, Phillipe. *Centuries of Childhood: A Social History of Family Life.* Trans. Robert Baldick. New York: Vintage Books, 1962.

Armstrong, Nancy. *Desire and Domestic Fiction: A Political History of the Novel.* New York: Oxford University Press, 1987.

Asad, Talal. *Genealogies of Religion* Baltimore, MD: Johns Hopkins University Press, 1994.

Azim, Firdous. *The Colonial Rise of the Novel.* New York: Routledge, 1993.

Barnes, Elizabeth. *States of Sympathy: Seduction and Democracy in the American Novel.* New York: Columbia University Press, 1997.

Barthes, Roland. *S/Z.* Trans. Richard Howard. New York: Hill and Wang, 1974.

Bayly, C. A. *Imperial Meridian.* New York: Longman, 1989.

Benezet, Anthony. *A Caution and Warning to Great Britain and Her Colonies; in A Short Representation of the Calamitous State of the Enslaved Negroes in the British Dominions; Collected from various Authors, and submitted to the Serious Consideration of all, more especially of those in Power.* Philadelphia, 1766.

Bentley, John. *Essays relative to the Habits, Character, and Moral Improvement of the Hindoos.* London, 1823.

Bottomore, Tom, Ed. *A Dictionary of Marxist Thought.* Cambridge, MA: Basil Blackwell, 1983.

Brennan, Matthew C. *The Gothic Psyche.* Columbia, SC: Camden House, 1997.

Bruhm, Steven. *Gothic Bodies: The Politics of Pain in Romantic Fiction.* Philadelphia: University of Pennsylvania Press, 1994.

Buchanan, Claudius. *Christian Researches in Asia.* 1812.

———. *A Memoir of the Expediency of an Ecclesiastical Establishment for British India.* 1806.

Burgett, Bruce. *Sentimental Bodies: Sex, Gender, and Citizenship in the Early Republic.* Princeton, NJ: Princeton University Press, 1998.

Burkhalter, Holly. "Humanitarian Intervention: A Forum." *The Nation.* May 8, 2000: 21–26.

Chatman, Seymour. "What Novels Can do that Films Can't." *On Narrative.* Ed. W. J. T. Mitchell. Chicago: University of Chicago Press, 1980.

Clough, Patricia. *Auto-Affection.* Minneapolis: University of Minnesota Press, 2000.

Comaroff, Jean and John Comaroff. *Of Revelation and Revolution: Christianity, Colonialism and Consciousness in South Africa.* 2 Vols. Chicago: University of Chicago Press, 1991.

Cowie, Leonard. *William Wilberforce, 1759–1833. A Bibliography.* New York: Greenwood Press, 1992.

Davis, David Brion. "Quaker Ethic and Antislavery International." *The Antislavery Debate.* Ed. Thomas Bender. Berkeley: University of California Press, 1992. 27–64.

———. "Reflections on Abolitionism and Ideological Hegemony." *The Antislavery Debate.* Ed. Thomas Bender. Berkeley: University of California Press, 1992. 161–179.

De Certeau, Michel. *The Writing of History.* Trans. Tom Conley. New York: Columbia University Press, 1988.

———. *The Practice of Everyday Life.* Trans. Steven Rendall. Berkeley: University of California Press, 1984.

Derrida, Jacques. *Archive Fever.* Trans. Eric Prenowitz. Chicago: University of Chicago Press, 1995.

———. *Of Grammatology.* Trans. Gayatri Chakrvorty Spivak. Baltimore, MD: Johns Hopkins University Press, 1998.

———. *Points: Interviews, 1974–1994.* Trans. Peggy Kamuf, et al. Stanford: Stanford University Press, 1995.

———. "The Ends of Man." *Margins of Philosophy.* Trans. Alan Bass. Chicago: University of Chicago Press, 1982. 109–136.

Donzelot, Jacques. "The Mobilization of Society." Eds. Graham Burchell, Colin Gordon, and Peter Miller. *The Foucault Effect.* Chicago: University of Chicago Press, 1991. 169–179.

———. *The Policing of Families.* Trans. Robert Hurley. New York: Pantheon, 1979.

Douglass, Frederick. *Narrative of the Life of Frederick Douglass, an American Slave.* Ed. Houston A. Baker, Jr. New York: Penguin, 1986.

Duff, Alexander. *Explanatory Statement Addressed to the friends of the India Mission of the Church of Scotland, as it Existed Previous to the Disruption in May 1843.* Edinburgh: John Johnstone, 1844.

Eagleton, Terry. *The Ideology of the Aesthetic.* Cambridge, MA: Basil Blackwell, 1990.

Ellis, Markman. *The Politics of Sensibility.* New York: Cambridge University Press, 1996.

Embree, Ainslie Thomas. *Charles Grant and British Rule in India.* New York: Columbia University Press, 1962.

Equiano, Olaudah. *The Interesting Narrative of the Life of Olaudah Equiano, or Gustavus Vassa, the African, Written by Himself.* Halifax, 1814.

Ferguson, Moira. *Subject to Others.* New York: Routledge, 1992.

Fleenor, Juliann E., Ed. *The Female Gothic.* Montreal: Eden Press, 1983.

Foucault, Michel, *The Archaeology of Knowledge.* Trans. A. M. Sheridan Smith. New York: Vintage, 1972.

———. *Discipline and Punish.* Trans. Alan Sheridan. New York: Vintage, 1979.

———. "Governmentality." Trans. Colin Gordon. *The Foucault Effect.* Eds. Graham Burchell, Colin Gordon, and Peter Miller. Chicago: University of Chicago Press, 1991. 87–104.

———. *History of Sexuality: An Introduction.* Trans. Robert Hurley. New York: Vintage, 1990.

———. "History of Systems of Thought." Trans. Donald Bouchard. *Language, Counter-memory, Practice.* Ithaca, NY: Cornell University Press, 1977. 199–202.

———. "Nietzsche, Genealogy, History." *The Foucault Reader.* Ed. Paul Rabinow. New York: Pantheon, 1984. 76–100.

———. "Society Must be Defended." Trans. Robert Hurley. *Ethics.* Ed. Paul Rabinow. New York: The New Press, 1997. 59–65.

———. "What is Critique?" Trans. Lysa Hochroth. *The Politics of Truth.* New York: Semiotexte, 1997. 23–82.

Foy, William Henry. Ed. *Christian Researches in India; With the Rise, Suspension, and Probable Future of England's Rule as a Christian Power in India.* London, 1858.

Fox, W. J. "A Discourse on the Occasion of the Death of Rajah Rammohun Roy." London, 1833.

Freud, Sigmund. "The 'Uncanny.'" *Collected Papers.* Ed. and Trans. Joan Riviere. Vol. 4. New York: Basic Books, 1959. 5 vols. 368–407.

Gallagher, Catherine. *Nobody's Story: The Vanishing Acts of Women in the Marketplace, 1670–1820.* Berkeley: University of California Press, 1994.

Gilroy, Paul. *Black Atlantic.* Cambridge, MA: Harvard University Press, 1995.

Colin, Gordon. "Governmental Rationality. An Introduction." Eds. Graham Burchell, Colin Gordon, and Peter Miller. *The Foucault Effect.* Chicago: University of Chicago Press, 1991. 1–51.

Habib, Irfan. "Processes of Accumulation in Pre-colonial and Colonial India." *Indian Historical Review.* 16.1–2 (July 1989–January 1990): 137–148.

Haggerty, George. "The Gothic Novel, 1764–1824." *The Columbia History of the British Novel.* Ed. John Richetti. New York: Columbia University Press, 1994. 220–246.

Hall, Lesley, and Roy Porter. *The Facts of Life: The Creation of Sexual Knowledge in Britain.* New Haven, CT: Yale University Press, 1995.

Hansard's Parliamentary Debates from the Year 1803 to the Present Time, Published under the superintendence of T. C. Hansard. London: 1813.

Hardt, Michael and Antonio Negri. *Empire.* Cambridge, MA: Harvard University Press, 2000.

Hartman, Saidiya V. *Scenes of Subjection: Terror, Slavery, and Self-Making.* New York: Oxford University Press, 1997.

Hensman, Rohini. "Women's resistance to authoritarianism." *Women and Politics in the Third World.* Ed. Haleh Afshar. New York: Routledge, 1996. 48–72.

Hobsbawm, Eric, and George Rudé. *Captain Swing.* New York: Norton, 1975 (1968).

Holt, Thomas. *The Problem of Freedom: Race, Labor, and Politics in Jamaica and Britain, 1832–1938.* Baltimore, MD: Johns Hopkins University Press, 1992.

"Humanitarian Intervention: A Forum." *The Nation.* May 8, 2000: 21–26.

Hunt, Lynn. *The Family Romance of the French Revolution.* Berkeley: University of California Press, 1992.

Hunter, Ian. "Aesthetics and Cultural Studies." *Cultural Studies.* Eds. Lawrence Grossberg, Cary Nelson, and Paula Treichler. New York: Routledge, 1992.

Inden, Ronald. *Imagining India.* Cambridge, MA: Blackwell, 1990.

Kaplan, Fred. *Sacred Tears: Sentimentality in Victorian Literature.* Princeton, NJ: Princeton University Press, 1987.

Kopf, David. *The Brahmo Samaj and the Shaping of the Modern Indian Mind.* Princeton, NJ: Princeton University Press, 1979.

Laqueur, Thomas. *Making Sex: Body and Gender From the Greeks to Freud.* Cambridge, MA: Harvard University Press, 1990.

Levinas, Emmanuel. *Basic Philosophical Writings.* Eds. A. Peperzak, S. Critchley, and R. Bernasconi. Bloomington: Indiana University Press, 1996.

Macdonald, John. *Statement of Reasons for Accepting a Call to go to India as a Missionary.* Glasgow, 1839.

Marshall, David. *The Surprising Effects of Sympathy: Marivaux, Diderot, Rousseau, and Mary Shelley.* Chicago: University of Chicago Press, 1987.

Marx, Karl. *Capital, Vol. 1.* Trans. Ben Fowkes. New York: Knopf, 1981.

———. "Merchant Capital." *A Dictionary of Marxist Thought.* Ed. Tom Bottomore. Cambridge, MA: Basil Blackwell, 1983. 332–333.

Mason, Michael. *The Making of Victorian Sexuality.* 2 Vols. New York: Oxford University Press, 1994.

McCarthy, Thomas. *Relationships of Sympathy: The Writer and the Reader in British Romanticism.* Aldershot, UK: Scholar Press, 1997.

McClintock, Anne. "Gender, Race, and Nationalism." Ed. McClintock, A. et al. *Dangerous Liaisons.* Minneapolis University of Minnesota Press, 1997. 89–112.

———. *Imperial Leather.* New York: Routledge, 1995.

Mill, John Stuart. *The Subjection of Women.* Ed. Wendell Robert Carr. Cambridge, MA: MIT Press, 1970.

Mullen, John. *Sentiment and Sociability: The Language of Feeling in the Eighteenth Century.* New York: Oxford University Press, 1988.

Nietzsche, Friedrich. *On the Genealogy of Morals.* Trans. W. Kaufmann and R. J. Hollingdale. New York: Vintage, 1989.

———. *The Will to Power.* Trans. W. Kaufmann and R. J. Hollingdale. Ed. W. Kaufmann. New York: Vintage, 1968.

Owen, David. *English Philanthropy, 1660–1960.* Cambridge, MA: Belknap, 1965.

Piggin, Stuart. *Making Evangelical Missionaries, 1789–1858: The Social Background, Motives, and Training of British Protestant Missionaries to India.* Sydney: Sutton Courtenay, 1984.

Poovey, Mary. *A History of the Modern Fact: Problems of Knowledge in the Sciences of Wealth and Society.* Chicago: University of Chicago Press, 1998.

————. *Making a Social Body : British cultural formation, 1830–1864.* Chicago: University of Chicago Press, 1995.

Prakash, Gayan. *Another Reason.* Princeton, NJ: Princeton University Press, 1999.

Prince, Mary. *The History of Mary Prince, A West Indian Slave, Related by Herself.* Ed. Moira Ferguson. Ann Arbor: University of Michigan Press, 1997.

Radcliffe, Ann. *The Mysteries of Udolpho.* Ed. Bonamy Dobrée. New York: Oxford University Press, 1998.

Richardson, Samuel. *Pamela.* 2 Vols. New York: Dutton, 1962.

Said, Edward. *Culture and Imperialism.* New York: Knopf, 1993.

Sanchez-Eppler, Karen. *Touching Liberty: Abolition, Feminism and the Politics of the Body.* Berkeley: University of California Press, 1993.

Schiebinger, Londa. *The Mind Has No Sex?* Cambridge, MA: Harvard University Press, 1989.

Sen, K. C. *Keshub Chunder Sen in England.* Ed. Prem Sunder Basu. Calcutta: Writers Workshop, 1980.

————. *Lectures in India.* New York: Cassell, 1901.

————. *Viveka o Vairagya (Conscience and Renunciation).* Trans. J. K. Koar. Calcutta: Navavidhan Publications, n.d.

Sharpe, Jenny. "'Something Akin to Freedom': The Case of Mary Prince." *Differences* 8:1 (1996): 31–55.

Sheriff, Mary. "Fragonard's Erotic Mothers and the Politics of Reproduction." *Eroticism and the Body Politic.* Ed. Lynn Hunt. Baltimore, MD: Johns Hopkins University Press, 1991. 14–40.

Shyllon, F. O. *Black Slaves in Britain.* New York: Oxford University Press, 1974.

Smith, Adam. *The Wealth of Nations.* New York: Everyman's Library, 1991.

Smith, Samuel Stanhope. *The Lectures, Corrected and Improved which have been delivered for a series of years, in the College of New Jersey; on the subject of Moral and Political Philosophy.* 2 Vols. Trenton, NJ: 1812.

Spivak, Gayatri Chakravorty. "Deconstructing Historiography." *Selected Subaltern Studies.* (New York: Oxford University Press, 1988).

————. *A Critique of Postcolonial Reason.* Cambridge, MA: Harvard University Press, 1999.

Starr, G. A. "Sentimental Novels of the Later Eighteenth Century." *The Columbia History of the British Novel.* Eds. J. Richetti, J. Bender, D. David, and M. Seidel. New York: Columbia University Press, 1994. 181–198.

Stocking, George. *Victorian Anthropology.* New York: Free Press, 1987.

Stoler, Ann Laura. "A Sentimental Education: European Children and Native Servants." *Fantasizing the Feminine: Sex and Death in Indonesia.* Ed. Laurie Sears. Durham, NC: Duke University Press, 1995.

————. "Sexual Affronts and Racial Frontiers." *Comparative Studies in Society and History.* 34:2 (July 1992), 514–551.

————. *Race and the Education of Desire: Foucault's History of Sexuality and the Colonial Order of Things.* Durham, NC: Duke University Press, 1995.

Todd, Janet. *Sensibility: An Introduction.* New York: Methuen, 1986.

Trumbach, Randolph. "Erotic Fantasy and Male Libertinism in Enlightenment England." *The Invention of Pornography: Obscenity and the Origins of Modernity.* Ed. Lynn Hunt. Cambridge, MA: MIT Press, 1993. 253–282.

Vergès, Françoise. *Monsters and Revolutionaries: Colonial Family Romance and Métissage.* Durham, NC: Duke University Press, 1999.

Walpole, Horace. *The Castle of Otranto, A Gothic Story.* Ed. W. S. Lewis. New York: Oxford University Press, 1996.

Walvin, James. *Black Ivory.* Washington, DC: Howard University Press, 1992.

Watt, Ian. *The Rise of the Novel.* Berkeley: University of California Press, 1957.

Wesley, John. *Considerations upon Slavery.* London: 1774.

White, Hayden. "The Value of Narrativity in the Representation of Reality." *On Narrative.* Ed. W. J. T. Mitchell. Chicago: University of Chicago Press, 1980.

Wiegman, Robyn. *American Anatomies: Theorizing Race and Gender.* Durham, NC: Duke University Press, 1995.

Williams, Raymond. *The Country and the City.* New York: Oxford University Press, 1983.

———. *Marxism and Literature.* New York: Oxford University Press, 1985.

Wolffe, John. *God and Greater Britain: Religion and National Life in Britian and Ireland, 1843–1945.* New York: Routledge, 1994.

Wright, Caleb. *Lectures on India.* Boston, 1851.

Young, Robert J. C. *Colonial Desire.* New York: Routledge, 1995.

Index

222   *Rule of Sympathy*

Watt, Ian 64
Wesley, John 75, 92, 124, 125
Whytt, Robert 23
Wilberforce, William 118, 123, 142,
   145–147, 158
Williams, Francis 41
Wollstonecraft, Mary 86
Woman 24, 25, 35, 39, 45, 90, 99,
   162, 165

and Civilization 25, 35, 99,
   139–140, 141, 149
See also Gender, Sympathy, Gothic,
   Aesthetics
Wright, Caleb 141

Young, Edward (Graveyard Movement)
   72
Young, William 118